DATE DUE			

Also By Robert MacNeil

People Machine:
The Influence of Television on American Politics

THE RIGHT PLACE
AT
THE RIGHT TIME

THE
Right Place at
THE
Right Time

ROBERT MACNEIL

LITTLE, BROWN AND COMPANY / Boston — Toronto

FIRST EDITION

The author is grateful to the following companies for permission to quote material noted below:

NBC Radio for a special report by Robert MacNeil on the funeral of Winston Churchill.

NBC News for excerpts from *The Huntley-Brinkley Report* for September 29, 1964.

Cinecentrum for excerpts from the documentary *The Dutch Connection*.

Library of Congress Cataloging in Publication Data

MacNeil, Robert, 1931–
    The right place at the right time.

    I. Title.
PS3563.A2365R5 813'.54 82–99
ISBN 0–316–54290–3   AACR2

070.924
M23r
125747
aug 1983

MV
Designed by Janis Capone
Published simultaneously in Canada
by Little, Brown & Company (Canada) Limited

PRINTED IN THE UNITED STATES OF AMERICA

To my mother, born Margaret Virginia Oxner,
and my late father, Robert Auburn Stuart MacNeil.

Contents

THE RIGHT PLACE
AT
THE RIGHT TIME

Introduction

O<small>N A HOT SATURDAY</small> in midsummer 1966, with my wife
and children and some friends, I drove out of Manhattan for
a picnic on Jones Beach. As we approached Long Island, our
expressway intersected with one coming from Kennedy Airport and the traffic merged with ours. A gray hearse slid
smoothly into the next lane and the traffic flow kept us side
by side for a few minutes.

In the hearse we could see a coffin with the Stars and
Stripes covering it. We all looked at it and nobody said
anything.

My insides chilled at the sight. The contrast between our
happy-go-lucky carload of kids and picnic food and relaxed
adults, with what I supposed that cargo to be, dismayed me
utterly. My imagination would not leave what might be under
the flag, inside the service casket, inside the rubber body
bag, freshly arrived from Vietnam. What pieces of a young
man were sweeping home to some community on Long Island
on a day when everyone was thinking of the beach, or a cool
beer in the shade?

The hearse swung away from us at the next exit. I drove on,
not talking about it for fear of upsetting the small children,
but with a strong impression that this body was being spirited,

almost smuggled, back into the United States, like contraband. There was something too mundane, too private about this manner of reentry. Given the death toll in Vietnam, running then at roughly one hundred a week, this must have been a very common sight. In each community, locally, people would know. But nationally, who knew? America as a nation heard the body count on television, but the consequences remained largely invisible. At least that was my sudden feeling about it. That feeling cast a shadow over the day and it remained with me.

On another Saturday, several months later, we were in the editing rooms at NBC, viewing the film rushes just in from Vietnam.

An American infantry unit on patrol in a forest was trapped by artillery fire from their own side. A salvo came screaming into the trees and exploded all around them, the fragments ripping into foliage and men. The NBC cameraman was there through it all. He filmed a very young GI who had just been hit. His legs below the knees were nothing but ribbons of bloody flesh. His agony was indescribable. He was screaming obscenities at the medics, who had yet to reach him. He clawed the earth with his fingers. He bit into the ground with his teeth. It was unbearable to watch. When it ended there was silence, and one of us, the executive producer, the film editor, or I, said, "Well, we can't use that on the air." No one disputed him. It was obvious.

There was more. In another place U.S. troops had killed a number of Vietcong. The film showed the Americans cutting the ears off the dead as trophies. The NBC correspondent explained that this custom had become increasingly common. The GIs had picked it up from the Montagnard tribesmen.

The camera followed a U.S. sergeant as he took a straight razor out of his knapsack. He reached down, pulled the dead man's ear away from his head, then slit it off. The razor severed it as easily as a piece of soft cheese. The sergeant folded his razor and put the ear away in his haversack.

Watching it made the executive producer feel sick. We talked about the propriety of running it. We all agreed it was significant, but we also agreed when the producer protested: "We go on the air at suppertime."

He referred it to an executive higher up in NBC News, who said not to use it. It seemed a reasonable, commonsense decision at the time. But I thought about it later and suddenly realized that we were sanitizing the war. The medium that *was* the war to most Americans, the medium commonly thought to be turning the country against the war, was systematically making it tolerable for family viewing at suppertime, like an adventure serial.

And then there was the young Vietnam widow, on a raw November day in New Hampshire, who broke down and cried in my car. . . .

Vietnam became something of an obsession with me, possibly because I did not cover it in person as I had in other trouble spots of the sixties — the Congo, Algeria, Berlin, Cuba. I experienced it vicariously, as the American people did, on television. But I felt more strongly about Vietnam than any of the other crises. The war that preoccupied me was the war as it was perceived in America and what those perceptions were slowly doing to America. Nothing since the Civil War so rent the fabric of American society and its institutions. And the instrument which conveyed it all, subtly transmuting the action and reaction, not merely a messenger but a catalyst of change, was my own profession, television.

By any measure my own career was going swimmingly. I was thirty-five. I had been a correspondent with NBC for six years, three of them overseas, two in Washington. I was now getting additional seasoning and recognition in New York as the anchorman for a daily local program and a weekly network one. Someone "up there" clearly had his eye on me and was bringing me along. Indeed, I had had so many different assignments and my career had moved so rapidly that I never really paused to ask myself what it was all about.

Fast movement feeds one's vanity. If my precious self is being whizzed around the world at the speed of sound, if my person is being subjected to greater and greater professional acceleration, what I am doing must be important. It must be meaningful. Add to that the exhilaration of being paid more than one ever expected, one's self-contemplation is not likely to be very critical.

Vietnam blew that complacency out of me. Not all at once, but gradually, the anguished questions the war produced in me changed my outlook. That gave me a critical perspective, on my profession and on my own development as a journalist.

ONE

The Reluctant Reporter

I STUMBLED INTO JOURNALISM. I was not pushed; I did not choose it; I had no burning sense of vocation. I thought I was going to be a naval officer, an actor, a playwright — in that order. Through a series of accidents I found myself becoming a journalist, even more accidentally a television journalist; the driving motive being expediency, the need to make a living. I never ceased to think in the early years that I would leave it as soon as I struck gold as a playwright. That never happened, although it remained a convenient escape fantasy.

That was typical of many of the people I worked with in the 1950s in London, especially the young "colonials" like myself, from Canada, Australia, New Zealand, South Africa, and a few from the United States. Most of us carried around fanciful notions of being a new generation of literary émigrés from our cruder lands. We submitted to the drudgery and discipline of wire service work, secretly comforting ourselves that we were honing our literary skills. Back in our bed-sitting-rooms in Earls Court or thereabouts, each of us had a novel or a play in progress. There were older men among us who successfully practiced journalism, as it were, with their left hand, and their creative writing with the right. By their example, journalism seemed a worthy and practical antechamber to one's true lifework.

Gradually, however, a sense of professionalism betrayed me; I began to take pride in my advancing skills. Competence was a pleasure in itself but also rewarded with promotion. When you are repeatedly failing in the field you have chosen, the wounds to your self-esteem can be healed by recognition in another. In my case, recognition in journalism made journalism more interesting. It led to travels and adventures I would never otherwise have experienced. It led to better jobs and more money. So, drop by drop, the creative juices I had reverently reserved for my own writing were surrendered to the daily craft of journalism.

Looking back, I can measure the transition by my changing attitudes to George Orwell's essay "Confessions of a Book Reviewer." For years, I identified totally with that shabby figure in his cold bed-sitting-room, "pouring his immortal spirit down the drain, half a pint at a time." My advancing journalistic competence drew a veil between him and me. I viewed him more distantly and complacently — although on reopening the book just now to check the quotation, I felt a pang of remorse, as for a deserted friend.

In Fleet Street, where "immortal spirit" is heavily diluted with alcoholic spirits, I also imbibed my fill of traditions. But they were craft traditions. The lead to a story had to be crisp and graphic. Facts had to be checked. You could not say more than you knew for certain or could pin on some good authority. When in doubt, leave out, get around it somehow. Be first but be right but be salable. It was like learning to be a good carpenter: saw a straight line; don't bend the nail when you hammer it in. It was in no way philosophical.

That background did not prepare me for the heavy earnestness of American journalism when I first encountered it: the diplomatic correspondent who wore the dignities of a secretary of state; the political reporter pregnant with wisdom on reforming the system. I had little preparation for this journalism, burdened by its own self-importance and its quasi-constitutional mystique. I recognize the need it fulfills in the cumbersome American political system, but have always felt personally detached from it.

My ganglia do not quiver when someone mentions the First

Amendment. I grew up in a country, Canada, and worked for sixteen years in another, Britain, where I never felt my civil liberties infringed by the absence of a First Amendment. Indeed, by becoming politically aware as I did in the early 1950s, I thought it a decided advantage not to be living in a country which permitted a demagogue like Senator Joseph McCarthy to trample on its freedoms. One can argue in which system the private individual's basic liberties are better protected. There are sound arguments for relief from the draconian libel laws in Britain and from the Official Secrets Act. There are good grounds to argue that American journalism is too sheltered to admit its own trespasses. I make the First Amendment point only to indicate that I did not absorb the true faith from birth.

Furthermore, I did not go to a school of journalism. All I ever wanted from the colleges I attended in Canada was as many English courses as possible. In Britain journalism schools were almost unknown and in the 1950s university graduates were still rather grudgingly admitted to Fleet Street. So I did not come factory-equipped, as they say of cars, with a body of theory about journalism. That has been a weakness from time to time, when I had to admit to myself that I really didn't know what I was doing — or why. But it meant that I also missed another opportunity for indoctrination in the myths and rituals of the craft. I was not programmed with as many stereotypes.

The cumulative effect of all these factors has left me ambivalent about journalism: extreme pleasure in the life it offered; pride as I found I could practice it successfully; growing doubts about how it is practiced. I think my unorthodox entry has given me some detachment, some freedom to look for new forms, to criticize existing forms. I have not felt compelled to genuflect before what exists and is sanctified merely because it is successful.

That detachment, however, was hard earned. Most of what I now hear flatteringly described as my "career" was spent in a state of controlled anxiety as I was forced to learn various parts of the trade by the sink-or-swim method. It was anxiety to stay afloat.

The wonderful thing was that various employers were willing to pay me to travel around the world, eat well, stay in pleasant hotels, meet unusual people, and be where exciting things were happening, while I learned. That is very nice work if you can get it. If you can manage to be a foreign correspondent, that is just icing on the gingerbread.

In the late 1970s, someone reported that there were currently 65,000 young Americans studying journalism, roughly the same number as there were jobs in the news business. Woodward and Bernstein can probably take credit for swelling the enrollment by making heroes of the reporters in *All the President's Men*. I would hate to add to the overcrowding even a little but I can't keep the secret. Being a journalist, a reporter, is simply wonderful.

It is a lifelong license to follow that most basic human trait, curiosity. It is also a dilettante's license. It is permission to probe and delve into whatever interests you as thoroughly or as superficially as you like; and then move on. Temperamentally, you may be as inconstant as a butterfly or as painstaking as a scientist who studies butterflies — and make a good living in journalism either way. You have a license to ask virtually any human being almost anything. You have a license to penetrate and intrude into the private lives and rituals of all the peoples on earth. You have a lifelong excuse to be a sidewalk superintendent, watching human beings work. When I was a child I was constantly told that it was rude to stare and bad manners to ask too many pointed questions. I have spent thirty years as an adult doing both as much as I pleased.

But beyond the mere permission to witness, journalism also permits you to share the experience of many professions, to live them vicariously — historian, archaeologist, detective, prosecutor, diplomat, soldier, spy, explorer . . . the list is endless.

So is the parade of characters and the flow of plots — the raw material of an endless serial novel, not requiring the awesome talents of a Dostoevsky or a Dickens to execute. Journalism is a license to dabble at the margins of great writing, without the risks.

Much of that life is funny. Sometimes it is frightening. Those are the personal experiences which it is usually considered unprofessional to report. So are the mistakes we all make but hide to maintain the illusion of infallibility. They are the sort of stories reporters like to tell each other. This is a book of the stories I tell people, if they ask me.

They are not intended as definitive accounts of events I covered. On really big stories, reporters, like soldiers in a battle, know only the part that is happening in front of them. Most of my stories describe the part that was happening in front of me. Looking back, I am chastened to discover how little I often knew of what was really going on. Sometimes I'm pleased to find that I had the essence of it, that I had stumbled into the right microcosm.

TWO

White Christmas

I HAD THE KIND OF apprenticeship in broadcasting that is difficult to acquire now: encounters with radio stations that let me do virtually everything, simply because I was a warm body who wanted to.

I had tried to run away to sea in 1951. Having completed two years of college I was very bored and broke. The great sea adventure fell apart but I happened almost immediately into a job as an all-night disc jockey. The station was CJCH, Halifax, the only station in Canada's maritime provinces that stayed on twenty-four hours a day.

The all-night job required me to turn up at 11:30 P.M. to pick some records; act as control-room engineer for the evening disc jockey from midnight until 1 A.M., then take over all alone until 8 A.M., when the cheery breakfast-hour boys arrived. Tradition required that I play current pop favorites (Teresa Brewer, Jo Stafford, Vaughan Monroe, Rosemary Clooney, Les Paul and Mary Ford) for the first hour, then do what I liked until 6 A.M., when country and western music was obligatory for the farmers.

I played a lot of classical music and recorded drama, largely because they were the only material that existed in those days on long playing or transcription records. Everything else had to be played on 78 rpm, which meant changing the disc and making an announcement every three minutes or so, a chore that seriously interfered with my reading. Penguin Books were just then bringing out new comprehensive editions of Aldous Huxley, Evelyn Waugh, D. H. Lawrence, and such, and I was getting through one paperback a night, provided I wasn't interrupted too often by having to make inane announcements like, "And now, the wonderful music of Les Brown and his Band of Renown" — and other whiz-bang phrases filched from the professional disc jockeys.

Occasionally, I operated something of a counterculture corner, reading long narrative poems on the air, doing skits imitative of a talented Canadian called Max Ferguson, reading chapters of books I liked, and playing whatever classics then existed on LP.

Very quickly I acquired some skills in the minor corruptions of that very minor corner of show business. There was a commercial to read once a night for an all-night diner. Properly handled, they delivered satisfying payola about 3 A.M.

The radio station was housed in a prefabricated penthouse built on the roof of the Lord Nelson Hotel, a solid red brick structure, eight stories high, overlooking the Halifax Public Gardens. There was a young man who worked all night as a baker in the Lord Nelson kitchens, who was hopelessly infatuated with the glamour of radio. Any night he was on duty, he sneaked upstairs for an hour or so just to sit and chat in his chef's outfit and watch me work. If he hadn't been there, I would have been reading for myself and doing minimum disc jockeying, but to impress him I had to be seen to be earning my forty dollars a week. The quid pro quo was a large tray of stunning food liberated from the hotel refrigerators. His taste ran more to elaborate pastries than mine but we got that sorted out.

Then there were the women who called up. Any radio announcer, especially an all-night disc jockey, knows them. In a seaport like Halifax, with thousands of men plying the oceans of the world, I heard from a lot of lonely ladies. Voices on the radio or on the phone play wonderfully into our erotic fantasies. They certainly played into mine, a twenty-year-old who felt he needed to catch up after years of boarding school.

Some women telephoned regularly and flirted safely from that distance. Others proposed more substantial fulfillment and, although I fantasized a lot about it, I never followed through, until there was one I finally couldn't resist. She called every night for months, usually at about 2:30 A.M. The budding novelist in me interviewed her subtly but ruthlessly until I thought I had her life more coherently in my mind than she had in hers. I don't know what quality makes a woman's voice sexy on the telephone, but she had it. She began by simply wanting someone to talk to because her husband was at sea, but the friendship ripened and she began to talk casually, then pointedly, about coming to see me.

She made dates to turn up on certain Saturday nights, then spent weeks apologizing for not having the courage to come. The more she hesitated, the more urgently I looked forward to the rendezvous.

Finally, one Saturday night in mid-winter she actually arrived.

But not alone. For moral support she brought her sister and brother-in-law. They were embarrassed about this tryst at 1:15 A.M. and stayed in the record library, two rooms away, where I could see them through the control room and studio windows. My phone date came into the control room. I was shocked. She was very fat and very drunk. Her face was very heavily powdered and the effort of climbing the two flights of stairs from the hotel elevator had forced little rivers of perspiration to cut channels through the powder.

My ardor evaporated the instant she came through the door, but hers did not. She sat down on the only other chair across the big record turntables from me, while I frantically managed to look busy. I thought she was collecting herself to go home (she had said she could stay only a few minutes) when she suddenly stood up and reached across the turntables to kiss me. Her body jolted the turntable legs and the sound arm went skittering across the record that was playing on the air; the big control-room speaker amplified the noise to a thunder.

I rushed to the control console, turned down the volume,

cued up another record, and let it roll. The lady pursued me into the horseshoe formed by the turntables and the control console. She was very big and determined and she was all over me. I was wondering what I could do to regain control of the situation — and of the radio station — when her sister and husband burst into the room and pulled her away. They got her out of there and I decided there must be a safer way to meet amorous women.

There was also a constant barrage of phone calls from people who wanted me to play certain records. It wasn't a request program, but I obliged now and then. Christmas Eve, 1951, produced hundreds of such calls, mostly from drunks and all wanting Bing Crosby's "White Christmas."

I was fed up with the song and fed up with being there all by myself on Christmas Eve, and just for the hell of it, for about two hours, I refused to play the record. Finally, to stop the phones ringing, I opened my microphone and said: "Okay, you win. Bing Crosby, 'White Christmas.' Once only."

I put the 78 on and cued up another disc, then headed for the men's room. To get there I had to leave the control room, cross through a small studio, through the record library, down a small hallway where the news ticker was located, out the front door of CJCH and into a door right beside it. I was used to making this run and getting back well within the time of a 78 disc and I noticed that "White Christmas" was unusually long, running three and a quarter minutes or so.

But the moment the station front door swung back, it clicked shut with a sound I was not expecting, but instantly recognized. I was locked out. I went to the bathroom, then tried the front door. It was locked. I put my ear against it and could hear, on the record library speaker, Crosby about halfway through the piece. He was all right.

I was terrified. I ran down two flights of stairs to the top floor of the hotel and rang frantically for the elevator. I thought the front desk might have a key to the radio station for emergencies. This was an emergency. In about forty-five seconds the disc would end and five thousand watts of power would be transmitting the amplified sounds of a needle oscillating at the end of the record, all over Nova Scotia.

The sleepy elevator operator finally came and took me down to the lobby. I raced to the front desk but they had no key. "What's the matter up there?" the night clerk asked. "Lot of people phoning about some trouble up there."

I ran back to the elevator, woke the operator a second time, got out on the top floor, and raced up the stairs. I didn't need to put my ear to the door to hear *Clunk-CLUNK, Clunk-CLUNK, Clunk-CLUNK* coming from inside.

Desperately, I looked around for a way to get in. At the top of the stairwell was a small window, high up on the wall. By balancing on a radiator, and a small ledge, and climbing a pipe, I got my fingers onto the windowsill and pulled myself up. The window was heavy and hinged horizontally but I crawled out and suddenly realized there was a snowstorm going on, with freezing wind driving the wet snow into my face. There was about eighteen inches of roof space outside the prefab construction of the station, and it was about nine inches deep in snow. Pressing my back against the wall, I edged gingerly all the way around the station, with nine stories of snowy space just past my toes. When I came to the window of the control room, I broke it with my elbow and got inside.

The telephone rang by lighting bulbs on the control console and they were all flashing wildly. I sat down at the console, turned down the pot (volume control) for "White Christmas," which stopped the horrible *Clunk-CLUNK.* Then I opened my microphone and said: "All right, here's what happened," or words to that effect, and told the story.

I didn't get fired. It was too hard to get anybody else to take that job.

A few weeks later I stumbled into my first big news story, although I scarcely knew enough about journalism to call it that.

Part of the disc jockey routine was to read a five-minute summary of the news every hour, obtained from a teleprinter maintained by British United Press which ran a service edited for radio. All that was necessary was to remember a few minutes beforehand to go down the hall; rip off the latest "Five Minute Summary"; and make sure you could pronounce the proper names before you opened the microphone, adopted your "news" voice (resonant and important-sounding), and let fly to the waiting multitudes. It is known in the trade as "rip and read" news and it is as close as many radio stations ever get to journalism.

One morning in January 1952, on the way to the men's room I passed the teleprinter and something was different. It was chattering away hard enough to make it tremble and it was ringing bells furiously. I had never heard it do that before so I stopped and looked. It rang more bells and I read "BUL-LETIN — KING GEORGE VI DIED TODAY."

I tore off that piece of paper and walked back into the control room, wondering what to do with it. Some faint stirrings of journalistic instinct made me realize that I should get that information on the air. But it was only ten minutes to seven. News time was at seven. In that fifteen-minute slot preceding the news every morning the station scheduled a syndicated talk by a Dr. Michaelson in Los Angeles. These appeared on fifteen-minute transcription discs. On them, Dr. Michaelson, with a very heavy accent, delivered impassioned appeals for various activities in Israel.

That morning, Dr. Michaelson was just getting warmed up. His subject was the neglect and desecration of certain Jewish graves in Israel. He used the word *graves* a lot and gave the *gr* a very wet, guttural sound, as though his adenoids and sinuses were bothering him.

It seemed to me either sacrilegious or, worse, commercially unsound to interrupt his sermon. But it also seemed imperative to let any Canadians I could reach know that the king was dead, since he was very much their king too.

There were clearly established procedures for such moments, laid down by the publicly financed Canadian Broadcasting Corporation. Somewhere, in a dusty drawer in all commercial radio stations, were elaborate orders to follow if the king or the prime minister or governor general died. In essence, they called for canceling all programming, playing somber music, and joining the CBC network as soon as possible.

I had never heard of any of that. So, I simply faded down Dr. Michaelson, opened the microphone, and said: "CJCH regrets to announce that King George the Sixth died today," then faded the voice of Dr. Michaelson back up. Nothing about "we interrupt this program for a special announcement . . ." or anything like that.

I went back out to the teletype machine and found "adds" to the bulletin and announced them the same way.

"The king died peacefully in his sleep, according to an announcement from Buckingham Palace."

Finally the station manager phoned from New Brunswick, where he was attending a radio convention, to ask what the hell I was doing. He told me where to find the procedures for broadcasting the deaths of kings.

I should have remembered this incident more often in the years since when I have found the antics of local station announcers somewhat embarrassing. You can't behave like Walter Cronkite if no one has ever taught you how.

THREE

Early Days in London

IT WAS LONDON THAT finally made me a journalist, and that city became the biggest single influence in my life, politically, culturally, emotionally.

Arriving in Britain at twenty-four, fresh from the provincialism of Canada, it really seemed, in Matthew Arnold's words, to lie before me "like a land of dreams, so beautiful, so various, so new."

The more I reflect on how London played on me, opening my eyes and ears and stimulating my curiosity in countless ways, the less I regret not continuing my education. London served me as a graduate school. It was my tutor in many things, but first and most practically, in the basic craft of journalism.

My first brushes with the craft were not very disciplined. It was October 1955. Commercial television was about to hit the airwaves, for the first time breaking the BBC's monopoly. It was creating its own news service, ITN (Independent Television News), and I talked my way in there on the basis of my TV experience in Canada, embroidered with a little delicate exaggeration. While I had done quite a lot of announcing and interviewing, I was not a trained reporter or writer, which is what they wanted. In the confusions of those early weeks, they hired me on a temporary basis for £9 a week.

I found myself a subeditor, without knowing what that was. With me on the news desk were Lynn Reid-Banks, who later wrote *The L-Shaped Room*, and Reginald Bosenquet, who was to become ITN's most enduring personality. We ran around London pursuing crazy stories, looking principally for ways to make the news more colorful and human than the BBC's bloodless product. So I covered the Old Bailey trial of a Soho gangster who had cut up a rival with a razor. We pursued the last entry in the telephone book, a Mr. Zzzu, until it appeared that the oddly named gentleman was a front for an elegant call-girl ring and we were called off the story.

I collected lots of color but didn't write in a crisp, direct news style, so my stories didn't look or sound like news to the grizzled Fleet Street veterans who ran the news desk. I didn't have the basic skills needed to convert raw material into a "story." When Emmett Till, a black teenager, was found murdered in Mississippi, I talked on the transatlantic phone to the local sheriff. I interviewed that colorful gentleman for fifteen minutes and reported to the editor that he hadn't said anything worth using. A few years later I would have seen the story in what he had said.

Also, I had to overcome shyness about accosting people, telephoning them or knocking on their doors. The night Donald Maclean and Guy Burgess, Britain's defector-diplomat-spies, surfaced in Moscow, I was sent to Maclean's mother's house. I loathed the idea of bothering her, of intruding on her shame. I climbed the stairs to her "mansion flat" behind the Albert Hall, my feet dragging with reluctance. I hated to ring the doorbell and nearly left, planning to say she wasn't in. But, I worried, some other reporter might get a quote from her and I'd be found out. With great embarrassment, I rang the doorbell. Lady Maclean opened the door herself. She looked frail and exhausted. She said sadly, as if talking in her sleep, "Please, go away. I have nothing to say," and closed the door. I galloped down the stairs, vastly relieved.

My embarrassment was worse the night the news broke that Princess Margaret had broken off her relationship with Group Captain Peter Townsend. For months their romance had kept the popular press buzzing and the "Establishment" papers clucking about the suitability of the queen's sister marrying a divorced commoner. The climax came when, after earnest consultations with the Archbishop of Canterbury, and presumably her royal conscience, the princess announced that there would be no marriage. The whole episode was so silly yet so revealing that I was writing a satirical play about it.

To some popular newspapers, the villain of this saga of the heartbroken princess was her brother-in-law, the Duke of Edinburgh. He was reported to have disapproved of Townsend and got the archbishop to talk the passionate and headstrong princess out of it.

The story broke on the evening of a Royal Command Film Performance, when the queen attends a movie opening, usually at the Odeon in Leicester Square, and young film stars who are to be presented to the queen compete to wear the lowest neckline. There is always a large crowd of Londoners outside, oohing and aahing as the Rolls-Royces disgorge their dazzling cargoes.

The news editor at ITN, formerly of the *Daily Express*, said to me: "Laddie, get down to Leicester Square. It'll be quite a story if the crowd boos the Duke of Edinburgh."

I got a taxi to Leicester Square and joined the crowd under the brightly lit marquee. Everyone seemed happy, jolly, and excited. I squeezed close to people to catch their conversation. No one mentioned Princess Margaret or Townsend or the duke. I went to a call box and telephoned the editor.

"I don't think they know about Margaret and Townsend breaking up," I said. "They certainly aren't talking about it."

"Well, tell them, laddie, for God's sake, tell them!"

He hung up. There was nothing for me to do but try, so, swallowing my embarrassment, I went back to the crowd and began.

"Excuse me . . ."

"Yes?"

"Did you hear about Princess Margaret breaking it off with Peter Townsend?"

"Who are you?" the first man asked, puzzled by my Canadian accent.

"I'm a reporter."

"Oh, I see," he said suspiciously and turned away.

I tried a few more people and got a few reactions like:

"Oh, really? Has she?"

"How do you know?"

"Oh, poor thing. What a shame."

But largely indifference.

Then the queen arrived, resplendent in a glittering tiara and white fur, accompanied by the supposedly hated duke.

The crowd went wild, cheering, applauding, waving, saying "Isn't she lovely?" "Isn't it nice?" — as warm a demonstration of popular affection as the royal family could wish. There was no hint of animosity to the duke. Clearly these people didn't read what the *Daily Mirror, Daily Sketch, Daily Express,* and *Daily Mail* were writing about the princess, or if they did, weren't living by the clichés Fleet Street thought they were.

I phoned the news editor and told him the crowd's reaction. He was very disappointed; worse, he made it sound as if it were my fault.

Eventually I became hardened to the business of approaching people. But I never overcame my instinctive distaste for concocting news.

It leads too easily to sheer invention. For example, suppose one person in the crowd *had* said something derogatory about the Duke of Edinburgh? But only one person. With the predisposition of the news editor and my desire to give him what he wanted, we could easily have "hardened up" the material, as journalists say, and featured that man. A reporter, fearing for his job, could simply invent more quotes. Or a diligent reporter might have doggedly gone through that crowd and wrung some more anti-duke material out of people. Reporting it would have seriously misrepresented the mood of that crowd.

In another sense, however, the editor was perfectly right. Suppose his sensationalist hunch had been correct and the crowd had spontaneously and unamimously jeered the duke.

It would have been quite legitimately a story. He was right to "cover" the event in case. I was right to be squeamish about becoming an *agent provocateur*.

Life was very different when I moved to Reuters at the end of that year. Like any news agency, there was the drudgery of constant output; and, as the oldest and most prestigious worldwide news service, Reuters suffered no tampering with its disciplines or traditions. From the first moment you entered the vast newsroom, with perhaps two hundred teleprinters and typewriters clattering away and scores of phones ringing on desks littered with copy, tea cups, files, pencils, cigarettes, and reference books, the institution made you feel suitably humble, grateful even to be there.

It was grueling. For six weeks, I spent eight hours a day writing newsbriefs, stories condensed into one sentence which newspapers run as column fillers. All the cables from around the world rejected by the copytaster,* who ran the world service, ended up as newsbriefs. Several times in a cycle he would shove a wodge of cables at the newest subeditor and cheerfully say, "MacNeil, hack us out a page of newsbriefs, like a good fellow."

It was wonderful training but it was awful. Most of the stories — sometimes amounting to a thousand words of cablese — were in the newsbrief file because there was something wrong with them. They required infinite checking and then, for a novice like me, painstaking writing and rewriting to reduce the essentials to one clear sentence. When they weren't right the filing editor handed them back for rewriting. Sometimes I spent an entire day on a dozen of those one-sentence items.

Deciphering cablese was difficult in itself. Radio teletype circuits were only beginning to come in, and most Reuter correspondents still filed by cable to avail themselves of the penny press rate, meaning one British penny per word for press messages cabled within the British Commonwealth. Not all Reuter

---

* The British term for the American slotman, who first sees all incoming news and decides what priority and length it deserves.

stringers in exotic foreign lands were totally at ease in English, which lent even more mystery to their cablese. Besides the normal abbreviations to save words, correspondents left the Central Desk in London to fill in many details. All names and titles had to be checked, as did ship tonnages, registry and position, all geographical place-names. All background to a story provided by the correspondent, however trustworthy, had to be checked against previous Reuter copy, unless the subeditor knew for certain that it was right.

I came out of that nightmare eventually. My trial period passed and, as a full-time subeditor, I began trying to master the Reuter style; to write fast, simple, yet graceful English, leaving no ambiguities.

The spring came on. The days grew lighter and outside the big newsroom window the dome and facade of St. Paul's Cathedral was a consoling presence, interesting in all lights. There were many other compensations for the grinding work on the battered old Royal typewriters which had to be up-ended on the crowded desks to make room to pencil edit your copy. Up-ending the typewriters frequently sent a mug of tea streaming across the desk to be collectively wiped up with absorbent copy paper. The mugs would be quickly refilled by the tea boys, bearing large enamel pitchers of hot tea, heavily pre-milked and sugared, from a steamy café across Fleet Street by the *Daily Express* building. Everyone drank seven or eight of those mugfuls a day, one's own china mug gradually turning brown like the inside of a teapot; the tea stirred always with a pencil wiped off with copy paper. Several times a day old ladies pushed trolleys around bearing custard tarts, sausage rolls, and cakes.

The so-called tea boys were elderly men, who also ran messages up and down the large room, and stood chatting and smoking by their station when not on an errand. One of them was Alfred Perlès, who shared with Henry Miller the adventures portrayed in the *Tropics* and subsequently published a delightful account called *My Friend Henry Miller*. Perlès was one of the compensations.

He was in his sixties, a short, balding, happy man with a constant smile; physically, a sort of scaled-down version of

Miller. He had a Zen-like quality of finding joy in any moment, curiosity in any conversation, delight in any friendship. He was a tea boy to give him pocket money and something to do each day. He was living with a handsome Scotswoman in Hampstead. We became quite friendly and sometimes I would walk across Hampstead Heath from Highgate, where I lived, to visit them; or my wife and I would go there to dinner. The specialty was jugged hare, a rabbit steeped for many hours and served with red currant jelly. Fred was very interested in food. He was also interested in wine, women, books, conversation, music, painting, architecture, and smoking. He had a collection of more than fifty pipes, and casually gave me one of his best, a Petersen with a silver band. Equally casually, he gave me a copy of Henry Miller's *Remember to Remember*, autographed to Fred, who had suggested the title.

Perlès not only gave the hungry literary pilgrim in me a glimpse into that immortalized life in Paris, he transmitted an attitude to life extrasensually, as a saint must transmit faith. Being with Perlès, you understood his and Miller's serene indifference to any social duty except to perceive the world clearly, consume its pleasures avidly, and communicate them joyously.

Another writer worked on the Central Desk, and I gradually became quite friendly with him. He was Hubert Nicholson, a gray-bearded man with Pan-like features. Five days a week he sat in the same place and wrote leads, the long roundups of the day's top stories for the next day's morning papers. Away from Reuters, he produced a series of well-received novels and poems. He came from the East Riding of Yorkshire, the lonelier, more desolate part of that great county, and two of his novels gave a vivid feeling of the people and the landscape: *Little Heyday*, the last summer before the 1914 war, and *Sunk Island*, a modern tale of dark passion. For nearly a year on the Central Desk we all lived vicariously with him through the traumas of a pending decision by Columbia Pictures to make a film of *Sunk Island*. We assumed that any moment, a call would come from his agent, vast checks would be written, and Hubert would vanish into clouds of fame and wealth. He deserved to.

I was nursing similar fantasies. I imagined a hundred times the moment when one of the more supercilious editors would suddenly encounter a review of a play of mine in the newspaper. "MacNeil," he would say, "funny, don't we have a MacNeil here? This chap's just written a smash hit. Best thing in the West End this year, Kenneth Tynan says." And suddenly it would dawn on them all that it was I, and at that precise moment I would stand up and say, "Yes, and I think I'll be moving along now."

While I waited for that improbable moment, I devoured Fleet Street and the nearer parts of the City of London, arriving hours early, or using meal breaks, to explore the historic little alleys that contained riches like Dr. Johnson's house.

One of my favorite amusements was to get off the bus a few stops before Reuters, by the law courts. I would go into any court and listen for an hour to whatever case was being tried, savoring the dry cadences of English barristers using the language to perfection.

Another was to explore gradually every Christopher Wren church in the vicinity, including every inch of St. Paul's.

One day as my bus swung around the Aldwych I saw a crowd gathered around the church of St. Clement Dane's, which sits in the middle of the road. It had been gutted by the German bombing, silencing one of London's best-loved sounds, the bells that played the ancient tune "Oranges and Lemons." The song, and the children's game that went with it, reached deep into London's history. Its verses recalled the seventeenth century, when ships carrying citrus fruit tied up on the Thames Riverbank nearby; when condemned people heading for execution at Tyburn were a daily sight in London streets.

I got off the bus and discovered that newly cast bells were being delivered to replace those lost in the Blitz. Several hundred people, lawyers from the Inns of Court, secretaries, journalists, businessmen, and workers, stood in silence as the new bells were placed on blocks of wood with their mouths upwards. Then, an old workman, who had come with the bells, picked up a wooden mallet and began striking them. He moved among the upturned bells and with perfect cadence struck them so that the old tune rang out sweetly.

Oranges and lemons,
Say the bells of St. Clement's.
You owe me five farthings,
Say the bells of St. Martin's

When will you pay me?
Say the bells of Old Bailey
When I get rich,
Say the bells of Shoreditch.

Two double-decker buses stopped at the music. I saw tears in the eyes of the Londoners around me, hearing the tune for the first time since the bombing. I have seldom seen Englishmen so frankly emotional. The bells had reawakened terrible and glorious memories. The war was still being absorbed.

Sometimes the bombing had produced delayed benefits. Right beside the Reuter building was one of Wren's prettiest churches, St. Bride's. It was a church of air and grace, befitting its happy role as a place for weddings, its spire resembling a wedding cake. It was also, officially, the journalists' church.

One night during the Blitz, I was told, a large German incendiary bomb fell into Fleet Street, and caught in the wires running between the *Daily Express* and Reuters. Before wardens could dislodge it, it blew up, and Wren's masterpiece was left a gutted shell. Gradually, in my years there, it was lovingly rebuilt, with subscriptions from all the journalists in Fleet Street. I often went in to watch the stonecarvers or the gilders at work. One morning as I passed through the churchyard, the rector called me over and said, "Do you want to see something interesting?"

At his feet was a hole in the grass where several ancient gravestones had collapsed into a subsidence.

Extra stone piled there for the restoration had fallen through the earth, revealing a medieval charnel house, whose existence had been unknown. He took me down into the vaulted chamber. There was daylight enough to see thousands of human skulls neatly arrayed on one wall; on another stacks of thigh bones piled like cordwood; in another pile shinbones, in another arm bones. Finally, there were tidy piles of finger and toe bones. There they had been, undisturbed for centuries, dry and safe, the bones of medieval Londoners. Faintly from the far end of the chamber I could hear the double-decker buses grinding down Fleet Street, making the ground of St. Bride's churchyard tremble slightly. People like John Milton and Shakespeare had perhaps walked in the churchyard overhead, before Wren built St. Bride's.

The rector was very excited for the anthropologists, whom he had already alerted. He said remains of Londoners before the plague and great fire of 1666 were very scarce. The bones were a treasure trove to those curious to know the physical size and health and diet of Chaucer's contemporaries.

London gave the impressionable North American thrilling intuitions of historical relativities, constant reminders of how close the past was, of how short the human effort had been. Here they were, these medieval bones, calmly waiting for Judgment Day and, damnit, in one sense they were nearly halfway back to the time of Jesus Christ. They had gone to their routine deaths before the discovery of America, before the discovery that Earth was not the center of the Universe.

FOUR

Britain:
Political Education

NINETEEN FIFTY-SIX was my first full year as a professional journalist and I cut my teeth on three of the biggest stories of the decade: Khrushchev's de-Stalinization speech, the Suez crisis, and the Hungarian revolution. At Reuters, even the lowliest subeditor got pieces of a big story to nibble. The senior subs wrote the comprehensive stories, trying in all major developments. But I got enough of a taste to feel part of these momentous events.

My attention had never been so concentrated on politics. As a result, I was politically awakened and the basic responses I discovered in myself have colored my political attitudes ever since.

A reporter can easily train himself to be impartial, even apolitical. He can quite successfully keep his opinions to himself; compartmentalize his feelings and prejudices, as a priest, or psychiatrist, or lawyer may do. If he does this for long enough, he may end up indeed apolitical, a man with no beliefs; or more likely, a man turned so cynical that he has no stomach for commitment. I have felt all of these tendencies in myself. Yet I know that a certain political current still runs in me, sometimes feeble, sometimes strong; and it was basically defined as I discovered my own reactions to the events of 1956.

I became aware that I was a political creature, that like a compass needle, I was responding to certain lines of magnetic force in the world.

The biggest shock was Suez: not the opportunism of Moscow, nor the sanctimonious interventions of Washington, not even Nasser's act of nationalization, but the Anglo-French invasion. Somehow, such cynical behavior by the French didn't surprise me; by the British, it did. I felt betrayed by the country I had adopted as a model of civilization and compassion. I had come to the fountainhead of our culture breathless with admiration, as many British colonials do, only to discover that my preconceptions were idealized or provincial and out of date. The experience awakened in me a dormant resentment of British colonialism. I was gradually persuaded that the forces that inclined me toward Britain subtracted something from my identity at home. I had grown up only half Canadian, because I felt more than half British.

The Suez crisis is very old and stale now. It is hard to remember what volcanic emotions it produced, what a decisive moment it was: a symbolic turning point in the retreat from empire of Europe's colonial powers and the consequent bursting of new nations like seeds from a ripe pod. There was international communism trying to ensnare them by sympathizing with their "oppression" and whipping up their impatience. There was the ambivalent interest of the United States, to hasten the divestiture of Europe's colonies, while trying to nurse the fledgling nations that resulted into the Western orbit. And in each of the colonial powers, like Britain and France, there were powerful political forces: some urging more rapid stripping away of colonies that were a tremendous economic and military drain; others just as vehemently resisting what they saw as the surrender of all "greatness." How would Britain or France remain world powers, able to sit as equals with the United States in the councils of the West, if they dissolved the empires that gave them world responsibilities? The answer was that they would not remain world powers and could not. That power was an illusion. Their equality in World War II was a moral equality, won by Britain for standing alone against Hitler from 1939 to 1941: wrested for France by the magnificent effrontery of Charles de Gaulle. That equality vanished with the end of the war, but it took Britain and France many years to accept their role as second-rank powers, dependent for their security not only on American might, but on American wisdom.

The "winds of change," as British Prime Minister Harold Macmillan later called them, were blowing hard in 1956, but their inexorable force was not understood. Suez changed that.

I was working on the desk at Reuters on July 26, the night the Egyptian leader, Colonel Nasser, announced the nationalization of the Suez Canal. It was a big story. For months we had been chronicling the events that drove the impulsive Nasser to this: his grandiloquent promises to eradicate Egyptian poverty as no leader back to the pharaohs had been able to, by damming the Nile at Aswan to increase the fertility of the Valley. His flirtation with Moscow finally caused the exasperated John Foster Dulles to rescind the American pledge of assistance. Now Nasser had reacted by grabbing for Egypt the great symbol of European colonialism, the vital waterway that linked Britain and France to the East; a waterway built by the French, half purchased by Disraeli for Britain, still jointly controlled by both nations. It was a gesture guaranteed to twist the British lion's tail and bring one last roar of imperial outrage. Which it did.

At Reuters that night, assignments were handed out rapidly: biography of Nasser, summary of events leading to nationalization, comments from British and other leaders. The desk was thinly manned. I was asked to turn out a rapid history of the Suez Canal. For an experienced rewrite man, able to gulp facts at a glance and quickly regurgitate some very presentable instant history, it would have been an easy job. I was too green. I ordered up from the Reuter library whatever they had and plunged into reading long detailed accounts and making notes, like a student. After an hour, the filing editor began asking where my first "takes" were. I told him I was still researching. He said I had better start writing: who did I think I was working for — the *Encyclopaedia Britan-*

nica? Obediently I rolled some copy paper into the typewriter, and typed in the slug and dateline. Then I stared for a long time, wondering how to begin.

What made it worse was that I was three days into one of my many efforts to give up smoking. Usually, I wrote everything with a cigarette burning on the edge of the desk. Now I kept reaching down automatically for the cigarette that wasn't there. Finally, after a second, less-friendly order to get my copy moving, I bummed a cigarette from another subeditor, lit it, and immediately started writing.

I was hooked on the Suez story after that. I was amazed at the reaction in Britain. It unleashed the most rabid nationalism, most sadly in Anthony Eden, the political hero of the Appeasement Crisis in the '30s. The ailing prime minister was drawing pathetic parallels with the glories of his past, when he resigned from the prewar Chamberlain government rather than countenance the further appeasement of Hitler.

I thought something had come unhinged in these sane Englishmen, whose greatest virtue was that they always acted temperately and in right measure.

On August 8, two weeks after Nasser's seizure of the canal, Eden made a broadcast to the nation. Both in his mind and in the country, it evoked something of Churchill's grand backs-to-the-wall broadcasts of wartime. I had mistaken the time and had left a pub too late with a friend, meaning to get home to the radio in time. But as we came through Earls Court, cars were stopped everywhere, their windows open, and small crowds had gathered to listen to Eden. There were so many, and the traffic was so still, that we could hear the speech almost uninterrupted from car radio on to car radio without stopping.

"This is a matter of life and death to all of us," Eden said. Then the echoes of the '30s: "The pattern is familiar to many of us. We all know it is how fascist governments behave and we remember only too well what the cost can be of giving in to fascism.

"We do not seek a solution by force," Eden concluded, "but I must make this plain: we cannot agree that an act of plunder which threatens the livelihood of many nations should be allowed to succeed."

It was immediately apparent to me that the analogy was absurd. It was far-fetched to compare Nasser's ambitions or power to Hitler's, but it also perversely ignored what was happening in the world. Nasser was a successful manifestation of the emerging wave of nationalism — often cocky, insufferable, irritating, but legitimized by the long history of colonial suppression, however benign. Nasser was legitimized in a way that American blacks were just beginning to feel legitimized in their protests against the remaining segregation: past inequities justified extraordinary remedies. The next year, President Eisenhower had to send federal troops to enforce the integration of Little Rock High School. But, the United Kingdom, staggering from one postwar economic crisis to another, did not have the power to impose its will.

I comfortably assumed that all this imperialist raving was theatrical "noises off" to impress the Tory party while a quiet and reasonable deal was struck. It was true that warlike preparations went forward. Reservists were mobilized, transport ships requisitioned. In September, sailing a chartered yacht off the south coast, I had seen scores of them, riding at anchor, waiting for a mission to the Mediterranean. But I never believed that Eden would actually go to war, would be the aggressor. In fact, all the heat of summer seemed dissipated by the interminable conferences of the fall.

When the moment actually came, I was stupefied. Israeli forces launched a surprise attack on Egypt. On the pretext of protecting the vital canal, Britain and France attacked Egypt. There was a strong smell of collusion, strenuously denied at the time, later confirmed. I remember the evening the British actually bombed Port Said, October 31, to soften it up for a parachute drop. I could not believe that these same Englishmen who had suffered so much the bombing of their own cities, only thirteen years before, could actually be dropping bombs on defenseless Egyptian civilians. I felt betrayed. I felt as many young Americans must have at the time of the Cambodian incursion and Kent State — politicized, radicalized with a political event engaging my emotions for the first time in my life.

The United States deplored the Anglo-French attack and tried to get a cease-fire. Hugh Gaitskell, leader of the opposition Labour party, broke with the tradition of political unity at home when troops are engaged overseas. He bitterly attacked the Eden government. Moreover, the publicly funded British Broadcasting Corporation gave equal weight in its overseas news bulletins to Eden's position and to Gaitskell's. That was unheard-of neutrality. The BBC was also reliving its World War II glories. The corporation said it had to maintain the credibility established in wartime as a worldwide voice of truth. That produced a storm of Tory vituperation against the BBC in Parliament, but the policy stuck.

One of my jobs during that political whirlwind was called Overnight Newspaper Milking. That meant culling editorials and news items from the British press and feeding them on the Reuters service to different parts of the world. It gave me a very complete feel for the range of opinions and passions. Nothing had so divided the British people and their news media as the Suez adventure. And for a generation, one's instinctive position on Suez became a litmus test of political identity.

The Suez experience trained my political ear; made it sensitive to the nationalistic hocus-pocus that grips nations at times of crisis, even sane nations like Britain and the United States. That is why, despite its vacuousness, I think the United Nations is useful. When rational men are moved to dangerous strategems in the grip of some nationalistic brainstorm, the U.N. is the right place for them to cool off.

But Suez played another role. It gave the Soviet Union some shelter from the full ferocity of world opinion, for the brutal suppression of the Hungarian revolution.

As Britain and France attacked Egypt, Soviet tanks rolled into Budapest and savagely crushed the Hungarian attempt to break away from the Soviet bloc and become a neutral independent state.

There was a tendency, which I shared, to transfer some of one's disgust and impotence over Hungary to Eden. If Britain and France had not distracted the world with their foolish and doomed exercise, the Kremlin might not have been able to "get away with" the savagery in Budapest, we argued. It was nonsense. President Eisenhower was not going to threaten war (especially on the eve of an election) to stop the Soviets from disciplining one of their own satellites. All Suez did was to let Moscow escape with only a share of the world's disgust, whatever that meant; while under the Cold War double standard, Anglo-French "imperialism" took a worse pasting from the Third World than the Soviet's.

Khrushchev secured his ends. Eden did not. Faced with an overwhelming vote in the United Nations General Assembly, Eden ordered a cease-fire on November 6. He was ill and emotionally close to nervous collapse. Shortly afterward he resigned as prime minister to be succeeded by Harold Macmillan.

There is an ironic footnote. In his memoirs, Eden relates that John Foster Dulles later asked him in amazement why he withdrew his forces before taking the canal.

Suez left me with a political identity and a sense that an important punctuation point had been reached in history. Whatever the traditional legalisms of property and rights acquired under colonial advantage, whatever indemnities or compensations might be argued, there was a logic in the rapid decolonization of the underdeveloped world; a logic as irresistible as it was in Boston in 1776, but with a far wider approbation in 1956; a logic impatient of niceties and of counsels of caution. There clearly had to be an explosion of fresh nationalism before the world could settle down into some mature understanding of interdependence.

It was easier, perhaps, for a Canadian to understand this, than for an Englishman or an American. If they delved into odd corners of their constitutional situation, Canadians could still find reason to smart under the colonial yoke. Through the British Commonwealth they had sympathetic access to the minds of West Indians, Africans, Asians, and Indians. Canadians were probably the world's least xenophobic nation. John Kenneth Galbraith, who grew up as a Canadian, once told me that he had "a very thin sense of nationalism." So do most Canadians. We are psychic bridges to many peoples. I slowly began to see the value of being Canadian.

Hungary at first thrilled, then sickened me. I could follow it minute by minute in the Reuter office down to the last desperate message from the Freedom Fighters in Budapest.

The uprising planted in me the conviction that has never left me: whatever contradictions might exist in our Western systems, they are as nothing beside the fundamental absurdity and inhumanity of the Soviet system. Time is ultimately on our side. Those absurdities eventually have to produce internal explosions.

This, of course, was the basic rationale for NATO and the Western policy of containing Soviet communism and, in Europe, it has been borne out by events, most recently in Poland.

The other conviction which dawned then was that it was essential that we in the West did not let our fear of communism, or the need to contain it, dilute the very values which made our system superior to theirs, the individual freedoms their system denied. That was a tendency the United States had only just experienced in the wave of McCarthyism.

My optimism in this regard got a tremendous boost from the other great event of 1956, Nikita Khrushchev's marathon speech denouncing the terror and repression of the Stalinist period. He made the speech in a tactical move to consolidate his own power at the last session of the Twentieth Party Congress in February 1956. The speech was secret but quickly leaked to the West. I processed some of that speech on the Reuters desk, first as leaks, later as official text. I then read the full 20,000 words as avidly as I was reading the contemporary Russian novels blossoming in the Khrushchev "thaw." It seemed that spring as though the Soviet system had some dynamic and capacity for peaceful change, however ponderous.

The bloody repression in Hungary came as a sobering check to my optimism but did not crush it.

I did not "cover" these events as I did later ones, on the scene, as a correspondent. But I was close enough to them journalistically to absorb the detail that a consumer of news has little access to. So, my first year as a full-time journalist left me with some discoveries and quickened perceptions which have colored the rest of my journey through the profession.

I found I belonged somewhere ideologically, which was comforting. I discovered that I was, instinctively, a liberal, as though I had been born with a gene that made my political vision sensitive to one color and not another. "Liberal" has a somewhat beaten down and despised connotation in the United States today. People shun the label, which is a pity. Liberalism in the classic sense is one of the great intellectual movements of Western civilization; its belief in individual freedom inspired the American Revolution. In the modern sense, liberalism has much to be proud of: not least the idea that government should create minimum conditions for a decent existence for its citizens. Western societies may quibble over the definition of "minimum conditions" — or safety net — but that aspect of liberalism remains a fundamental fact of life.

Instinctively, I find it more satisfying to belong with those people in all countries who put their trust in Man's best quality, his rational intellect and its ability to recognize and solve problems. It is distressing that the recent course of American politics has caused that trust to be ridiculed or dismissed as some sort of soft-headedness, inappropriate to a virile nation confronting the dangerous world. It will be unfortunate if being a "liberal" remains an embarrassment, if young Americans should begin to believe that conservatives are the only realists.

Each has its absurd extreme: liberalism tending to inspire foolish altruism and unwarranted optimism; conservatism leading to unbridled selfishness and paranoia. Taken in moderation, I prefer the liberal impulse: it is the impulse behind the great forces that have advanced mankind, like Christianity. I find it hard to believe that Jesus Christ was a political conservative, whatever views are espoused in his name today.

For all my instinctive liberalism, my experience of politics in many countries has not left me wedded to any particular political parties. Rather, I have found myself politically dining *à la carte*, on particular issues, seldom wanting to take the whole menu of one party's ideas. So I have always felt a bit of an outsider, a little detached. Whether that is an advantage for a journalist, as I can easily rationalize that it is, I can't be sure. What has made it easier to keep the professional part of me objective has been the experience of being pulled several ways on many issues.

One example is nuclear disarmament. This movement really began to flourish in the late 1950s in England, about the time that Khrushchev began to preach "peaceful coexistence" and realistic negotiations for nuclear disarmament began to be a possibility.

The British Campaign for Nuclear Disarmament started a tradition of Eastertime marches from Aldermaston, the British atomic weapons research center, to Trafalgar Square in London.

The philosopher Bertrand Russell gave his support, and his commitment moved me. He was in body then a frail old man but with the same indomitable spirit that had made him an advocate of unpopular causes for half a century. I had long admired his robust independence of mind and the clarity of his writing. He never minded flouting convention. He had the double self-assurance of great intellect and aristocratic background.

In the late 1950s, Russell acquired an American, Ralph Schoenman, as a secretary. I met Schoenman shortly after he had taken up his post. He told me that the first evening of his employment he dined with Lord Russell and his newly acquired and much younger third wife. Russell, then eighty-seven, sat at the head of the Georgian mahogany dining table, laid with the antique Russell family silver, and raised his glass: "I wish to drink a toast to longevity. I owe my longevity to intellectual stimulation — and fornication."

I found myself covering the Aldermaston marches, partly out of sympathy, partly because there was a Chaucerian appeal about walking through the English countryside in the spring-time; an appeal which could vanish rapidly when the march encountered freezing rains and straggled along main roads spattered by cars and trucks.

The practical trouble was that Russell advocated unilateral

nuclear disarmament, in Washington's eyes tantamount to inviting the Russians to occupy Western Europe without a fight. It was hard to dispute that argument, in the wake of events like Hungary and Khrushchev's threats to Berlin. Moreover, sympathy for Russell gave me trouble with another man I admired at the time, the Labour politician Aneurin Bevan. This lyrical and emotional Welshman, the most gifted speaker in the House of Commons that still included Churchill, was by now the Labour party's shadow foreign secretary. If Labour won the next election, as many thought it would, Bevan, the mercurial left-winger, would be foreign secretary of a key NATO government.

A furious ideological battle was raging both inside Bevan's breast and within the Labour party, a battle that continues to this day. One faction wanted to drag the party toward a Marxist, proletarian identity; the other toward a middle-of-the-road, Social Democratic position. Bevan's heart was with the left; his head, on this issue, with the right. At issue was whether a future British Labour government would commit itself to unilateral nuclear disarmament, thus gravely weakening the NATO Alliance.

It was one of the most exciting moments I can remember in politics. With one of those rare speeches that will ring in the ears of anyone who heard it, Bevan turned the Labour party around with sheer oratory. Even Churchill envied his gift and once told his doctor, Lord Moran: "When that fellow Bevan gets up he does not know what he is going to say and where he will end. But I have every word typed in front of me. An orator must be spontaneous."

Bevan was spontaneous all right, and Churchill had often been the target of the piercing phrases that shot from him in the heat of debate. Often, riding the waves of his lilting Welsh oratory, Bevan was slightly in danger of letting sound and emotion rush ahead of sense. But not this time. Rising after a parade of speakers clamoring for Britain to give up the hydrogen bomb, Bevan talked them out of it with every device of classic oratory, with scorn and wit and sympathetic understanding:

"Everybody argued about the horror that the hydrogen

bomb is in reality, but what this conference ought not to do, and I beg them not to do it now, is to decide upon the dismantling of the whole fabric of British international relationships without putting anything in its place . . . if you carry this resolution and follow out all its implications and do not run away from it, you will send a British Foreign Secretary, whoever he may be, *naked into the conference chamber*."

And the way he pronounced "naked" was at once so funny and so telling that the conference began to thaw.

"What you are saying is . . . that the British Labour movement decided unilaterally that this country contracts out of all its commitments and obligations entered into with other countries and members of the Commonwealth — without consultation at all. And you call that statesmanship? I call it an *emotional spasm*."

Those are the phrases the press picked up — "naked into the conference chamber" and "emotional spasm" — and they were quoted for years. But Bevan was not through. There were still hostile shouts from the hall. The part that brought them around was in a very different, unscornful tone and a passage that perfectly expressed what I then felt about the Cold War.

Bevan said: "I have thought about this very anxiously. I knew this morning that I was going to make a speech that would offend and even hurt many of my friends. Of course. But do you think I am afraid? I shall say what I believe, and I will give the guidance that I think is the true guidance, and I do not care what happens. But I will tell you this, that in my opinion, in carrying out this resolution with all the implications I have pointed out, you will do more to precipitate incidents that might easily lead to a third world war."

There were shouts of "rubbish" and "shame" and "oh" from the hall.

"Just listen. Just consider for a moment all the little nations, running one here and one there, one running to Russia and the other rushing to the U.S.A., all once more clustering under the castle wall, this castle wall or the other castle wall, because in that situation, before anything else would have happened, the world would have been polarized between the Soviet Union on the one side and the U.S.A. on the other. It is against that deadly dangerous negative polarization that we have been fighting for years. We want to have the opportunity of interposing between those two giants modifying, moderating and mitigating influences. We have been delighted because other nations are beginning to take more and more independent stands. We are delighted because the Iron Curtain has been becoming more and more pliable. We are delighted because nations of different political complexions are arising. We are delighted because the texture of international relationships is changing. . . .

"I know that you are deeply convinced that the action that you suggest is the most effective way of influencing international affairs. I am deeply convinced that you are wrong. It is therefore not a question of who is in favor of the hydrogen bomb and who is against the hydrogen bomb, but a question of what is the most effective way of getting the damn thing destroyed."

He won. The conference overwhelmingly voted with him. The Labour party remained respectable in American eyes and Nye Bevan, the left-wing rebel, was transformed into the cautious statesman. Labour lost the 1950 election to the brilliant Tory leader, Harold Macmillan, but Bevan had his moment in the sun.

I quote at such length, not only because the issues are still relevant today, but because no one can speak like that now. It is a masterpiece of rhetoric delivered ad lib. It deserves to be printed in a textbook on language; to be spoken aloud; to be studied for the poetry as well as the sense.

One's political heroes, like Adlai Stevenson, are seldom without flaws. Bevan had many: temper, inconsistency, laziness. But he moved and inspired people, and when he died of cancer in 1960, I drove two hundred miles to Wales to his funeral, to do a report for NBC but also because I wanted to go.

Bevan came from the coal mining valleys of Wales, rich in music and brave spirit. Both he and his father had been miners. His father died of miner's lung disease with no medical benefit to pay for treatment. That was one of the demons that drove Nye, and he became the architect of Britain's National Health Service in the postwar Labour government.

Later, there was a grand memorial service in Westminster Abbey. But the funeral service was in a small chapel in the village of Tredegar and the attendance was small because it was so far from London.

Bevan was an agnostic and they kept the ceremony very simple. There were a few prayers, then the congregation sat while a recording was played of the slow movement from Beethoven's Sixth Symphony, the Pastoral. It was very moving. My gaze left the front of the church and wandered out of the windows to the tops of the nearby hills, almost lost in a green mist. I fancied the music rising up and rolling over those hills into the next valleys, as Bevan's incomparable voice had done: as a boy when he walked those hills declaiming poetry; as a politician burning with indignation for the misery in these valleys; finally as the graying statesman, attempting, in his words, to "modify, moderate and mitigate: the madness of the nuclear arms race."

So, both as a journalist and as an emerging political being, I was born into the Cold War. It has kept rearing its ugly head these past twenty-five years. The Cold War was the one recurring event in my journalistic career. Whenever I thought it had ended (and I interred it several times) or could be ignored or was being exaggerated, there it was again.

The Cold War was an endless fund of stories, most of them of the dire, abstract variety that make good copy for the doomsaying newspaper columnists. There were fewer stories of the human dimension, where you could see what the tension was doing to people; not merely what it was doing to the careers of soldiers and politicians.

There were two events in which the Cold War very nearly became terrifyingly hot, Berlin and Cuba. By the accident of assignment, I found myself in both places. In those and in many other stories, the Cold War became a part of my life, to an extent I never really appreciated until I began to assemble stories for this book.

FIVE

Tangier

A<small>LTHOUGH</small> I <small>NEVER</small> set out to become a foreign correspondent, even a journalist, the thrill of it took a big surge
when I got my first assignment abroad as a special correspondent for Reuters. I had served on the desk for nearly five
years when the editor in chief asked me to go to Tangier,
Morocco, for two weeks. The story sounded dull enough, a
conference of the United Nations Economic Committee for
Africa, but the location seemed fabulous to someone as
travel-starved as I chronically felt.

In later years, one of the repeated excitements of jumping
off from London to cover a story overseas was the moment of
leaving the gloom of the British winter, bursting through the
clouds about Heathrow Airport into brilliant sunshine. Taking off for Tangier in January 1960, the effect was wonderful.
It was the first time I had ever flown anywhere; in fact the
first time I had been off the ground except for a demonstration flight. So everything of the experience was vividly new.
The BEA Viscount made a stop at Gibraltar and I had a chat
with Reuter's Gibraltar stringer before the short hop across
the Mediterranean to Tangier.

That wonderful, ripe, polyglot city dazzled all my senses;
exposed for the first time to Mediterranean light, to palm
trees, to the limpid airs of those southern latitudes, to mina-

rets, to veiled Arab women, I felt drenched by sensory stimulation: colors, smells, noises. Amid all those distractions, I
was very anxious to make all the right moves professionally. I
had never traveled on an expense account before: I worried
about every penny (or Moroccan franc) that I spent. I even
moved to a cheaper hotel because, to my parsimonious private
ways, the one I was sent to was charging too much. When I
got back to London and turned in my first expense report,
the managing editor, an otherwise stern Scotsman called Doon
Campbell, brought it back to me with the gentle observation
that I might look at it again. Translated by my less diplomatic colleagues, that meant, "For God's sake, pad it or
you'll ruin the fucking game for everyone else."

In other ways Reuters went to extraordinary lengths to save
money, and because of the habits developed there, I was repeatedly shocked at the profligacy I later encountered in American commercial television. One of the major costs of a wire
service is in correspondents' filing their messages back to head
office, and Reuters ran stringent controls to keep those costs
down.

The reason for my conference with the stringer in Gibraltar was to set up a procedure for him to receive my copy
and cable it on to London. From Gibraltar he could use the
penny press rate; cabled from Tangier direct, the same messages would have cost many times more.

Much wire service material moves without urgency; for
example, what Reuters called "curtain-raisers," long stories
describing an upcoming event, like the conference I was covering: which countries were attending, who the leading personalities would be, what the agenda was, what issues would
cause controversy. Dull stuff to the layman, but bread and
butter for a wire service which might have client newspapers
in half of the nations of Africa. A small African country would
gobble up pages of a speech by their own foreign minister,
which no one else would print. I was instructed to move all this
worthy but not very electrifying material the cheap way,
through Gibraltar. Anything urgent I could cable direct.

The cheap way was exotic and nerve-racking. I would write
my copy in the hotel, seal it in an envelope, then take a taxi

down to the harbor to the *Mons Calpe,* the ferry that crossed daily to Gibraltar. It was made famous by the movie *Captain's Paradise* with Alec Guinness. My orders were to find the First Officer and give him the envelope, which our man in Gibraltar would pick up at the other end. It wasn't as easy as it sounded. The Tangier harbor authorities took a lot of persuading, and bribing in the end, to be convinced that I was not smuggling something exotic. The policemen guarding the *Mons Calpe*'s gangway didn't want me going on board without a ticket. They required some lubrication as well. In the end, the effort was taking three or four hours a message, longer than the reporting and writing the stories, so I abandoned it.

The conference was interesting enough. The British representative was John Profumo, then a minister of state at the Foreign Office. With an eye to having his activities fully reported in Britain, he was very helpful about briefings and letting me see advances of his speeches. He was so solicitous of my well-being that I began to wonder if he were gay; he had that languid, soft manner of some well-placed Englishmen that outsiders can mistake for effeminacy. Just in case, I stayed primly on my guard. My suspicions seemed a bit ludicrous a few years later when the scandal over Profumo's affair with the beautiful call girl Christine Keeler rocked the Macmillan government.

The event that really excited the conference was the announcement that Belgium was giving rapid independence to its huge Congo colony. It was an electric moment in the modern history of Africa. Britain and France, with many African colonies, each had a timetable and a plan for independence through stages. The Portuguese had no plan for Angola and Mozambique; they hung on until events nearly destroyed their mother country. Belgium had no plan. There had been no preparation for independence. Belgium, in short, seeing the writing on the wall, was panicking and getting out. I didn't know it then, but only a few months later I would be seeing firsthand the human cost of Belgium's neglect.

I worked very hard to cover the conference well, suddenly noticing that what was so obvious on the desk in London was not at all obvious in the field. The neat, crisp lead which sprang from the cable and practically typed itself in London was often hard to find. I waded through acres of stodgy speeches trying to find a lead point; or, when I had found one, convincing myself that I wasn't irresponsibly hardening up or distorting the material. I would sit in my hotel room, at my very old-fashioned portable typewriter, imagining the easy jokes back on the desk when they processed my copy — the jokes I loved to crack with the others about this or that damn-fool correspondent "who can't tell his arse from his elbow." It was a very chastening experience, my first understanding that the contempt is mutual and traditional.

They must have let some of my copy through unscathed because one of them made what will undoubtedly be the only front-page newspaper lead of my life. The newspaper was the *Ashanti Pioneer* of Ghana and the by-line was, gratifyingly, set in type half an inch high.

When the journalistic thrills palled I made the most of being in such an exotic place, swimming in the Mediterranean, sampling the little restaurants, visiting diplomats in their homes.

Tangier was terrific for a would-be writer still rather deliberately and self-consciously amassing experiences. Through the centuries it had lived under Portuguese, British, Spanish, and Moorish rules. In the twentieth century it was an International Zone with a duty free port. That made Tangier the headquarters for the lively Mediterranean smuggling trade and by 1956 that had gotten so out of hand that the administering countries gave the city formally to the Moroccans.

So in 1960 it was still ripe with the flavor of all the cultures which had touched it. The Tangerines spoke Spanish, French, Italian, English, and Arabic interchangeably. There was a separate old Moroccan walled city, the Casbah, surrounded by modern European areas, but their lives intermingled.

In the early mornings, strings of donkeys carrying preposterously large bales of fresh mint would come into the city to furnish the perpetual mint tea drunk in the cafés on the fringe of the Casbah. As the donkey trains clattered through the European streets, the vivid minty perfume of their passing mingled with the other predominating odors: the eucalyptus trees, urine where the streets were used as lavatories, French coffee, Moroccan cooking oil, car exhausts, black and Turkish tobacco.

What drew me irresistibly was the Casbah, its narrow overhanging alleys teeming with clamorous, mysterious life. The local British all warned: "Whatever you do, don't go into the Casbah at night," which of course made it obligatory to do. The Fearless Foreign Correspondent couldn't very well admit he was afraid to walk into places that held no terrors for Humphrey Bogart, could he? After all! Besides, it was stimulating to live with a little tickle of danger — or what you thought was danger, which produced the same effect. If I understood Sartre, choices like that made you more aware of being alive. So I paid several visits to the Casbah at night, squaring up my shoulders in my trench coat to look a little huskier, imagining a curved Moroccan dagger insinuating itself between my shoulder blades.

The only daggers I saw were the ornate souvenirs the merchants implore you to buy. In the middle of a crowded alley, wiry fingers would manacle my arm, impel me into a cavelike shop walled with carpets, and there cajole, wheedle, and importune me to part with some francs. They were willing to spend hours at it, providing little cups of coffee, with a line of flattery and self-pity so inventive it left me breathless.

It was still quite a relief at night to walk back into the broader, well-lit streets of the European areas.

Those streets had their own perils after dark. In the Casbah all you were pestered to buy were things; in the European sector, it was flesh. You could not walk in the side streets without a taggle of small boys trotting along on the edge of the pavement, plucking at your sleeve and chattering on in one language after another — "M'sieu, gentleman, señor, signor, . . . you want girl, jeune fille, señorita?" The more you said no, the more ingenious and extreme their offers became.

I was being pestered by a handful of these urchins one night — each trying to outbid the other — and I was still some distance from the hotel. To escape them, I ducked into a little bar that looked inviting.

It was a narrow place, with small tables along one side and a bar on the other. Part of the wall behind the bar was covered with cuttings from British newspapers, especially the less-inhibited and popular Sunday papers like the *Sunday Dispatch* and the *Pictorial*. They all concerned the brushes with British justice by the man who kept the bar. He had enjoyed several criminal careers, most recently smuggling. He had jumped bail on that charge and was now a renegade, safe from extradition in Tangier. He paraded his career with considerable pride, as another bar-owner would his war record, and was willing to talk for hours while keeping your glass full, laughing at the Scotland Yard detectives he had outwitted, telling how he had nearly been nabbed a score of times. Most of the stories displayed behind the bar were the product of such conversations; apparently a stream of Fleet Street feature writers had wangled their fares to Tangier to look him up.

When after several evenings of dropping in for a drink his conversation grew a little repetitious, I noticed another feature of his bar. Each night a tall Moroccan in a striped djellaba came in out of the shadows with a mongrel dog following closely. He sidled up to the bar, keeping his hood up, and produced from the folds of his robe a package wrapped in newspapers. The owner paid him several thousand francs out of the till and the Arab and his dog left.

Then the bar-owner would unwrap the package on the bar. It was fresh marijuana — which he called "kif" — and his customers would gather around for a share, then retire to their tables to begin filling pipes and rolling cigarettes.

Most were young Americans who had "dropped out" in the most comfortable way — living on remittances from wealthy parents. There was quite a colony of expatriate "beatniks" at the time in Tangier, some clustered around the novelist William Burroughs, whose *Naked Lunch* was written there and became a cult book on some U.S. campuses.

The subcolony I had stumbled into was, or seemed, decadent in the manner of the 1920s more than the '60s. They were ostentatiously dressed. One very thin young man always wore a dinner jacket. He was an asthmatic and carried a glass vaporizing apparatus with him. The bartender would boil a kettle of water to fill it and the young man would breathe the vapors, while alternately smoking kif. His wife, a very beautiful girl in her late twenties, always wore an ankle-length mink coat tightly belted and buttoned up to the neck. Even in it, she shivered frequently until the marijuana relaxed her. Then one evening she opened the mink coat to reveal nothing but a bikini underneath. She claimed to be a painter, her husband a writer. They stayed awake all night and slept all day, getting up at 7 P.M. This was "breakfast." As the evening wore on, her husband's asthma subsided. They and their friends became more animated and voluble, but except for bitchy gossip about their families back in America, they had very little to say.

They annoyed and fascinated me; they aroused all my puritanical, work-ethic contempt, yet they made me realize how extremely sheltered my life had been so far. How was I, the developing writer, to know the world, when things like this were happening and I didn't know anything about them? A few years earlier I had read Aldous Huxley's *Doors of Perception*, which lent literary respectability to experiments with hallucinatory drugs, in his case mescalin. I carried a clear memory of Huxley's ecstasy on noticing, with his drug-heightened perception, the beauty of the folds in his gray flannel trousers. I was eager for such experiences, but dead scared to try them. So my contempt for these masquerade bohemians, living like elegant parasites, was modified by curiosity: what did the "kif" do to them? How did it make them feel? Was it addictive? Were their perceptions really heightened?

Finally, I rationalized that if the stuff wasn't killing them, once wouldn't kill me. I owed my experience bank a deposit.

So I finally joined the pipe smokers for an evening and got "high" fairly quickly. It had two effects. It made me think that I talked brilliantly, with a flow of imagery and command of vocabulary quite beyond the ordinary. If that inspired conversationalist really existed that evening, I would like to be him all the time. Unfortunately, he was an illusion.

With a superb sense of well-being, feeling lightheaded but not out of touch with reality, I decided I would leave and walked back to the hotel. There I noticed the other effect.

The bedspread in my room was of a drab, oatmeal color, rough grained, probably locally woven. When I turned on the light, it sprang at me in bright colors I had never noticed before. I was startled and, with a nod to Huxley, carried a corner of the material to the light. It was true; in the weave were threads of iridescent blue, red, and green, normally lost in the general drab effect, now insistent and obvious. Very interesting. I went to bed, slept well, awoke refreshed with no hangover, and immediately carried the bedspread to the window. The colors had retreated. By bending the fabric, I could just discern the colored threads but their effect was much diminished. Conclusion: that variety of marijuana greatly heightened my color perception. Still, the experience was slightly worrying; and I didn't go back to the bar.

Years later, when smoking pot became so common, I tried it twice in London. It must have been a very different variety. It made me ill. My career as a drug addict was very brief.

What Tangier gave me was a greatly heightened desire to travel. A few weeks later, back in London, I had a choice between joining the *Financial Times* of London, with little travel prospect, and NBC News, with a lot. I took NBC, with the added inducement of a lot more money.

The Congo

NBC QUICKLY FULFILLED the promise of travel: within a year I had covered stories in France, Portugal, Algeria, and Ireland, as well as many parts of Britain. But the most exotic early assignment, and the most daunting, was the Congo. I arrived in Elizabethville on September 15, 1960, feeling almost as out of place under the furnacelike equatorial sun as the hero of Evelyn Waugh's *Scoop*, somewhat apprehensive about the varieties of violence that had marked the brief independence of the Belgian Congo.

Released from colonial bondage, the raw and ill-prepared Congolese nationalist leaders began fighting each other for control of their vast, rich swath of Central Africa. With the European political veneer stripped away, they fell back on the ancient tribal and regional arrangements the Belgians had tried for a century to erase. But like so much else in the sixties, what gave the Congo the world stage was the arrival of the Cold War, which stimulated a new, aggressive phase in the development of the United Nations. It was further complicated by Western mining interests as determined to hold on to the Congo's mineral wealth as the politicians were to keep the Soviets out.

It was heady stuff and it was all manifest in the struggle over the province of Katanga (now called Shaba). Katanga sat at the northern end of a spine of incredible mineral wealth running down the center of Africa. Its development was heavily influenced by Union Minière de Haut Katanga, the giant Belgian mining consortium which extracted the minerals. Belgium gave the Congo its independence on June 30, 1960. Ten days later Katanga declared its own independence. To Patrice Lumumba, the emotional prime minister, it looked like a Belgian plot to carve off the richest part of his nation. He threatened invasion to end Katanga's secession but he had no transport and his mutinous army was too busy massacring the fleeing Belgians. Finally Lumumba appealed to Moscow, which sent him fifteen Ilyushin air transports. To his opponents this was further evidence that Lumumba was dragging the Congo into a Marxist dictatorship. President Kasavubu dismissed Lumumba, but the fiery Patrice went on pretending to be prime minister anyway.

Early in September came reports that the Congolese army had finally invaded Katanga, which prompted speculation about full-scale civil war. There were daily reports of atrocities against whites. All this convinced NBC that they had better have a correspondent there, a decision doubtless hastened by the fact that a *New York Times* staff correspondent began filing from Elizabethville. In those days, the television networks valued the news judgments of the *New York Times* more than their own. So by the time I got to Elizabethville, it had become a hot international dateline, overshadowing the turmoil in Leopoldville, the Congo capital, half a continent away.

Elizabethville was headquarters for the leader of the rebellion, Moise Tshombe, self-styled president of Katanga, who lived in the former governor's palace surrounded by Belgian advisers and experts. Appearances alone made Tshombe look like a puppet of the Belgians.

Elizabethville was also headquarters for the four-thousand-man United Nations force assembled by Dag Hammarskjöld, the secretary-general, with a multiple mission: to keep the Congolese from killing departing Belgians; to prevent civil war; and to keep outsiders like the Soviets from interfering with the Congo's independence.

Elizabethville was a pretty town to watch a war from. If the Belgian colonists really were more rapacious and exploitive than their British neighbors in Northern Rhodesia, the Belgians more than compensated in elegance. The Rhodesian Copperbelt towns were raw and frontierlike. Elizabethville was elegant and charming. It gave Union Minière, its chief patron, a human and gracious face. It had wide residential streets of comfortable bourgeois houses, like Brussels transplanted. The streets were arched over by canopies of blue jacaranda trees, cool against the equatorial glare. But most of the houses were empty and locked.

The small downtown area was more forlorn. The streets of two-story shops and restaurants, lined with scarlet flamboyant trees, were largely deserted. Display windows were empty, except for limitless supplies of Arrow shirts and Coca-Cola.

Most of the white women and children had fled. The whites who remained were Belgian officials in Tshombe's government, people keeping the mines running, and a community of shop and restaurant owners, some long-settled Jews and Greeks.

At night there was nothing to do. As the evening began to cool off, small groups of men meandered through the few downtown streets, looking in the shops with no merchandise, discussing reports of the fighting and the value of the Congolese franc. Once in the dusk there was a larger-than-usual crowd of men clustered together watching something. When I joined them I saw they were watching, gravely and without humor, two dogs mating. There was not much to do in Elizabethville, except leave, or wait and try not to be too frightened while waiting.

By contrast, the Grand Hotel Leopold II, named after the former king of the Belgians, seethed with life. It was the social, gastronomic, news, and blackmarket center of Elizabethville. All the correspondents stayed there, as did United Nations officials and various anonymous Europeans who may have been Belgian agents fomenting the Katanga rebellion, or CIA, or SMERSH, for all I knew. United Nations officers, in Swedish or Irish uniforms, ate there. African painters and carvers laid out their works for sale on the marble floor of the lobby, and shifty white gentlemen came looking for currency deals.

Fear was a major ingredient in those transactions, almost a commodity in itself.

The official exchange rate was around 65 Congolese francs to the dollar. Officially, the exchange was sealed. Ordinary citizens could not change their francs for dollars. However, the only way to get out of Katanga was to get together enough hard currency, in dollars, pounds, or marks, to pay for it. So the whites who had stayed to keep their shops or restaurants open were anxious to accumulate dollars — just in case. They wanted to be ready to leave fast.

The rate went up if the news was bad, if tribesmen loyal to Lumumba attacked a village nearer Elizabethville. If attacks were farther away, or were beaten off, the rate went down. The merchants listened carefully to the BBC shortwave news broadcasts but supplemented them by questioning reporters while changing their money in the Leopold II.

It was in the journalists' interest to have the rate go up. It is the same in every crisis. The foreign correspondents pay their expenses in the local currency. If you can buy that local currency at a rate above the official rate, you win. You don't have to cook the expense account quite so badly to pay for all the extra drinking most reporters do in such places. You may even turn a little profit.

But foreign correspondents rarely get the chance to manipulate the rate as they did in the Congo.

The more worried the moneychangers were, the more they were prepared to pay for dollars. One particularly unpleasant and greedy man inspired a group of British correspondents to find a way to make him more nervous.

They sat down and wrote a wire service story about a fictitious raid on a small white settlement. It was much closer to Elizabethville than any recent attack. The details were lurid and horrible.

They put the story on the teletype in the post office, and let it run through the machine, without transmitting it to London. Then they brought back the carbon copy, folded and unfolded a few times to make it look more real.

When the moneychanger turned up they asked him what the rate for the day was and he said 90 francs to the dollar. They said that wasn't very good, considering the news. He asked what the news was, and they, reluctantly, cautioning him that it wasn't official, showed him the carbon. The rate went up to 130 francs to the dollar and he went back to his store to get more money to change.

The British reporters tend to set the tone in these places. They joke a lot more and drink a lot more than their more earnest American colleagues. They appear not to take any of what is happening seriously. And they manage to give an air of having been not only there, but everywhere else, and having done all this many times. Especially practiced in a group, it is a type of behavior that hides a lot of anxiety. It also makes them very good companions, infinitely knowledgeable about food, drink restaurants, hotels, bars, nightclubs, and where the girls are, if there are any.

The popular British press still writes as extravagantly, as colorfully, and with almost as little regard for the facts as the characters in *Scoop*. Fighting news was not easy to come by in Katanga. United Nations press briefings were quicksands of bureaucratic nonspeak. Katanga government information was propaganda. To get action stories you had to go and find them, especially since the much-heralded Congolese invasion became more elusive by the day. In fact it began to seem less an official invasion than a reckless sortie by a few hundred irregulars inspired by Lumumba. But their presence excited warriors of the Baluba tribe to rise up and kill followers of Tshombe, who was of the rival tribe. Tshombe hurriedly scratched together a small army, led by Belgians, which dealt savagely with the Balubas whenever they could reach them. The United Nations tried to stop this killing, by closing all airports and refusing transport for Tshombe's troops, but that just made the U.N. hated by all sides.

Finding action stories meant hiring small planes for the day to fly to the northern towns where fighting was reported. Several reporters would pool resources for these flights and, if they were lucky, they saw or heard something that made a new lead. Sometimes it was a bit thin.

The London *Daily Mail* correspondent was a large, amusing South African, called Peter Younghusband. On one of these flights for news, he came back and found a hole made by a stray rifle bullet in one wing. Younghusband cabled and the *Mail* bannered, "I Was Shot At By Baluba Rebels." The *Mail*'s chief rival was the *Daily Express*. The next day the Express-man (as they were by-lined) got a cable from London in the *Scoop* tradition: "YOUNGHUSBAND SHOT AT. WHY NOT YOU?"

After several days of getting acclimatized, Louis Hepp, the NBC cameraman, and I decided we should make one of these forays. Baluba tribesmen were said to have taken over several of the small mining towns north of Elizabethville and were killing whites. Tshombe's forces, in turn, had carried out re-prisals, including mass executions. In one incident, which brought a personal protest to Tshombe from Dag Hammar-skjöld, Katangese soldiers rounded up sixty-eight people in a town called Luena, drove them off in trucks, and shot them with their hands tied.

With Gordon Martin of Reuters, we hired a small, twin-engine plane flown by a dashing individual who had been a fighter pilot with the Royal Air Force in the Battle of Britain. Surviving that experience apparently purged him of all ca-pacity to feel fear. He was an English-speaking South African, whose casualness about everything was both reassuring and disconcerting.

We took off at dawn, in time to make several stops before making it back to Elizabethville before dark, since the U.N. closed the airport at night. We also had to make it with the fuel we started out with since there was no place to refuel.

The flight north was glorious. I sat beside the pilot and held on my lap the Esso road map, fifteen years old, which was the only way of navigating. Roads were so scarce in the bush that they became major landmarks, when you could see them through the thick canopy of vegetation. The most reliable features were the lakes, leading up to Lake Tanganyika. From ten thousand feet their shapes came quite close to the Esso map.

We made several landings, one of them, improbably, on the top of a grassy hill. That involved swooping down into a valley and climbing the contour of the hill so that the wheels touched on the upward slope. We passed the crest at high speed and came to rest going down the incline on the other side. There was a tin shack with an outpost of Katangese soldiers loyal to Tshombe, but all was quiet.

Hepp, who looked like an officer in his khaki bush outfit, got the ragged band of soldiers to fall into line for his camera. An NCO obligingly put them through some rudimentary drill and then marched them up and down the top of the grassy hill while Hepp squirted away with his hand-wound 16mm Filmo. Eventually he had enough and we went into the shack to get a briefing from the Katangese officer about where the enemy was supposed to be. About thirty minutes later we came out into the scorching noonday sun, to find the wilting troops still marching up and down because no one had told them to stop. People will do a lot of crazy things in front of a camera.

Using the officer's information, we stopped next at Bukama where there had been heavy fighting. The pilot approached cautiously. We sighted a small airstrip about ten miles off, a thin red earth gash in the dense green bush. He gently descended and we made a pass at treetop level over the earth strip. We could see some burned-out huts which were still smoldering. Oil drums had been rolled out to prevent planes from landing, but the pilot decided there was enough room, if we really wanted to land. Privately none of us probably *wanted* to. It looked decidedly eerie, too empty and too quiet. But since this was the sort of thing we were spending $1,000 of NBC's and Reuter's money to find, we all said yes, and he circled for a landing.

We came in bouncing on the rough earth. No one emerged from the vivid green of the bush. We got out of the plane. The pilot took out a pistol, checked that it was loaded, and said he would cover us from the plane.

We walked from the plane to the nearest huts. The village was primitive and empty. The smoke was curling up from the ruins of the huts, utensils and personal belongings lying where they had been abandoned, but no bodies. The sky was an intense blue, the foliage livid green, the earth brick red, the sun achingly hot and bright. It was incredibly quiet; no cicadas, no insect noises. None of us said anything. It felt as though we were being watched from the trees.

From outside one of the huts, I picked up a beautifully carved and polished club, made from the root of a small tree. It looked like a nice souvenir and perhaps a weapon.

Then, from a great distance, almost inaudible, we heard a truck. It approached very slowly. We were all scared because there was no way of knowing who might be coming. The little hairs on the back of my neck tingled. My intestines felt as if cold water were running through them. We looked back toward the plane, judging the distance we might have to run. It was a good two hundred yards away and looked a very frail refuge.

We discussed whether it was worth running to the plane or standing where we were as if we had a right to be there and nothing to be afraid of. We decided to stay. The truck was now very close. I threw the ornamented club a few yards away in case it looked too aggressive. By the time the truck broke into the clearing, we were all holding our breath.

It was a large military truck, full of armed black men. It was not until they drove right up to us that we saw the blue and white badges of the United Nations. So we were safe. They were Ethiopian troops. Their officer said Katangan troops had rounded up all the people in the village by the airstrip and had driven them away, burning the huts. He also said there had been a big battle nearby with many killed and wounded.

We drove in their truck to the one-story cottage hospital in Bukama, which overflowed with wounded men and their families. Wives and children camped in the narrow intervals between the beds, cooking, talking, and nursing the patients.

The only person attending medically to a score of wounded men was a Congolese who told us proudly he had been an orderly, sweeping the floor and carrying out bedpans. When the Belgians left, he had put on a white coat and promoted himself to doctor. Now he was very proud of himself, and with good reason. After the battle he had dressed all the wounds himself. He took us from bed to bed, showing off his patients, some grinning with superficial wounds, some fevered and distant with graver injuries.

The heat and smell inside made us nauseous. The "doctor" kept telling us to take pictures so that "tout le monde" could see. He would bend over a patient, show us the bandage, then calmly rip it off so that we could see the wound it covered.

To escape from the smell, we convinced him that it was too dark inside to film. So we went outside while he made several special patients get out of bed and come into the blazing sun where we could take their pictures.

He was particularly happy about one young man. He made the fellow face the camera and when Louis started filming, the "doctor" pointed proudly to an X of adhesive tape on his patient's chest. With the camera running, he ripped off the tape showing a neat entry bullet hole. He then twirled the grinning patient around, showed us another adhesive X on his back, and pulled that tape off too, revealing a tidy exit wound.

Like a magician finishing a trick, he flourished his arms and talked rapidly in French about the miracle of the man who had a bullet pass within millimeters of his heart. I hope the young man survived all this ceremonial uncovering of his wounds.

We flew on to Manono, a small town where an Irish contingent of the U.N. forces had kept the Balubas from killing seventy Europeans huddled in a police station. The Balubas were in control of the town. They let us walk around and film them and we soon found ourselves in a crowd of young Balubas, armed with a motley collection of old muzzle-loading rifles, machetes, spears, bows and arrows, and, as a gesture to the twentieth century, bicycle chains attached to short sticks. They were friendly enough when we assured them we were not Belgians. Still it was reassuring to have an Irish captain and several soldiers with machine guns watching from a dozen yards away.

The leader was a young man with a Lumumba chin beard, wearing a tiger-skin hat. He had been a schoolteacher, but when he asked what country I came from and I said "Canada," he asked me: "Where is that?" He said again that we must tell the world that the young people of Katanga supported Patrice Lumumba against the imperialist conspiracy represented by Tshombe. He sounded as though he listened a lot to Moscow Radio's African service. But he was very friendly.

Flying back to Elizabethville in the late afternoon, we did not get shot at but we had other excitements.

We spotted a herd of wild elephants and swooped down to see them more closely. There were about fifty, led by an almost white elephant. From only a few hundred feet above them it was an amazing sight to see them galloping, as if in slow motion, silently, their huge ears flapping in the wind of their own speed.

We were late and the sudden equatorial dusk began to close in, turning the green landscape into a warm velvet blackness, broken by little pinpricks of light from cooking fires in the bush, as though the heavens had been turned upside down.

The pilot was looking more and more often at the fuel gauges. Sitting beside him I could see that both tanks were almost empty. The fat little indicator needles were trembling ominously near the *E*, yet nothing showed us that Elizabethville was near. Five minutes, then ten minutes more of droning on through the night, my eyes locked on the shivering dials.

What would it be like to crash-land in that blackness beneath us? Not pleasant.

Finally, a strong white light showed distantly among the fires. It was Elizabethville, but the drama wasn't over. The pilot radioed the standard I.D. and request for landing. But the control tower began an argument in French. The airport was closed at dusk. United Nations orders. No one could land. Our pilot argued that we were running out of fuel. We began slowly circling the airport, keeping the small white light in view. The fuel guage's hands touched *Empty*.

I was beginning to sweat. More argument from the tower about their orders to close. More increasingly angry replies from our pilot. We circled further, and finally the pilot told the tower that if they wanted the responsibility of killing a planeload of American and British journalists they were doing the right thing. More argument, then finally from the control tower a resigned, "Vous pouvez atterrir." All at once all the runway lights went on and we landed.

"Bit of a close thing, that," shouted our pilot, as though he had just landed a Spitfire after a brush with a Messerschmitt.

The worst part of Elizabethville was the P.T.T., the post office, which controlled the radio circuits. Some of the Belgians who knew how to run things had stayed but left some functions to bewildered Congolese with little technical training. It was a routine job to patch through the small radio booth to the transmission equipment that would carry my voice by shortwave to Brussels. (The Belgian P.T.T. would then, in principle, switch it through to New York.) But it was seldom done, and I finally got quite good at walking through their control room into the racks of equipment and putting the patches in myself when they weren't looking, which was a lot of the time.

That was only the beginning. I had to meet two prearranged New York circuits every day, timed to bring in material for the early-morning news programs, like the *World News Roundup* and the *News on the Hour*, and another for the afternoon. That meant lunchtime and dinnertime in Elizabethville. I would go to the P.T.T. with the stories I had written in the hotel, make sure I was patched through, go into the small soundproof cubicle, sit down at the microphone, and put on headphones. I then had to call the Brussels switching center until they answered. Whether the transmitter was not switched on, or not functioning, or the atmospherics were bad, or the operators in Brussels couldn't be bothered monitoring their ungrateful former colony, I never knew. I could sit there for hours, and often did, intoning:

"Allo, Bruxelles, âllo, Bruxelles, En-Bay-Say [NBC] Elizabethville, attendant New York. Allo, Bruxelles, âllo, Bruxelles," as the sweat rolled down and dappled the script, and strange shiny bugs crawled up the acoustical tiles on the walls. If I were very lucky, Brussels answered in about thirty minutes and put me through to New York, and NBC recorded my pieces and I went to the hotel to join all the newspaper and wire services reporters enjoying lunch or dinner.

Most of the time that didn't happen. It took one or two hours, sometimes three, to raise Brussels and reach New York. By that time NBC was no longer expecting the circuit and would therefore assume that I was coming up specially and had something hot. When I delivered the rather innocuous routine stories I had written only because there was a circuit to meet, they would shout across six thousand miles of short-wave circuit: "What the hell are you bothering us for with this stuff now? We're trying to take in Cleveland. They've got a big fire." I couldn't explain that I had been sitting for two or three hours trying to get through.

New York wouldn't cancel the prearranged circuits in case something very hot broke and I wouldn't be able to order one. I was too unsure of myself simply to ignore the times and meet the circuit only when I had something good. I doggedly met every one and I missed a lot of meals. I made up for them later.

I felt very green among the correspondents more seasoned at this kind of assignment, green and scared. It was one thing to court a little danger for the titillation of it in a place like Tangier. It was another to be surrounded by the potential for real and almost indiscriminate violence. So I lived through that assignment with a certain background anxiety.

Sometimes, fortunately, I got scared only when it was all over — like the incident on the run to Rhodesia.

Every so often a couple of correspondents would drive from Elizabethville to Northern Rhodesia, where the banks were open, to collect money cabled from the head offices and to shop for things you couldn't buy in the Congo, like liquor and cigarettes. Since the bars and hotels of the Copperbelt towns were inviting after the doomed, all-male atmosphere of Elizabethville, the trips had an R&R aspect as well.

The drive was a little hairy, one hundred miles of poor dirt road through bush country with scattered villages of mud huts. Some of the villagers were Lunda and some Baluba, and we were not very sure which was which or how to tell the difference. The evidence on the road was ominous. During the initial fighting after independence, the Belgians had fled in their cars toward the Northern Rhodesian border. Evidently, many never made it, because the hulks of their shot-up, burned-out vehicles still littered the roadside every few miles. You almost never met another car.

On one trip, our ancient Vauxhall overheated. We stopped and decided we needed to find some water. The bush around us looked empty, tall trees and thicker low vegetation punctuated with huge red earth anthills. But when our eyes got used to looking through the vegetation, we could see some huts a few hundred yards off the road. Since we had to have water to get the car going, we walked into the kind of village you see in the *National Geographic*, stamped bare earth around half-a-dozen huts of mud and thatch, the men idle, the children milling around, and the women working. One woman was grinding meal, using a hole in a felled log as a mortar and another heavy log with a rounded end as a pestle. We couldn't tell whether they felt any hostility toward us or not. They seemed indifferent, sullen, lethargic. I took some pictures and we found a man who spoke a little French. He got us some water in an old can and we drove off without any trouble, feeling very adventurous.

Some weeks later, I drove down the same road, with Erroll Friedman, a South African reporter for the Associated Press. We stayed overnight in Chingola, Northern Rhodesia, did our banking, and completed all the errands other reporters had given us. As we headed back, my rented Volkswagen beetle was loaded down with boxes of cigarettes, bottles of wine, toothpaste, soap, shaving cream, and other things we had been commissioned to bring back, as well as our luggage.

It was around noon, very hot, the sun directly overhead. We had seen no one on the road all day. I must have been drowsy from the heat because I rounded a curve a little too fast. The VW skidded and one of the wheels hit a rock. Very slowly, it seemed, the car began to roll over, while still going forward at about 40 mph. It did one complete revolution and, as the door on my side hit, jamming me against it with the weight of Friedman falling on top of me, I kept thinking, Well, this is it! Any moment now it's really going to hurt. This is it. But it never did hurt. The car came to rest on its side with my face lying in the dirt through the open driver's window. Friedman was jumbled up on top of me, apparently half knocked out and dazed. I pulled myself past him and out his window.

Outside, things looked very depressing. The wheels were still spinning in the air but every inch of the body was crumpled from the rolling over. Our bags and shopping were strewn forlornly back along fifty yards of road. There was thick red dust settling on everything.

There was no sound, except the high wheezing of the cicadas, and it felt as though there wasn't another creature within miles. Then I turned around and saw about a dozen black men standing in the bush just off the road, silently looking at the battered car. They were all armed, some with spears, some with very ancient rifles, and some with modern guns. Some wore African dress, others ragged trousers and shirts. They were sullen looking and unfriendly. It occurred to me that the nearest Rhodesian town was about fifty miles behind us, Elizabethville was fifty miles ahead, and there was nothing in between but bush.

I asked if anyone spoke English. There was silence, then one of the men wearing trousers spoke up in French. To make sure he understood from the start that we were not the hated Belgians, I explained that we were reporters telling the world about their glorious struggle for independence and that we'd had an accident, which was pretty obvious, and asked if he would help me. He muttered something and half of his warriors began picking up our fallen shopping — dusty bottles of wine, packets of fifty Rhodesian cigarettes — and piling them by the roadside. The others went over and very easily tipped the car back onto its wheels. They wrenched the door open and I helped Friedman out, still dazed, his hands covered with blood from holding on to the sunroof when the car went over.

The fenders were so dented in that they pressed against the tires. I felt the metal to see if it would easily pull away. It was burning hot from the sun and I couldn't budge it. But the leader, or headman, said something to the others. They applied very large hands to the fender, appearing not to notice the heat, and pulled it out effortlessly. I said that was great and could they do the others, and they did. It seemed best to keep them busy and I got the others to put all our cargo back in the car. I opened the compartment at the back and stared at the tiny engine.

The oil was clearly not in the crankcase where it should have been but seeping into the dust on the road. To look competent and busy I checked the dipstick. It showed nothing — obviously. Friedman sat back in the car to get out of the sun. The Africans now had nothing to do but stare at me unpleasantly, and, I thought, menacingly.

And then an amazing thing happened. In the distance we heard a car, the first we had encountered all day. It approached from Elizabethville, a very used-looking Peugeot. A white man was driving and he stopped. He was apparently Belgian. We exchanged one French phrase each.

"What happened?"

"We have no oil."

He glanced at the band of armed black men and at our car and me. He looked frightened, and his look made me feel uneasy. He said nothing, but reached over the seat of his car and produced a gallon can of engine oil. Almost simultaneously, he pushed it out the window into my hands, blew his horn to clear the way, and drove off very rapidly, sending up a cloud of dust like a red smokescreen.

It didn't occur to me just then that meeting one car on one hundred miles of empty road in the middle of Africa, with a gallon of oil, was straining the probabilities a bit. There was no time to think. It was too important to keep busy. Knowing perfectly well that the engine was hopelessly damaged by the accident I opened the compartment anyway, removed the cap, and slowly filled the crankcase. I put the empty can by the side of the road, closed the engine top, got in the driver's seat, and closed the door.

Just for the hell of it, I turned the key, and the engine started instantly. Unbelievable! The moment it roared to life, the Africans all started shouting at me and waving their weapons. The leader shouted at them. It felt very menacing. The leader was beside my door. I reached in my pocket and clutched all the money I could grab — Congolese, Rhodesian, British, and U.S., coins and bills. I held it out the window and the leader took it with both hands cupped. The shouting grew louder. Some of the men were leaning on the car. I put it in gear and drove forward, forcing them to stand away. I could hear the shouting grow louder still and I wondered if they were going to shoot. I couldn't see behind because the rearview mirror was at a crazy angle. The car wouldn't go higher than second gear, but we were away. There was a sharp bend about a hundred yards down the road. When we came to it, the front wheels wouldn't turn enough to make the corner. The fenders hadn't been pulled out enough. I had to reverse, go forward, reverse, go forward, three times to get around the bend, all the time expecting a crowd of furious Africans to come running after us. There wasn't time to look. We were few miles down the road before we began to relax.

A half bottle of red wine was rolling around on the floor at Friedman's feet. I said: "We need a drink. Can you open that?" Since there was nothing to open it with, he held the bottle with his raw and bloody hands and picked at the cork with his fingernails. Finally, he shoved it into the bottle. We each had several swigs of Mouton Cadet, which had not suffered from its adventures in the Dark Continent.

Very slowly, in second gear, taking every sharp corner in several bites, we limped back to Elizabethville. We pulled up in front of the Leopold II hotel to find the other correspondents looking very fresh, drinking gin and tonic on the terrace. Some of them came running over when the battered VW pulled up.

"You been ambushed?" a British reporter asked greedily, scenting a story to file. He looked disappointed when we said we hadn't been shot at, and went back to his drink.

But some of the others came into my room in the hotel and listened as I told them the story. I was sitting on the bed. They were standing around saying things like "my God" and "you were lucky," when two strange things happened. I suddenly became very frightened, actually shivering, and then I fell into a very deep sleep.

I felt fine when I woke later that evening but have never been certain whether the situation on the road had been truly dangerous or not.

The British consul's insurance company thought the car a total write-off, only worth scrapping. I thought it was a great advertisement for Volkswagen.

The Congo cost many of the principals their lives: Lumumba, Tshombe, even Hammarskjöld. Lumumba was shot in an alleged attempt to escape from army detention. There has always been a strong odor of CIA complicity. Tshombe survived many hair-raising adventures only to die in his sleep in Algiers in 1969.

Dag Hammarskjöld was killed in October 1962 when the plane flying him to Elizabethville crashed in a storm in Northern Rhodesia. I was sent to Sweden to cover his funeral. It took place where he was born, in the town of Uppsala, site of the university and of a soaring cathedral in pale red brick.

The route to the old cemetery was lined by university students wearing their white, peaked caps. In each curtained window a candle was burning. The gravesite was arched over with old trees, their leaves yellowing in the cool autumn.

The setting was as far removed in spirit from the fierce climate of Africa as Hammarskjöld's own austere personality from the flamboyance and passion he dealt with.

The Congo, renamed Zaire, was saved for the West. General Joseph-Desiré Mobutu seized power and has wielded it with authoritarian competence, and American backing, ever since. Katanga's secession ended and its mines are running efficiently. Whether that was quite the nature of the independence Hammarskjöld was intervening so controversially to promote is another question.

But I came away convinced that independence for these colonies was no political-science abstraction. I fancied I could see its effects in the eyes and the bearing of the rural Congolese who crowded into the open-air markets in Elizabethville. The women walked erect and proud, in noticeable contrast to the apologetic shuffle of the blacks only a few miles away in Rhodesia, then still a British colony. The difference may have been all of my imagining, but it appeared to me that lack of independence acted on people like a vitamin deficiency. Even if that were true only figuratively, it helped to explain many struggles ahead as the scent of freedom swept the continent.

SEVEN

France

THERE IS NO FRENCH BLOOD in my family, that I know of, but I feel an affinity for France often stronger than for my own country. Other places have palled on frequent visiting. Never France. To go there now is as entrancing to me as the first time, in July 1955, when I arrived at the Gare du Nord by boat train from England and took a room at a very cheap hotel across the street. It cost 500 old francs (about $1.75) a night, and the patron himself walked up five flights to deliver the *café complet* for breakfast. My future wife and I commuted between that hotel and hers, somewhat grander, near the Madeleine. The weather was golden, we were in love and really alone together for the first time with nothing to do for ten days but enjoy ourselves.

It is asking a bit much of a city to continue living up to an introduction like that. But Paris has never disappointed. Nor has the rest of France. I have made perhaps fifty visits, some as long as six weeks, some as brief as a few hours, and I still seize any pretext to go there.

The French have humiliated and patronized me, as they have every foreigner and each other. They have also treated me with extreme kindness and civility. I have seen what is squalid and brutal about France and, obviously, what is elegant, but I doubt that I will ever look at it quite objectively; I love it too much, as one is inclined to love things one can't quite attain, like real mastery of the French language.

My debt to journalism is incalculable when I consider how many times I have had to go there to work in the last twenty-five years.

I don't think I learned much journalism from the French. *Le Monde*, which every reporter admires and envies somewhat, is too austere a model for American and British newspapers. It makes even the *New York Times* seem racy and superficial. But I revel in the romantic clichédom of popular French crime reporting, in papers like *France-Soir*. They always begin with color and mood and then move on to the facts, or some semblance of them, with their unabashed preference for lurid crimes of sex in otherwise dreary provincial towns.

I used the style once quite successfully for the BBC in a documentary about the murder of a prostitute in Montmartre by an unemployed, lame stablehand. The story was really about his unprecedented legal plea that he was driven by a genetic defect, having two Y (or male) chromosomes, a syndrome he shared with some other violent gentlemen like Richard Speck, the Chicago killer of eight nurses. The piece was actually a fairly serious study of that condition, its incidence among violent criminals, and its validity as a plea of diminished responsibility. The producer, David Harrison, as keen a francophile as I, rationalized that we really should recreate the atmosphere and the crime itself, to draw the audience in, the British, *nom de Dieu*, being so besotted with sex and crime as a nation that they mightn't pay any attention unless we spiced it up. We had several marvelous days doing just that, living our own Simenon novel in the grubby side streets and bars off the boulevard de Rochechouart. We got a BBC secretary to don mesh stockings and black high-heeled shoes to play the victim. We got a sleazy café proprietor to show us at which table she had met the murderer and what was playing on the jukebox ("I'll Have the Last Waltz with You"). Harrison talked the police into racing their van up and down the crowded streets of Montmartre with a klaxon hooting. And of course, the weather being cold, we were often forced to fortify ourselves with nourishing meals and beverages in suitable restaurants, well known to the French film crew.

So many French situations are memorable because they begin or end with or revolve around eating something.

In the late spring of 1956, I took a walking trip in Normandy with Clare McDermott, a reporter in Reuter's Paris Bureau. We set out from Abbeville, heading south to hit Neufchâtel where we could get a train back to Paris.

On the second day out, we felt strong and the weather was fine, so we pushed on without worrying about finding a place to spend the night. In the late dusk we found ourselves in a very simple village with no hotel. We were famished and worried first about eating. The only hope was a small, unpretentious café and the *patronne* threw up her hands at being asked for dinner unexpectedly. But when we explained that we had walked all day, she softened, and said, "Let me see what I can do. Do you like soup?"

We could have eaten the red-checkered tablecloth while she was away in the kitchen, but she soon returned with two large bowls of mushroom soup. We got through that and half a loaf of fresh French bread washed down by red wine, and things were beginning to look up. She said, "I don't know what else I can give you. I have no food. Do you like eggs?" We said yes and presently she appeared with two *omelettes fines herbes*. She still looked worried and asked, "Do you like pâté?" A large chunk of *pâté de campagne* followed, then cheese, then an apple tart and coffee and calvados, it being Normandy and we feeling very expansive.

Between courses, the good lady stood by the table, her hands twisted in her apron, and asked where we came from, why we were walking, and so on. Like everyone else we met that week, her eyes lit up when she heard we were both Canadian. Canadian troops had liberated that stretch of Normandy countryside and she described the joyous moment when their tanks rolled down the street outside, the girls throwing flowers and kisses, the Canadian soldiers throwing coins to the children.

When we asked if there were an inn nearby where we could

spend the night, she said there was not but if we didn't mind staying in a nearby farmhouse, she was sure some neighbors would put us up. She put on a jacket and went out the back way leaving us alone in the café to finish our coffee and calvados. When she returned she gave us directions to a house down the road and said we could pay for everything in the morning.

The farmhouse turned out to be a fine old stone building with several wings. It was clearly a very prosperous farm. The kitchen where we were welcomed had a shiny new stove, refrigerator, and washing machine, the sort of large consumer goods still rare in Europe in the middle fifties.

The farmer was a ruddy-faced jovial man in his sixties, delighted to have visitors to talk to. He made us sit down at the large kitchen table and poured us small glasses of rum with a sugar cube in the bottom.

And then he began to talk. He talked for about four hours as we, already exhausted from walking twenty kilometers, got drowsier and drowsier. He kept the little rum glasses full, which didn't make us any more attentive. He wanted a fresh audience for a speech which, judging by his wife's expressions as she came and went, had already worn out the locals.

Like a lot of landed French peasants then, he was a communist as a protest against everything that the power structure was doing to France — big business, the church, the politicians, the military. His list of grievances was very long and required much arm waving. I missed a lot of nuance, partly through sleepiness, partly my inadequate French and ignorance of French politics. But I picked up enough to be amused by the paradox of this sturdy yeoman, secure in his place and land for generations, who thought he had something in common with the Soviet Union, where the evils of Stalinism were getting wide publicity that year.

What I clearly remember of him seemed far more representative of France. He knew we were Canadian and soon after we arrived he opened an antique desk. He came back to the table with a packet, which he unfolded ceremoniously. First he showed us the Croix de Guerre his father had won in the

Franco-Prussian war, then the Croix de Guerre he had won in World War I. He described it all with great pride. Then, as though just as valuable to him, he showed us about two dozen coins tossed by the liberating Canadian soldiers in 1944. He picked up and fingered them as though they were talismans, while describing very affectingly the scene of the liberation. The coins were all British, florins and half crowns and a couple of shillings. When we had looked at them, he carefully wrapped them up and returned them to the desk.

Somewhat later in the conversation, he came back to the coins. Of course, they were no longer of any monetary value, evidentally. We asked why he thought that. Because *"le roi est mort, non?"* He meant that the coins all dated from 1944 or before and bore the likeness of George VI, who had died in 1952, or his father, George V, who died in 1935. No, we said, that didn't matter, the coins of any king of England were still legal tender, no matter how long ago he died.

That was remarkable, the farmer said. It showed the extraordinary continuity of England's government, in contrast to the shambles and humiliations of France, with new governments every few months. So the coins were still useful as money? Well, no matter, he said briskly, they were souvenirs to be cherished like medals. He returned to the iniquities of the ruling circles in Paris.

Finally, at the very end of the evening, over a cup of *tisane*, an herbal tea designed to make us sleepy, he said, suddenly: "If those coins *are* still money, what do you suppose they would be worth?"

They came out of the desk again, out of their paper, we counted them up and told him the current rate of exchange between the French franc and sterling. A delicate ballet of courtesy, greed, and sentimentality ensued. The upshot was that McDermott and I each lugged off to bed a pocketful of heavy English coins, having given him a good equivalent in francs.

The bedrooms were sumptuously furnished, mine with a fine carved four-poster, an armoire, and other furniture to match. I slept wonderfully. In the morning, I opened the leaded casement windows onto a garden full of blossom and sweet smells. And to top it all a cuckoo began uttering its two liquid notes from somewhere nearby.

Following instructions, we returned to the café. Breakfast was a large bowl of *café au lait* that you ate with a soup spoon while dunking freshly baked bread. The *patronne* made us large pâté sandwiches for our lunch on the road and filled up the wineskin we carried for refreshment along the way.

We dreaded to look at the bill. We were on a very tight budget and had foolishly asked no prices in advance. But all she charged us for breakfast, lunch, the rooms, and dinner the night before was six hundred old francs each, about two dollars.

I remember that when people complain about how tight-fisted the French are.

If you enjoy strenuous walking, it is still a good way to see France. It is a much emptier country than visitors might think as they drag around the tourist sites in the congested cities or whiz along the overcrowded autoroutes.

Unlike North America, the scenery and character of the landscape change rapidly enough from district to district to offer variety to the walker. Much of the scenery is fabulous. The villages lie close enough to provide shelter, food, drink, baths, bed, and first aid for blisters, at humane intervals. It is a rare place in France where you can't find a good meal and a bottle of drinkable wine. Finally, France is extravagantly mapped, down to a scale of 1/25,000. That gives you more than three inches to the mile and even shows tiny footpaths and forest tracks where there are no roads.

I believe in civilized walking, no backpacking or camping out. I loved all that when I was a Boy Scout: now I don't want to carry all that backbreaking gear. Especially for hill and mountain walking, I prefer to go very light, one change of clothing in a small mountaineer's haversack, a few toilet things, and some paperback books. You also need a very good pair of boots and a stick for discouraging dogs.

In the late afternoon you descend to a quiet village to have a drink, take a room, soak the muscles in a hot bath, have a good meal, a chat with anyone who wants to, and fall asleep by ten o'clock. The next morning you are off by eight o'clock, well refreshed. Some little inns will even do your laundry overnight.

Traveling that light gives you a wonderful sense of freedom, the illusion that you are beating the twentieth century, seeing historic landscapes from the perspective of the men who shaped them.

Walking ingratiates you with country people and it amazes townspeople enough to make them treat you nicely. It lets you smell and feel the countryside. It frees you from the imprisoning effect of speed. If you see something that intrigues you, you merely stop and take your fill of it without anxious moments of slowing down, turning around, and finding somewhere to park.

If you walk over a piece of country, examining its wildflowers closely, feeling in your leg muscles the rise and fall of the land, bathing your aching feet in its streams, enjoying the play of its weather on your face and the perfumes the earth gives off, you will be attached to that piece of geography forever. Just looking at the map years later will bring back the proprietary glow you earned by expending yourself on it.

I retain that feeling for many parts of France and England that I have walked over. In each I have felt moments of sublime contentment, well worth the sweat and the aches that produced them. The Pyrenees are such a place for me, the chain of mountains dividing Spain and France. They have, as the Michelin guide says, "all the attractions of high mountains: jagged crests and snowy peaks, great amphitheatres laced with waterfalls, high lakes surrounded by pasture, forests of beech and fir, rushing torrents, deep gorges and rock defiles, alternating with cultivated hollows." I spent two weeks walking there in July 1970. Years before some reference in a forgotten book had lit a slow fuse in my imagination. (I have them still burning for places like the Isle of Skye, where I have yet to go.)

My headquarters was a small town called Ax-les-Thermes, a spa whose hot mineral springs attract people seeking cures for sciatica and rheumatism. It lies in a deep valley, where several rivers meet, the Lauze, the Oriège and the Ariège, the last giving its name to that department of France. Soldiers returning from the Crusades passed through Ax-les-Thermes. Many were suffering from leprosy and the special stone basin built for them over one of the hot springs is still there and still used.

The Lauze flowed just outside the french doors of my room in the Hotel de la Paix. Through them came the rustle of running water and the smell of pines. On the first day, I climbed about three thousand feet to the north of the town to have a picnic lunch. I stopped for breath on a grassy slope facing south, with a view down the valley, and got out the things I had bought in the small shops in the town: a sausage, bread, red wine, and a local cake made from nuts. I ate them slowly. The sun was warm but a faint wind cooled my face. The only sounds were the homemade bells tinkling on the cattle grazing in a meadow two thousand feet below and some skylarks screaming faintly in the warm air. A golden-colored hawk or falcon came sailing along the edge of the mountain below me. He stopped — actually stopped — in space, staying in one place almost motionless, riding the current of hot air rising from the valley. When he had seen what he wanted, he dived in an exact vertical with his wings closed, until he braked and snatched up some small creature and flew away.

I lay back to doze and my fingers felt something in the grass, wild strawberries, hundreds of them all around me, perfectly ripe, sweeter than any cultivated ones, all that I wanted reachable without moving my position. That was a good moment.

The next day, leaving my car and luggage at the hotel, I set off for a week of walking. At first I followed the icy little torrent that came by the hotel, climbing steadily through some woods, around a lake in a valley, then up another mountain to the north. It took many hours, up the bed of another river, through the woods fighting off flies, then zigzagging up the steep slope of grass. That turned to heather and rock and grew steeper until each meter of additional elevation was agony to the thigh muscles. But at one o'clock,

I came to the snow-covered crest called the Col de Quercourt and it was worth it all.

I took off my shirt and bathed in the cold snow, then filled my water bottle where the snow melted. I sat in the delicious cool wind at six thousand feet, eating French bread and semisweet chocolate, washed down with the icy water, not wanting to be anywhere in the world at that moment but there; looking south into Spain across a procession of jagged, snow-covered peaks, dazzling in the sun, or north where the mountains gradually subsided into the ancient plains of France.

But there were two villages beckoning from the next valley. I chose one, set off on a compass bearing, and, after descending for two hours through heavy woods, had the luck to fall into a small inn not shown in the Michelin. It was run by a Parisian for the ski season and empty now except for his family and some friends. They took me in and fed me wonderfully, lent me some slippers, and oohed and aahed a great deal about the hill I had come over, even getting out their own maps to verify it.

I went to sleep with the window open to the cold night and the Col I had climbed outlined in black against a sky blazing with stars.

There are many sharply contrasting facets in the French personality. I saw a notorious example of the cruel side when chance took me to Devil's Island in 1964.

Devil's Island was the most popular name for the prison colonies in French Guiana, where for a hundred years French justice stored the most intractable and inconvenient wrong-doers. It started as a move by Napoleon III to clean up French prisons; it degenerated into one of the most infamous exercises in penal history.

Devil's Island was one of a cluster of small islands twenty-seven miles off the coast of South America in the Caribbean. A sentence there was almost worse than a sentence of death. Prisoners called it *"la mangeuse d'hommes"* (the devourer of men). If they did not die from disease, or discipline, or execution, they were eaten by sharks when they tried to escape. The place became notorious when Captain Alfred Dreyfus, the army officer wrongfully convicted of treason in the scandal that shook France at the turn of the century, spent five years there in solitary confinement. Through the efforts of the novelist Emile Zola and others, he was finally exonerated and freed, but the name Devil's Island remained a symbol of horror.

The French government removed the last prisoners in 1946 and closed Devil's Island in 1951. To minimize publicity about the past, they carefully kept the curious away. I think I was the first reporter to go there with a film crew, but I'm not sure.

It was May 1964. I was heading north after two weeks in Brazil covering the revolution which overthrew President Goulart. I was doing feature stories for the *Huntley-Brinkley Report* and they wanted me to stop in and look at both French and British Guianas on the way.

French Guiana was sizable but almost totally undeveloped, used as a penal colony since 1852. Its capital was the sleepy town of Cayenne, a jumble of white stucco houses with red tile roofs. It is perched on the edge of some of the most exotic and unexplored jungle in the world, reaching back in the uplands to the steamy Amazon rain forest. Its economy was so lethargic, or so cripplingly dependent on metropolitan France, that even fresh produce, like lettuce, was imported. Cayenne was beginning to see better days: President de Gaulle had just made a personal visit and promised to make up for centuries of neglect.

While investigating that story, I fell in with Ben Cooper, one of several Americans who had discovered that the golden shrimp in the shallow waters off Guiana were bigger and sweeter than those in the Gulf of Mexico. The Henderson Company of Florida had set up a packing and freezing plant in Cayenne and was anxious that it be included in NBC's story on the local economy. Since it was the only piece of fresh business enterprise (and had an American angle), it was a legitimate part of the story and we filmed it.

He invited us in turn to lunch, where a Creole woman cooked some of his fresh shrimp in a hot mayonnaise sauce that I will never forget. The lunch turned into evening with friends who told the kind of stories about the interior of Guiana that I hadn't heard since the heavy diet of adventure books I consumed as a boy.

One couple described a journey to the plateau country several years before. Three days out of civilization, the French husband was bitten in the leg by a deadly snake. They had ampules of snakebite serum and immediately injected them above the bite. But he rapidly became delirious and developed a high fever. His wife was part Amerindian. As he was rapidly losing consciousness, she bit into the wound, sucked out as much envenomed blood as she could, then made him a poultice of leaves and moss. She left him there and paddled downriver alone for three days and nights to get help. She got it and he lived. He showed us a very convincing scar on his leg to prove it.

Even on the coast, on the outskirts of Cayenne, the wildlife was still pretty exotic. Their garbage was regularly visited by a jaguar from the nearby forest.

During that evening Ben asked if we wanted to go to Devil's Island. It had always been forbidden territory, but the current prefect of Guiana was a friend very interested in their shrimp business, and he might say yes.

I had an interview with the prefect the next morning. In the dry and disdainful way of French officials, he was rather suspicious of my motives, but he gave his permission.

That evening we had dinner in a small restaurant run by Raymond Vaudet, a former Devil's Island inmate, one of the few who had successfully escaped. Around the walls were primitive paintings explicitly depicting the gory horrors of the prison. One painting illustrated one of the enduring legends: the sea burial of a dead prisoner. The coffin was made with one end open and the funeral party went out in a boat. At six o'clock the chapel bell rang, sharks appeared, and the coffin was tilted up, so that the body slid out conveniently. The painting showed all these grisly details and the restaurant owner insisted, as do all other Devil's Island raconteurs, that the Pavlovian sharks would come simply from the ringing of the church bell at the hour of six.

We boarded the sixty-five-foot shrimp trawler early the next morning to catch the tide. It was a perfect morning to watch dawn in the tropics and nothing ever made me happier than being on the sea. But we came to a patch of water where the river, the tail end of the Amazon current, and the local tide all meet. It is shallow and the confused waters create an unpleasant rip. Very soon the cameraman, Gene Broda, was sick over the side. A few minutes later, the sound man, Jim Geraghty, showed a green tinge beneath his freckles and he was leaning over the side. I felt very solicitous and tolerant. I had been on ships all my life and had never been sick. I thought I could not be. But I was standing in the wheelhouse, having a turn at the wheel, when Wimpy, the skipper, offered me a cup of coffee. One sip and I felt a great oppression come over me. In two minutes I had joined the others at the rail. But that cleared it up and I spent the rest of the three-hour voyage helping Bill, a big-jawed Texan skipper who had come for the ride, prepare a huge Louisiana gumbo to simmer in the galley for our supper on the trip back after dark.

Devil's Island is the smallest of three islands called Les Isles du Salut (the Islands of Health) because they lie away from the mosquito-ridden swamps of the coast, out in the fresh airs of the Northeast Trade Winds.

That day they rose from the horizon like a tropical paradise in a travel brochure, thick with glossy vegetation crowned with feathery coconut palms. We anchored a hundred yards from the shore. The three islands were grouped so tightly that only a few dozen yards of water separated them and tidily kept their functions distinct: Royale, housing administrative offices; St. Joseph, the main prison island; and the small Isle au Diable, Devil's Island itself, where the political prisoners like Dreyfus were isolated from the murderers, blackmailers, forgers, and others transported here by the mercies of French justice.

A black called Joseph Jacob came out in a dugout canoe to the shrimp boat. He lived on the mainland and paid the

French authorities a fee of about a hundred dollars a year for the concession to harvest all the fruit that grew on the islands. Since they teemed with breadfruit, coconut, limes, and mangoes, he was on to a good thing; but he had to commute across thirty miles of open ocean in his homemade canoe and outboard motor to do it. Today he was staying on the islands and agreed to give us a tour of his domain.

We got into his canoe with the camera gear and I put my hand into the turquoise water to feel how warm it was. Joseph suddenly slapped my hand with his paddle, shouting "Raquin" (shark), and I hastily withdrew it.

As soon as we came close to the lee of the shore and out of the sea breeze, the heat was oppressive. Before we landed, the noise of the prison island enveloped us; the dry wheezing and buzzing of cicadas and other insects made a din so loud that it weighed as heavily on our spirits as the heat. In the absence of men, the insects had taken over. So had the tropical vegetation.

We were met on the shore by a lieutenant of gendarmes, the official French government presence on the islands and its entire population, except for visits by Joseph. These officers were rotated every six weeks. During their stay, they lived alone in the former commandant's house, with nothing but the shortwave radio and the ghosts of the past to keep them company. The young lieutenant, very neat in his khaki summer uniform and black kepi, warned us insistently not to swim between the islands, no matter how hot we felt. He said that the gendarme officer stationed there immediately before him had ignored that advice, and had been lost to the sharks — just out there! He pointed a few yards from shore toward the other island. The sharks had also eaten a crewman from another shrimp boat which went aground. We got the message.

The prison was on a hill at the top of the island. Leading to it was a causeway made of large squared stones laid by convict labor in the nineteenth century. It rose in gentle steps into a green gloom made by the jungle that had begun to reclaim it. A maze of vines, creepers, and tendrils hung from the overreaching trees and had to be moved aside as we mounted the staircase, with Joseph in front hacking listlessly with his machete to cut a pathway. The noise of the cicadas grew louder and the heat more crushing. The ground finally leveled off and Joseph said: "There is the prison," pointing with his machette. I could see nothing in the green shadows. Only when I pushed a few feet farther through the dangling vines could I discern the shadowy outlines. It looked like a Beau Geste fortress, with crenellated battlements and an ornate studded door as the main entrance.

We walked through it and the courtyard to the main cell block. It was beautiful and appalling. Long rows of cells faced each other, conventionally open with bars to the front, but also open to the skies, with gratings of bars in place of ceilings. That enabled the guards patrolling on balconies above to see into any cell. But it also left the inmates to the mercies of grilling suns and drenching rains. These cells were now beautiful in a way; vines and jungle plants had captured them, flowing in green profusion through the bars. In some cells, lime trees had planted themselves, presumably from seeds dropped by prisoners on the earthen floors. Mature trees had entwined themselves in the ceiling roof bars and were heavy with fruit.

We filmed all this then moved into another building, the dreaded Réclusion Disciplinaire — solitary confinement cells for prisoners being punished. Those small, boxlike cells were also observed through open gratings, from a catwalk. The wretches confined there were fed bread and water every three days through small hatches in the front. The prisoners had to maintain absolute silence — some for years.

Everywhere were written messages of hope or desperation; and calendars, penciled, dug, scratched into the walls.

To me, what intensified the terrible echoes of suffering that filled the imagination were the frequent tantalizing glimpses outside. Through the bars were vistas of indescribable loveliness, of shiny palm fronds restless in the breeze against a dazzling ocean.

We filmed everything in sight, then descended to the sad graveyard, the resting place of prison guards and members of their families; their fatal illnesses faithfully inscribed on their headstones — yellow fever the most common. One felt sorry for them, too, loyal servants of the French Republic, trying to wrest some family life from this monstrous environment, burying their wives and young children. At least they had enjoyed the dignity of burial and were not fed to the sharks as dead prisoners were. We visited the commandant's house and had a beer with the gendarme. Underneath it were dark punishment cells for particularly difficult prisoners. As we filmed, I did "pieces to camera," where possible standing in suitably grim settings, which could be used as narration for the other film sequences.

On the way back to the boat, we heard a tremendous noise of grunting and squealing and came across a herd of wild gray pigs, whom Joseph was feeding. He sat on the ground with a pile of coconuts, chopping them open with his machete and throwing them to the hairy pigs who gobbled them up. The pigs roamed the island freely and lived on fruit and roots when Joseph wasn't there to open the coconuts. Occasionally, he said, smiling, one of them accompanied him back to the mainland "like this," and he drew his machete blade across his throat picturesquely.

The light had begun to fall and we had to leave. It was a relief to get into the canoe and pick up the fresh air from the sea, to climb back aboard the shrimp boat and survey the islands from a distance.

Human cruelty has many dimensions but this seemed a particularly beastly form: punishment sadistically administered, on a par with the Gulags of the Soviet Arctic.

Some American entrepreneurs wanted to convert Devil's Island to a tourist resort. The French government kept refusing, citing the menace of the sharks. But I wondered whether they did not mean the embarrassment of the past.

As the tropical dusk fell, the powerful diesels of the shrimp boat soon left the islands astern, small hummocks of black against a horizon white with stars. It was a wonderful night, with a calm sea. We ate the skipper's chicken-shrimp gumbo, then lay in the bows looking up at the stars, but I kept feeling a shudder of pity for the seasick wretches who had crossed these waters in chains as cargo for the Islands of Health.

Five years later I read *Papillon*, Henri Charrière's amazing tale of imprisonment and escape from Devil's Island. In it he says, "I could never have imagined that a country like mine, France, known to the world as the mother of liberty, the land that gave birth to human and civil rights, could have created, even in French Guiana, on an island no larger than a pocket handkerchief, lost in the Atlantic, an installation as barbarously repressive as the Réclusion on St. Joseph."

France always seems richest in crisis. The French wear political turmoil like a perfume, and a hint of violence in the air sharpens the national personality. It is as though, born of violence as a modern nation, made an empire through violence, there is in the national spirit, as they say about the wine Sancerre, *un petit arrière-goût de poudre de feu,* a little aftertaste of gunpowder. Of the Western nations only the French can still put zip and panache into military display, like the Bastille Day parade on July 14, a sense of gaiety and dash, a romp with bright uniforms and gleaming weapons, the excitement of small boys playing with colorful lead soldiers.

None of the other Western nations is quite as vicious in using force. The British bring it out hesitantly and use it, particularly on civilians, very gingerly. The French come out crisply in great strength and *bang!* no sentimentality. Then they wipe up the blood, reopen the cafés, and talk about it all, vehemently, animatedly before, finally, subordinating all considerations to a good meal.

The violent resistance to the pull-out from Algeria provided a running series of crises in the early '60s. One autumn night in 1962 I covered a protest rally in a hall on the Left Bank. After hours of fiery speeches the crowds came pouring out of the hall into the narrow streets and the CRS (Compagnie Républicaine de Sécurité) were waiting for them. The CRS are specially trained riot police with a well-deserved reputation for brutality. Journalists knew not to quarrel with the CRS.

I was in a small street, being pushed along by the excited crowd that filled it like a swollen river, right to the walls of the buildings. They were chanting the familiar *"Algérie française! Algérie française!"* and motorists began picking up the rhythm on their horns — *"beep-beep-beep, BEEP-BEEP"* — until the noise echoing off the old buildings was deafening. Suddenly the crowd behind me became agitated and started to move faster. A French reporter said: "CRS, making a charge." At the rear of the crowd, a squad of CRS was charging with batons, clubbing and beating those in the rear. That made everyone run faster, pushing all of us, scrambling to stay on our feet, choking the already jammed street. Then someone shouted: *"Attention en avant!"* The damned CRS were also charging from the front. I could see their helmets shining and the batons flailing down. That made the front of the crowd crush back hysterically. Some still chanted defiantly, *"Algérie française."* Everyone tried to find a way out to avoid getting beaten up as the two squads methodically squeezed the crowd, like snowplows approaching from opposite directions. That was frightening enough, but on top of it they started exploding tear gas grenades. Bodies swirled away from the exploding canisters, like flocks of disturbed pigeons, jamming themselves against the crowds farther out. And still the CRS charged and clubbed. I wormed and squeezed through the constricted bodies to one side of the street where I could see a recessed doorway. I had just reached it when I saw a gendarme, not CRS, an ordinary policeman, raise his rolled-up cape. That is a serious weapon. Sewn in the hem are lead pellets. Swung artistically, the cape can fell a man. I crammed myself back into the doorway and the cape, intended for my head, fanned past my nose and the charge went by, littering the street with fallen people nursing cracked heads.

I left my doorway to look for some better shelter. The street opened into a little square, with a statue on a stone plinth. The crowd and the police were rushing back. In the dark I climbed up onto the statue, stepping first on a shadow I thought was stone — but it was soft and it groaned, a body left from the first charge. I crouched in the shadow of whatever famous individual the statue memorialized while the battle surged around the base. Eventually, it moved on and I left.

It all seemed quite unnecessary. It only made everybody madder at the government represented by the sadistic CRS.

It would have been smarter police work to let the crowd simply disperse. Instead, after the first charge, angry demonstrators started fighting back, picking up stones or bottles, anything they could find, and hurling them at the CRS, who, of course, became more aggressive in defending themselves. So the small streets between the boulevard St. Germaine and the river were treated to a night of running skirmishes in which lots of people, CRS and journalists included, got hurt; and the popular newspapers the next day made it look like a pitched battle. That probably had the effect of making other Frenchmen think that the opposition to Algerian independence was stronger in France than it really was, with the obvious consequence of making it stronger.

I was also in Paris when the generals in Algeria revolted against de Gaulle.

Incredible as it now seems, we lived through one night, April 22, 1961, actually expecting that rebellious paratroopers from Algeria might land on Paris to try to overthrow de Gaulle and take over the Republic.

The crisis air was palpable that night. The city's adrenaline was up. Parisians seemed to be afraid and to enjoy being afraid at the same time.

It was a Saturday, and one of those warm April nights in Paris that songwriters enthuse over. The sky was clear and full of stars. The streets were packed, the restaurants and sidewalk cafés jammed. The girls in the Champs Élysées wore blouses and dresses but no coats. They crowded excitedly around the tanks ranged under the chestnut trees below the Rond-Point, where the stamp dealers set up on Saturday mornings. The soldiers, equally excited to be in the most fashionable part of Paris on such a night, leaned out of their tanks, smoking and flirting with the girls. People brought them drinks and coffee. Clusters of people gathered near car radios for news. There was an aura of nervous gaiety.

The preparations were serious enough. President de Gaulle had blocked the runways of all airfields with trucks to stop the rebel troops from landing. Gasoline supplies at army bases were cut off to stop other units from joining the revolt. Paris was a city under siege. Busloads of troops and gendarmes waited in the side streets, ready for an attack on the Élysée Palace where de Gaulle grimly waited it out. In the place de la Concorde I saw a column of twenty tanks, followed by armored cars and truckloads of heavily armed soldiers, mobilized in case of attack on the National Assembly or the government ministries behind it on the Left Bank. The courtyard and front steps of the Assembly bristled with policemen carrying their short machine guns at the ready.

I kept up a steady flow of radio reports to New York all evening. I would go out, scout down the Champs Élysées, around the place de la Concorde to the National Assembly, then back through the Faubourg St. Honoré, passing the front of the Élysée Palace, then up to the NBC office at 52 Champs Élysées to write and broadcast another report before going out again.

Of course, the paratroopers never came. Around midnight, my taxi driver said, "They won't come now. They've left it too late." And it was difficult to tell how much he and the people in the streets of Paris that brilliant night were secretly a little disappointed, as though the gland of anarchy locked in every Frenchman had been stimulated but not used.

The Generals' Revolt collapsed but the diehards in Algiers kept up a fierce resistance for a long time and I made several trips to Algeria as the war approached its climax. Many pieces of the story had previously passed through my hands as subeditor at Reuters. I had lingered, horrified, over evidence of rebel atrocities circulated by French propagandists to sway world opinion. There were photographs of pregnant women disemboweled; men mutilated, some decapitated, some further dishonored by having their penises cut off and stuck in their mouths. Gradually, we also learned of the French response — systematic torture of prisoners, the victims placed naked on metal bedsprings, with electrodes applied to their genitals. It was no game.

But in front of all that, like a glossy restaurant façade hiding a pestilential kitchen, was the city of Algiers; dazzlingly beautiful, a heady collision of the French and Arab cultures.

From a distance, flying in from France, it looked like a gigantic Greek amphitheater that had been pillaged for its marble. Its white cubist buildings nestled into a curve of hills, down to the glittering Mediterranean.

The very flight from France in those days was full of atmosphere. The Air France Caravelle was then a new plane, built and flown with all the confidence and dash of modern French technology. As you crossed the coastline of Metropolitan France at Marseilles, the pilot would say: "We are now leaving *la métropole* to fly over the Mediterranean. In thirty-five minutes we shall be landing in the Department of Algeria." The fiction that the festering colony was actually a part of France (like Guadeloupe or Martinique legally remain today) was becoming increasingly threadbare. But the words also got you inside the French skin for a few moments, a feeling for that sense of empire that all Frenchmen grew up with and were now painfully jettisoning in what seemed like an endless parade of humiliations — the Nazi occupation; the political chaos of the Fourth Republic's twenty-three governments; the disasters of Indochina; the disgrace of the Suez adventure.

But in Algiers, it was still all hubris. Fashionable, sensual Algiers, a provincial city only because it was not Paris. Next to the rue du Faubourg St. Honoré, the rue Michelet in Algiers was the most elegant street I had ever seen. It was protected from the sun by trees that had not only been pollarded but squared so that their dark green foliage formed thick rectangular umbrellas over the sidewalks. One by one, the trees disappeared, when shop fronts were blown up with plastique explosives. But the street survived; the smart shops, the bars, and the restaurants remained open.

In a crowded lunchtime you would hear a shot nearby, turn a corner, and find elegantly dressed women stepping daintily but indifferently over a body in the gutter, still warm, the blood trickling away, his FLN or OAS assassin perhaps lurking confidently a few feet away, while the distant klaxons of the police and the ambulance ooh-aahed closer.

I remember the *pieds noirs* women, elegant and unapproachable. I remember the wonderful rich syrup of smells that steeped the air of that exciting city, combining many scents —

Gauloise cigarettes, *café filtre*, garlic, French perfumes, all mingled with the inevitable North African odors.

I never got to know it really well, neither the pleasures of Algiers nor the story. Like many "firemen" I was in and out and, consequently, it was all a little bewildering. To tell the truth, most of it is a little bewildering to the foreign correspondent who moves around a lot. The trick is to keep your employer and your competitors believing that you know precisely what you're doing.

Most of the time I didn't know, but I learned not to let it show. I learned to report the piece of the story in front of me, confident that the pundits or historians would sort out the context.

On one quick visit, I flew in from London and got into the center of Algiers early in the evening. I checked in, as usual, at a little hotel called the François 1er and went out to dinner with Paul Davis, an NBC stringer who was a cameraman and reporter. I was very tired, barely able to stay awake through the meal and long enough to get back to my bed at the François 1er.

I was deeply asleep some hours later when the phone rang and a voice said excitedly: "Listen, you can hear the shooting! All hell has broken loose. Listen!"

And, indeed, through the phone I could hear a lot of gunfire. I was still feeling drugged from sleep. I said, "Just a minute, let me go to the window." In bare feet I crossed the tiled floor and quickly opened the full-length doors onto the cool night. Yes. I could hear machine-gun fire, a lot of it, sounding just a few streets away. I knew Paul Davis lived in another part of town, up in the hills. If there was fighting there too it might be a general uprising.

I ran back to the phone. "Yes, I can hear it outside."

"You mean it's happening in Algiers, too?"

"What do you mean, in Algiers? Where are you?"

"Who do you think this is?" asked the voice.

"Paul Davis," I said.

"It isn't Paul. It's John Cooley and I'm in Oran."

John Cooley was a first-rate correspondent for the *Christian Science Monitor* and he freelanced for NBC. Since he specialized in the Middle East, he always knew a hundred times more than I did. I felt a little foolish standing there. Oran was hundreds of miles away to the west.

"Just a minute," I said. I went back to the window. Yes, there it was, a loud rhythmic, staccato sound from the street. But you had to have a strong power of suggestion to think it was machine guns. Directly across the little street from my window was an old mosque, converted for use by the French army printing press. In the middle of the night its presses were clacking, clicking, and clanking away full blast. I closed the doors, shutting out the sound, and went back to the phone.

"There isn't any gunfire, here. It's the goddamned printing press across the street."

"You'd better get some sleep," Cooley said generously and hung up.

As I drifted off, I wondered what NBC would have thought if I had excitedly transmitted a tape recording of a printing press as the sound of gunfire. Would they have known the difference?

They did get some authentic gunfire from me, however, very soon.

I had come on that trip in case there was trouble on November 1, 1961, the seventh anniversary of the Algerian uprising against France. The French authorities had forbidden any demonstrations. An estimated forty thousand soldiers and police were mobilized in Algiers and the army made a *quadrillage*, squaring the city off into small, manageable sectors controlled by barbed wire, checkpoints, and armed soldiers.

All over town the atmosphere was very tense, foreboding. The air was overcast and humid, a little chilly. Small groups of correspondents drove in their rented VWs from area to area, looking for incidents. We were passed grudgingly through the checkpoints by the tough French troops. The French army was still smarting about de Gaulle's decision to let Algeria become an independent nation. In Algiers, these sinewy, lean-cheeked, Gauloise-puffing characters were not amused by the foreign press.

They showed their animosity that day by dropping canisters of nausea gas from a helicopter into a group of press cars near the cemetery. The helicopter was circling above a small nationalist demonstration and dropping gas bombs to subdue them, which it did very effectively. The gas made you want to vomit instantly and it took the fight out of everyone. We happened to be a little distance from the others when the helicopter buzzed us and lobbed a gas canister down among us. We got our VW moving, but the car next to us wasn't so lucky. The canister exploded and the reporters began leaping out the doors and being sick in the road. We got enough whiffs to feel nauseated but not actually sick.

Then something happened that made us sick in another way.

Passing through several checkpoints in the *quadrillage*, we came to Dar El Kef, a suburb of scrubby hills, one of them surmounted by a grim, modern apartment complex. Far up on top of the hill, there was a crowd of Moslems waving banners and mounting one of the forbidden demonstrations. When we got out of the car, we could hear on the wind the high-pitched "you-you-you," the wailing cry of Algerian women.

A company of soldiers began moving up the hill, obviously to stop the demonstration, and I decided to go with them. They fanned out and began climbing the hill in a long line, with me right behind them and a BBC camera crew some distance away. The wailing and cheering and taunting grew louder as we climbed and I turned on my small Ficord tape recorder.

Just before we reached the top of the hill, there was a rattle of heavy machine-gun fire from the apartment building. A couple of men close to me, including the French lieutenant, were hit and fell. I threw myself in a small gully near him, while his troops hit the ground, pointed all their weapons at the huge concrete building, and opened fire. The entire front of the building was crowded with people, standing on the balconies that jutted out from every apartment. Most of them were women and children merely watching the demonstration. The barrage of rifle and machine-gun fire lasted about a minute. When it stopped, there was an echo in the moist air, then a moment of silence. Two donkeys, tethered nose to tail, startled from their grazing, went hee-hawing down the hill in crazy stumbling circles. The silence was followed by an incredible burst of screaming and wailing.

A jeep raced up the hill on a dirt track. A colonel jumped out and greeted the wounded lieutenant, who was bleeding profusely from a bullet in his upper thigh. To stop it he was squeezing his thigh with both thumbs on the pressure point. But when the colonel got out of the jeep and saluted, the lieutenant raised his bloody right in a smart salute, said, "Bonjour, mon Colonel," and returned his hand to the wound.

The French medics applied a tourniquet, put him on a stretcher, and drove down the hill. I walked up to the crest of the hill with the shocked troops. There was awful bloodshed. Official figures later said three dead and nine wounded. There were many more. Women and children had been hit. A man came running to me, his eyes crazed, holding a little boy of three or four. A large bullet had torn open his thigh. His skin had turned white beneath the natural dusky color. You could see both colors. His eyes were vacant. He was moaning "Maaam . . . maaam . . . maaam." The man showed him to me wildly for a moment, then ran to the French army medics. They were now treating the civilian wounded as tenderly as their own troops.

The air was filled with shrieks, and then more gunfire. I went with the maddened troops searching for the rebel machine gunners. When they came to a locked door in the apartment building, they gave it a burst of machine-gun fire and kicked the door in, not caring what was behind.

I kept feeling, "I am not here. I am disembodied. I am looking at all this in a dream." Yet I could smell the people, the cooking odors in the building, and the aftersmell of the gunfire which lingered in the humid air outside. I felt nothing. Some mechanism kept my own emotions locked away behind much simpler professional preoccupations. The soldiers did not find the rebel machine gunner.

I got to the studio downtown and fed my tape to NBC in New York, with an appropriately sententious commentary. I knew what I was supposed to feel and I knew precisely how much of that conventional emotion could leak through in commentary.

I don't know whether other correspondents operated the same way. It was something we never discussed directly, this adopting of conventional emotion to color one's copy, pulled from the same grubby bag of clichés all journalists in a hurry use. It was something more subtle than the code we all acknowledged that reporters were tough guys, hardened by exposure to everything. It would have been far too complicated, as well as being considered unprofessional, to have explored our own feelings, to have filtered the event through our own sensibilities. That became fashionable only in the New Journalism a decade later. The pace and deadlines of daily journalism left us no time for such exquisite stuff. Also, the sensibilities brought to bear by New Journalists were largely unremarkable, clichés in themselves. They wrote clichés of clichés.

Without really knowing what I was doing, I fell easily into the same facile professional amorality as my colleagues. I put at the front of my mind the thought "this is a really good story," and next to it the thought "how do I get it out?" All the while, I was telling myself, half-consciously, that the reality of these events, the living of them, was being safely deposited in a bank of experience that I could later draw on. The lack of such a body of lived adventure, I told myself, was why my attempts as a novelist and playwright had been so callow. There was time; the emotions would catch up later. Like Wordsworth, I could recollect them in tranquillity. But they never catch up, really, those emotions. And the reporters' best insights as to what the story *means* are usually shared privately over drinks and meals with the only other people who will understand them, fellow reporters.

I know I was sickened by that incident. It was wanton violence — on both sides. But at what level was I really distressed at having witnessed it? Certainly not the professional level. I was exhilarated that I had stumbled into the "best" story of the day.

By that evening when eight or ten of us went out to an ornate, tiled restaurant in the Casbah, my spirits were high.

We sat on huge cushions, eating wonderful cous-cous, with a lot of strong Algerian red wine, finding, as usual, a lot to laugh about, like the memory of our colleagues leaving their breakfasts on the roadway thanks to the nausea gas.

De Gaulle magnificently survived the revolt by the French Algerians. He survived, by a hairsbreadth, their attempts to assassinate him. But his extraordinary courage and vision could not survive the materialist revolution of 1968. His ability to reawaken the French to a sense of their glory and purpose as a nation had become irrelevant. Under his leadership France had surged out of the enervating postwar malaise to claim its share of the prosperity of Western Europe. But as French society leaped onto the materialist escalator, many were left behind. So were some common liberties in de Gaulle's paternalistic constitution. By 1968, the catalogue of grievances was very fat, and when students infected by the new worldwide radicalism started a protest about conditions in the French universities, they catalyzed a revolution that swept de Gaulle from power.

In the French tradition, they played out their revolution in the streets of Paris and some provincial cities. Again to an onlooker it produced that heady mix of danger and heroics that put the French on their mettle. The student quarter around the Sorbonne and the boulevard St. Michel became a besieged city. *Les événements* became a way of life. Streets were barricaded with cars, paving stones, furniture, even — sadly — venerable sycamore trees cut down from the sidewalks of the Boul' Mich. They were defended against repeated CRS attacks. The students hurled Molotov cocktails and stones. The CRS replied with tear gas and baton charges. For days, the smell of tear gas never left the quarter. From their command posts inside the Sorbonne, student leaders ran printing presses for leaflets and posters and organized demonstrations. The medical students in white coats and armbands took care of the wounded with a shuttle of small cars as ambulances, with the famous Odéon national theater a major first-aid station, its stone columns plastered with posters.

I came into Paris to do a report for the BBC just as the

students were on the verge of victory, on May 25, 1968. With a film crew I had brought a car across the English Channel by ferry because everything in France — even gas stations — was shut by the general strike. With extra jerry cans of gasoline to keep us going, we drove to Nantes in Britanny and filmed violent demonstrations there. De Gaulle made a broadcast to the nation and no one in Nantes paid any attention. For seven hours, the CRS charged the workers and students with batons, and swooped overhead with helicopters dropping tear gas, while the demonstrators, made angrier by each attack, threw more stones and bottles. Amazingly, no guns were used, on either side, in any French city.

The workers' demands were a measure of the different world. In a small village, la Montague, I attended a rally by strikers from a government arsenal. Besides higher minimum wage, shorter working hours, better health and social security services, they wanted access to the universities for their children. At the Renault automobile plant outside Paris, young strikers were demanding a week's vacation in winter. They already had four weeks in summer.

We drove on to Paris Saturday evening to complete our half-hour report for a transmission to London Monday evening. Only essential services — gas, electricity and water — were running. Everything else was stopped — the metro, buses, trains. The streets were swarming with excited people, drinking in cafés, eating in restaurants, looking at the wreckage of the battles the night before; burned out cars, felled trees, garbage and smashed windows.

While waiting for the evening battles to begin we ate in a favorite restaurant, Le Méditerranée, in the place de l'Odéon. The plate-glass windows were shattered. There was an exploded tear-gas grenade in a corner on the floor. Everything reeked of tear gas. The electricity dipped or went out now and again. Yet the restaurant functioned: waiters took orders, delicious food appeared; the bread was fresh, so were the flowers; the tablecloths were perfectly laundered. No amount of political turmoil had interfered with the wine. Very little interferes with the wine.

. . .

When de Gaulle's successor, Georges Pompidou, died, in April 1974, I did a BBC program from Paris, assessing his impact. As a studio we used the Tour d'Argent restaurant. Its big windows gave a splendid backdrop of Notre Dame and the Seine, and also overlooked Pompidou's apartment across the river.

In scouting the location, David Harrison, the producer, and I were invited to tour the wine cellars of this famous establishment. We did so reverently. They reached out incredibly far under the streets, and neither war nor civil catastrophe had disturbed the steady collection and husbandry of the restaurant's wines.

In one bin, for example, there was a shelf of a favorite St. Julien, Gruaud-La rose 1865. Above it the same wine, vintage 1866, above it 1867, and so on, year after year to the newest.

During the Nazi occupation, the manager told us, other establishments had fearfully moved their wines to safety in the country, just as the priceless medieval stained glass of Notre Dame was removed and stored. Not the Tour d'Argent. They had simply left the wines where they lay. German officers used the restaurant. If they knew enough to ask for a certain wine they were served it. If they did not, it was not offered. Was that not collaboration? we asked. The manager, a young man, shrugged: who benefited in the long run? The few discriminating Germans who drank some good wine? Or posterity?

Pragmatism in the defense of property is no vice to the French; when buttressed by the morality of sound marriage lines, dowries, and well-drawn wills, it becomes quasi-religious in its virtue. Take the case of the two living descendants of Napoleon Bonaparte.

June 1969 was the two hundredth anniversary of Napoleon's birth, giving the French another occasion to consider the colossal achievements and villainies of the little Corsican. His influence lives everywhere in modern France — the administrative system, legal structure, financial organization, educational institutions, road network, and system of weights and measures. The glory of his imperishable legend is still tangible everywhere in French architecture, statuary, painting, furniture, decorative objects, and street names, with incidentals like the Arc de Triomphe thrown in.

The Bonaparte mystique had been instilled in me from early childhood by my maternal grandmother, who was romantically fascinated by him. She had collected many Bonapartist mementos, notably an ebony snuffbox with his figure in ivory relief on the lid. She had a reproduction of a painting showing Napoleon in Hell, confronted with the mutilated bodies of the victims of his conquests. And finally, she made me repeat, until I knew it by heart, the plea made before he died, exiled by the British on the Island of St. Helena, in 1821.

> *Mes amis, quand je suis mort, placez*
> *mes cendres au bord de la Seine, au milieu*
> *de ce peuple français, que j'ai tant aimé.*
>
> *My friends, when I die, place*
> *my ashes beside the Seine in the middle*
> *of the French people whom I have so much loved.*

That is inscribed overhead as you enter Napoleon's tomb, descending from the eerie blue light of the Church of the Dome into the open crypt where the emperor lies under tons of red marble, inside six coffins.

While working for the BBC in London, I was also hosting a series for National Educational Television, the predecessor of PBS, called *International Magazine*. Maggie Weil, the producer, wanted a piece to mark the Napoleon anniversary and her researcher turned up two Bonaparte descendants, both in Paris but living very different lives.

Bonaparte had doubts about his ability to father a child, since his empress, Josephine, had produced none. A plot was concocted to prove that he was not the infertile one. A luscious courtier, Eleonore Denuelle de la Plaigue, at eighteen seductive and dark-eyed, submitted herself to be confined under rigid surveillance in a pavillion of the Murat estate at Neuilly.

Although harassed by great problems of state, the emperor found time to be with her, and presently news came that she was pregnant. There were ugly rumors that Count Murat got to the pavillion first, but the child produced so closely resembled Bonaparte that all such treasonous doubts were dispelled.

The child's birth was registered "absent and unknown father," but Napoleon openly adored the boy whom he named Charles Leon, using the last syllables of his own name. Between campaigns, he played with him in the Tuileries. He made Charles a count and left him a fortune.

Count Leon gambled it away. His son went bankrupt trying to be elected to the National Assembly, and Leon's grandson, Gaston Leon, spent his life as a Paris bus driver.

When I met Gaston in June 1969 he was eighty-two, retired and ill, living on a small pension in mean, dark rooms in a modest suburb called Le Raincy.

He had little to say but his wife, an amateur artist, had plenty: she was bitter and voluble about the neglect of Napoleon's great-great-grandson. She had the head copied from one of the famous David portraits of Napoleon. Her poor copy hung on their shabby wall. What was extraordinary, and haunting, was to look from the portrait to the feeble old man: in the power of the eyes, it was easy to imagine that you saw his ancestry.

When his neighborhood, Le Raincy, celebrated the anniversary of Napoleon's birth at their summer festival, the aged "Count" Leon was given the place of honor.

Things were rather different for His Royal Highness, Prince Louis Jerome Victor-Emmanuel Leopold Marie Napoleon, whose connection with the Emperor was slimmer but legitimate. He was the great-grandson of Napoleon's youngest brother, Jerome, erstwhile king of Westphalia. Somehow, that branch of the family knew how to hold on to things. They married into the Belgian royal family, and by 1969, Le Prince Napoleon had it all: wealthy businessman; Legion d'Honneur for fighting with the French Resistance; a number of opulent homes, including a palatial apartment where I met him in the fashionable Sixteenth Arrondissement of Paris.

The appointment was made by the Paris branch of J. Walter Thompson Public Relations. I was met at the entrance by a footman in black wearing white gloves. When he introduced me to the prince he bowed, then left the room walking backwards.

The prince was a commanding figure, well over six feet, very tall for a Frenchman, an athletic fifty-five. But what bowled me over was what the man possessed in that one apartment. In the entrance foyer was the vast oil by David of Napoleon crossing the Alps at St. Bernard: a copy by David himself. Behind the desk was David's *Napoleon in His Study*, also a copy by the artist. The highly ornate desk was the emperor's; so was the inkstand, and the walls were lined with Napoleon's own books. There were small memorabilia everywhere. A museum could mount a Napoleon show from that one room. The prince had the name and he had the goods. Everything authentic. He also had more than his share of Napoleonic imperiousness.

The questions, in French, had been submitted through J. Walter Thompson, a stipulation often accepted by journalists when the prey is big enough. The prince sat at the desk of his great-granduncle, the emperor, as solemn as an archbishop. He must have been watching the press conferences of President de Gaulle on television and decided that was the appropriate style, patronizing and magisterial. He behaved as though he were a legitimate monarch, awaiting restoration to his own throne.

The answer which revealed all this came in response to several questions: did he feel any special responsibility towards France? did he have any political ambitions? would he like to take over the country? did he feel the present Republican system of government was the right one for France? — all questions asked as much for ironic effect as for substantive answers.

The questions had a current point. The student riots of '68 had convulsed the nation and had been followed by the departure of General de Gaulle. The stability and continuity de Gaulle had given France seemed over. Instead there were nervous reminders of the instability and political impotence of the Fourth Republic. A man of the prince's lineage and confidence might be forgiven for fantasizing a little.

He probably didn't get interviewed very often — if ever — on television, so he may have thought that speaking thus to American television was making a statement to the world.

With great solemnity, he said, "At times like these, it is incumbent on all Frenchmen of position, especially someone bearing a name like mine, to hold himself in readiness, to serve France if the nation should call on him." Almost precisely what de Gaulle had said while waiting in the wilderness to return to power.

When I left, he was still sitting at the desk of the emperor — holding himself in readiness.

But the only call he received was from a French women's magazine, which put his picture on the cover.

Gaullist grandeur had its victims. One was freedom of speech on French television.

I have a souvenir from the events of 1968, a poster painted with great verve. It shows Marianne, the symbol of France, looking out of a television set. Her mouth is blotted out with a white rectangle. The white rectangle means censorship in France, and the journalists of ORTF, the state television service, were heavily censored.

On a given day, ORTF newsmen were literally instructed by various government ministries in what to say on the news. The news bulletins were heavily slanted toward the official position, and contrary views either did not appear or were given very cursory treatment. Opposition politicians, if shown at all, appeared without sound, with a newsman's commentary over it.

It was a humiliating situation for the journalists and scores of younger ORTF newsmen joined the movement that eventually led to de Gaulle's retirement. Their protest brought substantial reforms.

The caption on the TV poster read: *Pas de rectangle blanc pour un peuple adulte.* I had it framed and hung on my office wall during the years when the Nixon White House was trying to abort news programs on public television in the United States.

EIGHT

The Berlin Wall

THE PHONE ALWAYS RANG in the middle of the night. Often for agonizing seconds I couldn't remember where I was: was this the room in the Hotel Metropole in Brussels, where the windows were over there and the phone on the right side of the bed? Or the Gallia in Paris with the desk there and the huge wardrobe opposite? Very worrying when the night is dark, the velvet curtains are heavy, and you cannot tell instantly by the feel of the bed or the smell of the room what city, or even what country, you are in. A panicky feeling.

This time, it was the Kempinski Hotel, Berlin, the night of August 12/13, 1961. The Berlin crisis had been mounting for months. I had arrived the evening before to cover NBC's Berlin bureau for a few weeks to free Piers Anderton, the resident correspondent, to work on a documentary.

The Saturday evening had been quiet, marked only by the announcement that the highest number of East German refugees ever to flee in one day, 2,662, had reported to the West Berlin reception camp. I had eaten dinner in the hotel and gone to bed early.

"This is the news desk in New York," said the voice on the phone. "What do you know about the East Germans closing the border?"

"What?"

"The AP and Reuters say they've started closing all crossing points right through the city. They've closed the Brandenburg Gate."

"I don't know anything about it," I said, "but I'll go and find out." In the dark mood of crisis that summer, such a move by the Soviets, acting through the East Germans, was very ominous. It quite literally could have meant the beginning of nuclear war.

I hung up, turned on the light, and discovered that it was 4 A.M. Sunday, making it 11 P.M. Saturday in New York, which explained why they sounded so alert.

Outside the Kempinski I got a taxi and headed for the Brandenburg Gate, the most famous landmark on the line separating the Soviet Zone, or East Berlin, from West Berlin, comprising the three zones controlled since World War II by the other conquering powers, the U.S., Britain, and France.

The sky was just beginning to lighten as we passed the Tiergarten, replanted after the wartime destruction, its new trees still only big saplings. With an East-West showdown over Berlin inevitable, it was still an open question whether the woods that were slowly regenerating there would eventually shelter Marxist or capitalist lovers or some hybrid of the two. I kept thinking, How extraordinary that I am here!

West Berlin was a terrible irritant to the Kremlin; an island of freedom and prosperity 110 miles inside the bleak empire behind the Iron Curtain. Stalin tried to starve the two million Berliners into submission by blockading all land supply routes in 1948. The United States and its allies saved the city with the historic airlift. For fourteen months planes flew in every few minutes carrying vital necessities, from coal to food. The Soviets finally removed the blockade.

A decade later the new Soviet leader, Nikita Khrushchev, returned to the offensive. In 1958 he demanded that Berlin be made a demilitarized free city and threatened to sign a separate peace treaty with East Germany. That would have forced the Western powers to give up their rights in West Berlin and to recognize East Germany as a legitimate nation, instead of merely the Soviet Zone of occupation.

In January 1961, with John Kennedy just entering the

White House, Khrushchev renewed the threat. He repeated it in such bellicose terms when he met Kennedy in Vienna in June, that U.S. planners began actively considering the prospect of a nuclear war over Berlin.

Kennedy himself said: "All Europe is at stake in West Berlin," and on July 25, the president raised defense spending, called up some reserves, ordered new weapons and an enlarged program of civil defense — all as a signal to Khrushchev of his determination not to be driven out of Berlin.

As the tension mounted, thousands of East Germans panicked. It was escape now to the West or risk being imprisoned forever behind the Iron Curtain. The usual trickle of refugees turned to a flood: young, old, skilled workers, housewives, doctors, engineers — human resources East Germany desperately needed. The hemorrhaging had to stop. Now, apparently, just before dawn on a beautiful summer Sunday morning, the Communists were making their move.

My taxi reached the Brandenburg Gate. The huge columns and heroic statuary dwarfed the few people standing underneath. It made the moment seem insignificant in comparison with the history that had swirled through there. Where the armies of Napoleon Bonaparte had marched in triumph, scruffy members of the Volkspolizei (People's Police) now strutted. Workmen were unloading large concrete tubs of flowers and lining them up, side by side, across the openings of the gate, blocking the two roadways. At first sight it looked almost a joke, a wall of flowerpots. But a few hundred yards away, other workers were erecting a fence of concrete posts and barbed wire.

There were very few people about: a handful of journalists, some photographers, and West Berlin policemen to witness this bizarre moment of history.

The outrageous extent of the Communist plan was not fully apparent. In the next few hours, the East Germans continued running temporary barbed-wire barricades through the city. They ordered the thirty-five thousand East Berliners who worked in West Berlin to abandon their jobs. Subways and elevated railroads were stopped at the border. Telephone and telegraph communications between the two halves of the city were cut. Two battle-ready Soviet divisions ringed Berlin just in case.

It was not until several days later that the first prefabricated cement blocks appeared, first across the Brandenburg Gate, then the Potsdamer Platz, and on along the twenty-seven-mile sector border. Only then did it become clear that they were actually building a wall. That is when the full shock hit.

Standing there, in the growing light, trying to drink in the detail, it was difficult to grasp what these first simple actions might lead to. Would the Western powers try to knock the barricades down? If they did, would the Soviets move their tanks on West Berlin? Would desperate East Berliners rise in open revolt as they did in 1953, right at this spot, swirling through the Brandenburg Gate until they were crushed by Soviet tanks? Would President Kennedy intervene? If he did, would the whole world go up?

Thinking some of these staggering thoughts, I took my taxi to the NBC office to broadcast to New York. Part of my complex reaction was simply exhilaration: to be there, at this moment, was incredible luck. But in addition to that selfish thought, another emotion added to the journalistic adrenaline exciting me.

Berlin had haunted me long before I ever got there. I came to it with overheated expectations and ambivalence. My late boyhood spanned the Second World War. My father and uncles and friends' fathers were at sea in the Royal Canadian Navy hunting German submarines. All our games were war games in which Germans were the villains to be hunted, or killed, or escaped from. One New Year's Eve, I had been taken to a midnight movie. Before the feature a documentary on German-occupied Russia was shown. The camera was on a vehicle moving slowly along a winter road. From every telegraph pole swung the frozen body of a Russian man or woman hanged in some mass savagery. It seemed there were hundreds. The scene went on and on and on. The images never left me. Years later, walking the streets of Berlin for the first time, I looked into the eyes of every man old enough to have been there and asked myself: Could he have been one of the executioners?

Yet my mother's father was a Nova Scotian of German descent; Hanovarian, we were frequently assured, very "peaceful Germans," as he certainly was. He happened to marry a lady from Tennessee, my grandmother, who had been strenuously educated in Europe. She spoke some German, recited its poetry sentimentally, and loved to recall the elegance of Berlin before World War I. She tried hard to stuff German (as well as French) phrases into my head when I was too young to resist, and some of them had stuck.

My fascination with the Germans caught fire at sixteen with the Señora Pardo de Zela. She was the wife of a South American diplomat and she came twice a week to give German lessons to six of us who had been excused from Latin for incompetence. It was a boys' school. The señora cut quite a swath in our fervid imaginations; arriving in the late winter afternoons, walking crisply down the main corridor, leaving a trail of perfume on the stale, over-centrally-heated air. With the snow piled deep outside and the temperature twenty below zero, she would enter our classroom bringing a waft of cold but scented air with her; take off her fur coat, smooth her blond hair, and perch on the master's desk, revealing a comely stretch of stockinged knee. Her perfume dominated the wet wool smell of winter classrooms and she had my undivided attention. Thus transfixed, I imbibed a strange mixture of German language and erotic fantasy, both augmented when I later acquired a German girlfriend.

When I finally got to Berlin, the city still bore enough scars from the war to make its horrors tangible. Neat mosaic sidewalks suddenly ended in a tangle of weeds where a street had been bombed into oblivion. Solitary villas stood as the only relics of rich neighborhoods. The symbol of renascent Berlin was the stark ruin of the Kaiser Wilhelm Memorial Church, rising like an accusing skeleton bang in the middle of the flashy Kurfürstendamm. The ruins of the Reichstag fire, Hitler's first atrocity, were intact.

For the insatiable literary pilgrim, there were echoes of Isherwood's Berlin of the '30s. You could still, if it amused you, spend late evenings in a *Tanzenbar*. Somewhat overweight ladies, their ample white skin squeezed into black

Merry Widow corsets, made themselves available to dance or otherwise divert you, to old music, in dim tinted light. It was not vicious, not even exploitative, merely nostalgic for something I had only read about.

And in the cafés on the Kurfürstendamm, sitting at the rear, usually alone, dressed in tailored black, sat the widows of former Nazi officers, nursing cups of *Kaffeeschokolade*. They were silent and elegant, perhaps still known to their friends as *Frau General* or *Frau Oberst*.

The past haunted the present — and me. Every street, every glimpse from a car window, seemed like a scene from the movies I had so hungrily devoured in my college years. It was an adventure just to be there. The history that had dominated my youth had been made there in Berlin. Now it was happening again.

West Berlin authorities feared that the situation might explode. The next day, Monday, it became even more tense. Thousands of West Berliners converged on the Brandenburg Gate, whistling and jeering. The East Germans brought up armored cars and high-pressure water cannon. When their own police wouldn't let them near the gate, the West Berlin crowd threatened the Soviet War Memorial, a few hundred feet inside West Berlin. Two lonely Soviet soldiers stood guard. The crowd could have torn them to pieces. West Berlin police formed a chain and forced the crowd back a quarter of a mile.

That night I heard that one line of the elevated railroad was still operating through to East Berlin, so I decided to go in early the next morning to get the feel of the situation before it was too late.

A student named Klaus from the Free University was helping NBC as a messenger and interpreter and he agreed to go with me. I was a little apprehensive. I had been into East Berlin on other trips and been depressed by its shabbiness but not worried about safety. This was different. A number of Western newsmen had been detained for straying just inside the border. I wanted to explore deeper into the city.

So we felt a little like spies as we boarded the S-Bahn at 7 A.M. at the Zoo station in West Berlin for the short ride across the sector border to the Marx-Engels Platz.

No one checked our papers. Klaus had his ready in case. He told me it was lucky that he had just renewed his *Reise-buch,* the travel document West Berliners carried instead of a passport. It later became critical that he added one detail. The stupid authorities, he said, had put the renewal stamp on the wrong page of the folded document.

I was still using a Canadian passport issued in 1952, which described me as a radio announcer. Since I had nothing else to identify me as a journalist, I decided to be a tourist, with my Zeiss-Ikon camera around my neck.

It was a gray morning, chilly for August, giving the Soviet Sector an even drearier cast than normal. From the Marx-Engels Platz we began wandering away from the border to get a sense of the mood in East Berlin. There was nothing unusual. We walked through the Alexanderplatz and into the soulless Stalinallee, the wide boulevard adorned with stolid Soviet-inspired architecture. We looked in shop windows at the uninspiring goods. I bought some postcards and sent them from a post office. I took a lot of touristy pictures, including some of a bombed-out church left as a neglected ruin.

Gradually we wandered back toward the border. Near the Friederichstrasse, we found a large concentration of Soviet-built tanks parked in an empty bombsite. Against Klaus's advice I took about six pictures. All morning I had felt very conspicuous. Now, when I raised the camera to focus on the tanks and squeezed the shutter-release, it was as though I were raising a gun and firing it. But no one seemed to take any particular notice of us. Policemen passed, alone or in groups, but we were not stopped.

We had started before breakfast and we were both getting very hungry. We put off eating anything because we planned to have a long lunch in a state restaurant where we could observe people in a more leisurely way and listen to the conversations.

Around noon we came out into the Unter den Linden, the

grand avenue leading to the Brandenburg Gate on the East Berlin side. The Volkspolizei were keeping people well away from the gate. There was a small crowd, including a lot of young people, openly arguing with the police. It was the only manifestation of anger we had run into. We melted into the crowd, listening, but not taking pictures in case it attracted too much attention. The Volkspolizei behaved unprovocatively and the crowd gradually dispersed.

We set off for the restaurant, so hungry that we had even begun discussing what we would eat. We had just entered one of the side streets running south from the Unter den Linden when two men in plain clothes appeared from behind, muttered, *"Polizei,"* and ordered us to go with them. My pulse accelerated rapidly. They guided us into a nearby office building and down to the basement.

It was swarming with policemen and regular East German soldiers. Many offices opened off the corridor and they took us immediately into one of them. It looked like a makeshift operations headquarters, with several desks pushed together, maps spread out, and officers bent over them. As we entered, they turned and we saw that there were high-ranking Soviet as well as East German officers. They looked surprised. A civilian in a leather jacket and turtleneck sweater hurried forward and said harshly, "Not here! Take them out of here!"

One of our escort bundled us outside. He took my passport, Klaus's *Reisebuch,* and my camera, and went back inside leaving an armed policeman to guard us.

Along the wall opposite us soldiers were lining up, their rifles on slings over their shoulders. Behind the wall was a kitchen. The delicious smell of wurst and sauerkraut filled the corridor.

Thinking there was nothing to lose, I got up and joined the line of soldiers, who obligingly made a space. Klaus, still sitting on the bench, looked horrified but the guard seemed unperturbed. I was almost at the steamtable and congratulating myself that whatever happened I was going to have a full stomach, when the office door opened and the plainclothesman shouted angrily at me to sit down. He spoke so rapidly that I understood only the order and the word *schiessen*, meaning shoot. I whispered to Klaus, "What did he say?"

"If they move again, shoot them." With that, fear rapidly replaced hunger as my dominant concern.

After fifteen minutes or so, we were taken outside and put into the rear of a van. It drove to the headquarters of the Volkspolizei, a very large old building off the Alexanderplatz. The van stopped in a broad courtyard and as I got out and looked around I felt as though I were in a movie about people being rounded up by the Gestapo. It was frightening.

We were taken up three flights of a wide wooden staircase, the walls lined with white tiles. A long corridor with a creaky wooden floor, dimly lit by low-wattage bulbs, opened to the left and we were taken down it to a door that was open. They told us to wait in a large room, empty except for a dozen straight chairs and a table. Very little light came through the barred window.

Klaus and I sat down to wait. "This is not so good a place to be," he said. "Perhaps we could be here a long time."

A surly-looking Vopo was posted at the door to guard us. Once more I thought of all the Gestapo films I had seen. The Volkspolizei uniform, though a different color, was identical to the World War II outfits; the tight-waisted tunic with leather belt, jodhpurs sticking out from the thighs, and the knee-high boots. This fellow acted as though he had seen, and relished, all the same movies I had.

We were talking quietly when he showed up and immediately shouted at us to keep silent. A few minutes later, we lit cigarettes and he roared at us: *"Rauchen verboten!"*

A long time passed. Gradually, more people joined us, all miserable-looking individuals, whose whispers and clothes told us they had been caught trying to escape to the West.

Once each newcomer had exchanged a few words, he became silent, turning his thoughts inward. How to let his relatives know? Would he go to prison? It would be quiet for a few moments, then someone would whisper a question and get an answer. Then several people would answer and conversation developed until the young Vopo stormed back into the room shouting for silence. Twice he took his pistol out of the holster and brandished it menacingly; then, holding it by the barrel, crashed the butt on the table for emphasis. He carried on so extravagantly that I wondered if he were quite sane.

An elderly couple came in, leading a child of three or four, perhaps their grandchild. They carried many parcels and were wearing winter overcoats. They looked thoroughly exhausted and frightened. The little boy began to play cheerfully on the floor with a toy car, making *rrrm-rrrm* and *beep-beep* noises. His little voice was the only noise in the room. Everybody watched him and his grandparents. It got darker, and the single weak bulb hanging from the ceiling made the room seem more forbidding.

The little boy got up and said: "I'm hungry." His grandmother reached into her string bag and offered him a banana. "No, I want some sausage," he said petulantly. "We have no sausage," she said. He took the banana and went back to his car on the floor. It grew darker. More people were put into the room, until the newcomers had to sit on the floor against the wall.

The Vopo left the room. Klaus and I started whispering about what we could do. The policeman came back suddenly and caught us talking. He lunged forward, grabbed Klaus out of his chair, turned him to the wall, and, with his hand at the back of Klaus's head, pushed his face violently against the wall. He shouted: "I told you no talking! It will be worse next time!" He stormed off, presumably having to oversee several more rooms down the corridor.

Klaus's face was running with tears, from the pain of having his nose banged against the wall.

On top of being very hungry and needing to go to the bathroom, I was angry. I got up and went to the door and shouted down the hall in my very simple German: "You must send someone to speak to me. I am not a German citizen. I am a Canadian citizen and you have no right to keep me here!" The effect was somewhat spoiled because halfway through the speech I forgot the word for "citizen" and had to ask Klaus, who nervously whispered, "*Burger*," without turning away from the wall. I shouted the same sentiments in English and then went back to my seat, very hot in the face, intercepting worried glances from all the eyes in the room.

I was beginning to think it had produced no results when a plainclothesman came to the door and took us both down the hall. There we were separated and I found myself in a little office, sitting facing a desk with one uniformed police officer and one civilian. The questions were coldly polite and in English. My passport was in the civilian's hands and he verified all the details. He asked me what I was doing in East Berlin. I said I was visiting West Berlin and had decided to come and look around. What was I looking for? Nothing in particular, I said, just interested in what a tourist wants to see.

His expression changed. "Then why did you take pictures of tanks?"

So, I thought, they have developed the film.

"Just because they interested me."

"Why should you be interested in panzers?"

"No particular reason."

"For whom are you taking these pictures of tanks?"

"What do you mean?"

"Who is paying you to take these pictures of panzers?"

"No one is paying me."

This went on for half an hour or so, until he told me to go back to the waiting room. Klaus was also back, but we couldn't discuss the questioning.

There was another long wait, aggravated by hunger and an overfull bladder.

Night fell outside and the wan light threw depressing shadows under everyone's eyes. The little boy had been dozing with his head on his grandmother's lap. He woke up and said fretfully, "*Ich wunche Wurst.*"

"We have no sausage," the old lady crooned at him. "Have another banana."

But he began whimpering: "When are we going home? When do I see Mummy? When are we going?" And the grandparents exchanged terrible looks with each other and with the rest of us.

The possibilities began to look quite stark. Many Westerners had been accused of spying on evidence slimmer than they had on me. Some had gone to prison for years. It was a real possibility. It was stupid not to say from the start that I was a journalist and get whatever immunity that might give me. I would do so the first chance I got.

It came about two hours later, around 10 P.M. By that time we had been sitting for some nine hours, unable to go to the bathroom, eat, drink, or smoke. The next interrogation made it worse.

It happened in the same office but with two different men, both in civilian dress. One asked the questions, the other, a heavyset man in a turtleneck, merely listened. As he did so he ate appreciatively from a big bowl of thick soup, and munched a piece of dark bread.

As soon as they started I said:

"I should have told you from the beginning. I am not a tourist. I am a reporter from NBC News in New York. I have been assigned temporarily to Berlin. I came to East Berlin today as a reporter."

"Show us your accreditation, your identification."

Since I had deliberately left everything identifying me with NBC back at the hotel, I told them they could telephone the office in West Berlin, or London, or New York, to check.

"You were taking pictures for NBC?"

"Not really, just for myself."

"Who will you sell these pictures of panzers to? The CIA?"

"No."

"How much does the CIA pay you for each picture? One hundred dollars?"

"No one is paying me for the pictures."

"Then why did you take pictures of panzers?"

"Because I wanted to."

"Do you come from Canada?"

"Yes."

"In Canada, if you saw panzers in the street, you would take pictures of them?"

"If I wanted to, I would."

They laughed at each other, the soup eater and the questioner.

"Do you expect us to believe that? In Canada you would take pictures of panzers without permission?"

I began to feel the rigidities in their thinking and it worried me.

"So, you must tell us. Who is paying you for these pictures and how much will they pay you for each one? Who is paying you to come here as a spy?"

It went on and on in circles until they sent me back to the waiting room again, very discouraged. This time Klaus was not there.

Another long wait, punctuated by the arrival of Johnny Tiffin, a CBS cameraman I knew from London. He said they had picked him up at the Brandenburg Gate. Then the guard shouted at him to shut up. So Tiffin shrugged, lay down on the table, pulled his trench coat collar over his eyes, and went to sleep.

Close to midnight, Klaus had not reappeared and I was taken for another bout of questioning.

They made me repeat the story again, then said: "We have verified that you are a reporter for the American television, NBC, and we think it is right that you should go back to the Western Sector in a little while."

I felt enormously relieved.

"However, we have more questions concerning your friend, the West Berliner. There are some irregularities."

They asked me what I knew about Klaus, where I met him, how long I had known him, what he did, how many times he came to East Berlin. I told them the little I knew but began to wonder whether they had stumbled onto some part of Klaus that I knew nothing about. Berlin was full of characters leading very complicated lives. It teemed with spies.

I was so eager to get out of there that I found myself rapidly entertaining some unworthy thoughts; rationalizing that it would be all right to leave Klaus there and get help to him from West Berlin. I was shocked how the temptation crept over me. It also occurred to me that West Berliners had very little status in East German eyes. If left behind, Klaus could disappear for a long time.

I asked: "What are the irregularities?"

"His papers are not in order — among other matters."

The interrogator held up Klaus's *Reisebuch*, almost triumphantly. "You see, the *Reisebuch* is even out of date. We will have to investigate. It is better that your friend stays here until the investigation is completed. But you may go."

"But the *Reisebuch* has been renewed," I said. "He showed me this morning. They stamped it in the wrong place. If you turn it over, you'll see the renewal stamp."

He did so with bad grace, scarcely acknowledging that he saw the stamp. "Well, there are other things we need to investigate about him," he said, a little lamely, I thought.

I said I would wait while they did. The man shrugged indifferently and I found myself back in the waiting room. This time Johnny Tiffin was gone.

Fifteen minutes later I was called in and found Klaus with them.

"We have no more reason to detain you. You may both go. There is just one thing." He pulled my camera out of a drawer. "Please remove the film from the camera."

Astonished, I did so, realizing they had not developed the film and the only way they could have known what I had taken pictures of was by following us all morning. In a rather puny gesture of defiance, I exposed the film to the light as I removed it, and gave it to them.

The interrogator turned very gracious. He escorted us downstairs, chatting amiably, and showed us where to catch the S-Bahn near the Alexanderplatz.

Few things have given me as much joy as getting out of there. We were well over the Sector Border, through the police checkpoint, and the train was curving around toward the bright lights of West Berlin, before I remembered the shadowy figures still sitting in that room and the little boy who wanted wurst. Those people had no immunity.

When we got back to the NBC office, we had a celebration.

The experience affected me in two noticeable ways. Thereafter, I took more seriously the necessity to oppose Soviet totalitarianism. I also became a much fiercer defender of civil liberties in the West.

The emotional jolt I had received and concern for my own safety quickly subsided into contempt for a regime that could treat its own people that way. The hopelessness that emanated from those captured East Germans, the thuggishness of the guard, all made a profound impression. Freedom from arbitrary arrest, freedom of political thought, freedom of movement, became more than nice abstractions.

No one understood this better than the West Berliners. The next day, Wednesday, the anger and bitterness at the apparent indifference of the Western powers produced a staggering turnout for a rally at the Schöneberger Rathaus, used as a town hall. More than a quarter of a million people jammed the square in pouring rain to listen to Willy Brandt, the mayor of West Berlin. From the steps all you could see was a vast landscape of multicolored umbrellas, broken by banners and signs demanding Allied deeds, not words.

That was the theme of the message Brandt told the crowd he had sent to President Kennedy. The president responded by sending Vice-President Lyndon Johnson to Berlin and by ordering another army battle group into West Berlin.

On Saturday I covered LBJ's arrival at Templehof Airport and followed him on a triumphant tour with Willy Brandt. Johnson waded into the crowds, shaking hands and scattering ball-point pens as though he were running for Brandt's job. The back of his neck turned such an alarming shade of purple from these exertions that I was afraid he was about to have another heart attack. But nothing stopped him.

On Sunday morning I got up at 3 A.M. and flew to Hanover to come up the autobahn across East Germany with the U.S. Army battle group. No one knew whether the East Germans would stop them at the Helmstedt checkpoint, where the autobahn crossed into East Germany. To reach there in time, NBC had arranged a car with a driver to take me from Hanover to Helmstedt. I found him right off the plane, an elderly man who looked at me, horrified, and said, "*Blut*." I went into the airport men's room and found that in my hasty shaving in the middle of the night I had made a deep cut which apparently had been bleeding ever since. My neck and my shirt collar were soaked in blood. It looked as though someone had tried to cut my throat and botched it. I washed my neck but there was no time to do anything about the bloody shirt. So we took off for Helmstedt in a very ancient Mercedes, which still managed to purr along at more than 100 mph and got to the checkpoint in good time.

The fifteen-hundred-man battle group was just going through when I got there. No difficulties. But it took me half an hour to get through, the East Germans insisting on a full transit visa to cross the German Democratic Republic.

With that, we sped after the battle group and eventually came into Berlin just behind it, to a delirious welcome from the emotional Berliners and LBJ himself.

For several weeks, the Wall became my life. I kept going back as it grew and reported at all hours to NBC. Piers Anderton returned to handle the television assignment. As the junior correspondent, I did the radio.

Unlike many foreign stories, where journalists tend to work in packs, I worked this one alone. I patrolled the Wall constantly, through the French, British, and American sectors, day and night. I drove as close as I could get through the tangle of dead-end streets, parked my rented Volkswagen, then walked along a stretch of Wall until I found something. It was a reporter's dream. Every time I went I picked up a story.

I ate few organized meals, ducking into bars for a draft beer while telephoning, stopping at a wurst stall to buy a sausage with sauerkraut or chili sauce or curry. I slept very little; it was too exciting.

Some stretches of the Wall became more intimate and poignant for me than the grand public spaces like the Brandenburg Gate or the Potsdamer Platz. The most touching was the Bernauerstrasse, in the French Sector. The street ran southwest to northeast. The Soviet Sector line ran along the south side. As the East Germans began extending the Wall to the Bernauerstrasse, they did not actually build a wall. They used the walls of existing houses, merely bricking up the windows and doorways, first on the ground floor, then upwards.

In the first few days, people on the upper stories leaned out of their windows and watched themselves being gradually immured in East Berlin. Their friends, and often parts of their families, lived on the other side of the street — in the West. But their houses and their possessions, their homes, were in the East. They watched as the tide rose to cut them off.

I watched one woman weeping helplessly from the second-story window. That evening she was still there as the yellow sunset shone down the street, burnishing the brownish-red brick of the row houses. The next day she was not there. She had jumped from her window to be in the West. She was killed on hitting the pavement. I got there soon afterward, just as someone was placing a tin can of flowers on the spot. Others followed. Soon it became a custom all over the city, these little shrines to people who had died escaping.

In those early days there were also joyous escapes: a young Vopo, watching for his moment, simply leaped the barbed wire, then put his machine gun on the pavement, tearing off his helmet and shouting, "I'm free!" When Willy Brandt visited the scene at the Brandenburg Gate, one East Berliner ran straight to him across the no-man's-land, sure that the East Germans wouldn't dare shoot at the mayor of West Berlin. But many *were* shot and the shrines grew more numerous and more elaborate.

I kept coming back to the Bernauerstrasse. The tragedy seemed so palpable there. One afternoon, as I walked close to the bricked-up houses, I heard a grating noise, like a stone moving. I looked down and saw a hand move a brick in a basement window. I pretended not to see and walked on. Sometime later, I sauntered back. Another brick was loose. I went away to another part of the Wall and came back a few hours later. The hole was much bigger, so I assumed that someone had got away.

One night, I stayed up and patrolled the stretch of Wall in the American Sector, to see what the troops did. They had moved up in force, and every few blocks you came on a cluster of tanks blocking the crossroads, their guns aimed into East Berlin.

By 3 A.M. it was raining. For a while I didn't find very

much. I drove, parked, got out, talked to the troops, drank their coffee, said goodnight, and continued on. Then I came to a point where a bridge carried a street over a canal. The Wall blocked the bridge about halfway across. Several tanks marked the intersection. I chatted with the men, their helmets and ponchos glistening in the streetlights from the misty rain. I was about to move on, when someone said, "Captain! The radio says the general's coming. Be here any minute." That created a flap. They woke up the guys who were dozing, put guns into the hands of men who should have them, doused the cigarettes, put away the coffee, and generally stiffened up. Indeed, a few minutes later, jeep headlights appeared out of the gloom and out stepped no less a figure than the deputy commander of U.S. forces in Europe, General Charles D. Palmer. He was wearing a helmet. He chatted with every soldier. Everyone was terrified and elated that he was there. And I was impressed. There is always something very tender about a senior officer doing rounds in the middle of the night.

The general glanced at the bridge with its stretch of Wall and asked: "They all quiet over there?"

"Yes, sir!"

"Well, I'd like to have a look."

He walked up the rise of the bridge, with the captain and a sergeant carrying a flashlight, and me. You could sense the protective shifting and cocking of weapons behind us.

We came to the Wall in the middle of the bridge. It was about chest-high. The general told the sergeant, "Shine your light over there."

The beam hit the derelict buildings on the other side of the canal. Then it swept down along the immediate other side of the Wall and we all leaned over to look. Directly beneath us, it suddenly revealed two Volkspolizei, sound asleep, leaning comfortably against each other in the shelter of the Wall. The general leaned farther to take a good look. As I watched him, a streetlight illuminated the front of his helmet. A large drop of water collected on the lip of the brim and fell right onto the sleeping face of one of the Vopos underneath. Both men awoke with a great start, scrambling for weapons and helmets, trying to orient themselves in the glare of the flash-light.

The general laughed and walked down the bridge and laughed some more. Everyone in that small U.S. Army group laughed delightedly with the general.

Our imaginations were fevered enough to make me toy with the phrase "Could World War III begin with a raindrop falling on the face of an East German policeman?" Fortunately, I resisted that temptation.

I decided to spend another night along the canals farther south, in the industrial part of Berlin. Some East Berliners had been escaping to the West at night by swimming the canals. Some had been shot.

My VW had broken down and been replaced with a well-used Mercedes. It growled through the dark maze of streets as I kept getting lost and had to stop to read the map. Several times I stumbled into the border without meaning to. Finally I found the bit of the Teltow Canal I was looking for, in Neuköln. I parked the Mercedes and walked to the towpath, which was overgrown with bushes and trees. My plan was to patrol that towpath all night, hoping that something would happen.

The first thing that happened was that I got frightened out of my wits. It was very dark but I was strolling along, enjoying the mild night, congratulating myself on my enterprise, when I heard low voices approaching. I took several steps into the bushes to hide. But there was a sudden snarling and two large dogs sprang at me out of the night, forcing me to the ground, pinning my chest and panting over my face. I was terrified. Then a man's voice spoke a command in German, the dogs retreated, and a flashlight shone down at me.

"*Was tun Sie hier?*" For a few seconds I thought I might have inadvertently crossed the border in the maze of inter-secting canals and that these were East Germans. But they turned out to be very large West Berlin policemen, both wearing ankle-length, belted rubber raincoats. I scrambled up, trying to remember the words for American television.

"*Amerikanische Fernsehen,*" I stammered, pointed out my

tape recorder, and got out my press credentials with Willy Brandt's signature. They relaxed, told me to be careful not to get shot from the other side of the canal, and left. It took me about fifteen minutes to reassemble enough courage to carry on with my plan.

The other side of the canal looked like the perimeter of a concentration camp, which in a sense it was. On the higher ground, above the towpath, there was a new chain-link fence with thick coils of barbed wire on top. Searchlights shone along the fence at intervals. Pairs of Vopos carrying rifles slung over their shoulders patrolled constantly.

They were close enough when they passed that I could hear them talking. The smell of their cigarettes drifted across to me. I stood very still and tried to merge into the shadows. I didn't want to get shot by some nervous Communist trying to do his duty.

The night passed very slowly. I got cold and damp. I kept visiting a small West Berlin police outpost on a bridge nearby, to check whether anyone had come across. No one had. The East Germans had mounted a very ancient machine gun, with tripod legs, at their end of the bridge, pointing west.

There was only one moment when the quiet was broken. A couple of hundred yards along the canal, there was a splashing in the dark. I began running toward it. There was a shout from a Vopo. A dazzling searchlight switched on and swung down to the water. Rifle bolts clicked. But there was nothing there. Ducks perhaps. Or a person too terrified to leave the cover of the bank. I waited for a long time until all the ripples disappeared. But nothing came.

These incidents made wonderful atmosphere and color stories. They addressed the human problem of the Wall. Its political essence was more elusive, caught up as we were with the emotions of the Berliners, aware only of the small piece of the picture directly in front of us. Because that piece often carried such powerful emotions, I, for one, had to make a huge effort to fit these scenes into the overall strategic picture. I came supposedly well fitted for it, fresh from frequent briefings at Number 10 Downing Street and the Foreign Office in

London. But I found it most difficult to be snatched emotionally from the role of detached diplomatic correspondent, to street reporter dealing with the human realities.

Both perceptions coalesced for me in one incident. It was Sunday, August 27, and the Wall was now two weeks old. I drove along it, stopping to look at the reactions of West Berliners spending the Sunday gazing wistfully across the Wall into the East; watching young workers adding more concrete blocks to raise it higher.

Whether from nervousness or shame, several bricklayers I watched were deliberately building a sloppy wall, placing the blocks and sloshing the mortar carelessly, making only superficial effort with their trowels to finish the pointing neatly. It seemed to me that they worked grudgingly and very self-consciously, under the contemptuous eyes of the West Berliners, some standing only a few feet away, uttering a stream of insults.

I stopped to watch such a scene near the Friedrichstrasse, the only crossing point left open to the Western allies, and later known as Checkpoint Charlie.

An East German loudspeaker truck came along to bolster the workers' morale and counter the hazing from West Berliners. Its enormous loudspeakers battered the ears with insulting slogans and songs. The crowd of West Berliners grew bigger and angrier. They started jeering at the Communists, trying to drown the blaring loudspeaker by chanting: "Warmongers! Warmongers!" A U.S. Patton tank rolled up and the West Berliners cheered. Heartened by its presence, they redoubled their shouting at the Communists.

Then, on the Eastern side an armored car with a high-pressure water cannon in the turret came around the corner. The West Berliners roared their disapproval. Men and women together snatched up handfuls of small paving stones and flung them at the Communists. A hail of stones fell on the armored car, clanging off its sides and turret. The water cannon fired several powerful jets of water into the crowd, which scattered. But the West Berliners, obviously delighted to vent their frustrations physically, re-formed and kept up the stoning, driving the masons away from the Wall. The demonstration now involved more than a thousand people and there was increasing danger than the East Germans would open fire with bullets, not water.

A U.S. Army Infantry company moved in to break it up. Soldiers wearing bulletproof vests lined up along the Wall, cocking their rifles whose fixed bayonets pointed to the sky. Then they firmly pushed the angry West Berliners back several hundred yards.

I had been taking pictures from on top of a piece of road-building machinery. I got down and ran over to the U.S. officer in charge and accosted him rather hotly about why American troops were protecting the East Germans.

He was a very competent looking colonel and gazed at me coolly. "I'm not going to start World War Three," he said, "just to let these Berliners throw stones at Communists."

His name was John R. Dean of San Francisco, a veteran of World War II and Korea. I wrote a piece about that incident and it restored some perspective for me.

As long as the Communists had done nothing more than seal off the territory they already controlled, East Berlin, it was a humiliation but there was nothing the U.S. and its allies could do, short of nuclear war.

All that Khrushchev had done was to further assert the division of Europe agreed by Roosevelt, Churchill, and Stalin at Yalta in 1944. That reality was finally sanctioned by the Helsinki accords in 1974.

If the Communists had attacked West Berlin, as all the fearful scenarios of that summer imagined they might, Kennedy would have had to respond. Early in the planning, Defense Secretary McNamara pointed out that rapid escalation to full nuclear war was almost inevitable. That realization caused Kennedy to make an important change in the policy of massive nuclear retaliation inherited from the Eisenhower and Dulles years. He ordered a build-up of U.S. conventional forces, to permit a more flexible response — short of nuclear war.

For all the heartbreak and pain it caused, the Berlin Wall may have done mankind some service. It removed a dangerous source of friction between East and West. It advertised in the crudest way to the impressionable Third World that a Communist state like East Germany could survive only if it became the jailer of its own people. And it helped to give the West a modified deterrent strategy needed for the era in which nuclear terror was approaching balance.

I understood very little of this at the time. All I knew was that for a few weeks that summer I had lived where World War III could have started.

NINE

Stories from Britain

IN LATE SEPTEMBER 1962, a Super Constellation airliner of Flying Tiger Airlines, filled with U.S. servicemen and their wives, had engine failure on a flight to Europe. The pilot had to ditch at night, in the open Atlantic, six hundred miles west of Ireland. With superb handling and discipline, fifty-one of the sixty-six people on board got out and into life rafts. Three of them died of exposure, leaving forty-eight survivors. Ships of many nations were diverted to search for them and the rescue became a very big story. Newsmen from all the media in Europe descended on Shannon Airport in Ireland to get the first survivor stories. NBC sent me with a film crew from London.

First, four survivors and twelve dead bodies were landed from the Canadian aircraft carrier *Bonaventure*. A West Point instructor, Major Richard Elander, said there had been absolute silence and no panic as the plane ditched. He and his wife, Lois, had held hands. He said he had told her, "We've had a good marriage. It doesn't matter if we die." And she had said: "Sweetie, it's been a wonderful life. I'm so glad I married you." The plane struck. Her back was broken and a shoulder dislocated. But her husband got her out of the plane and into an overcrowded life raft. For six hours he held her face above water. Gasoline and salt water burned their skin. The raft tossed and heaved on gigantic waves. Some of the survivors were seasick, some had dead bodies lying on top of them. Some sang "The Battle Hymn of the Republic."

That was very moving stuff, told by the young major standing by his wife on a stretcher. But because forty-five more survivors were still to arrive, all the newsmen stayed on.

My cameraman was Chris Callery, an engaging Irishman and a close friend who had been with me in many scrapes. The sound man was an older, eccentric Englishman named Digby Jones, a legend throughout NBC. He looked like a slightly mad scientist, a "boffin," thin, balding, peering through thick spectacles that were always falling down his nose or broken and held together with bits of camera tape or fuse wire. He was reputed once to have found electric current in the Sahara desert, when camera batteries failed, by sticking two wires into the sand.

Digby had been a wireless operator during the war and one of his amusements was to monitor the shortwave frequencies. One evening, while we were waiting at Shannon, he stayed in his room with his earphones on while Chris and I went to dinner. We had been talking for days about the Shannon Estuary lobster we heard they served in the excellent airport restaurant.

The lobster had just arrived on the table when Digby burst in, disheveled and agitated. He had picked up an emergency message from the freighter *Celerina*, which was carrying a group of survivors to Antwerp. There had been a fire on board and several people were injured. The captain wanted them and the air crash survivors taken off. They had arranged a rendezvous with the Irish Coast Guard for 8 A.M. the following morning, ten miles due south of Cork.

We looked around the dining room. Many of our competitors — CBS, ABC, CBC, ITN, BBC and others — were there, stuffing their faces with the innocent pleasure of all camera crews who know they are being paid to do it. We could scoop them all!

We left quietly, the lobsters still on the plates, and raced to the hotel. We threw the camera gear into the car and set off into the night for Cork, about a hundred miles away.

We stopped once, in Limerick, to call the Gàrda, the Irish National Police, to ask if it would be possible to rent a fishing boat in Cork the next morning. They apparently misunderstood and assumed we were some official party. Every village and small town we came to, there was the Gàrda officer standing in the road, with a flashlight, waving us through, some even saluting. It may have helped the illusion that we were driving a Ford Zodiac, famous as the "Z Car" of the fabulously popular British TV police serial.

All went well until we stopped in one dark village to ask directions. I got out of the car to stretch my legs, missed the curbstone in the dark, and sprained my ankle badly. I could almost hear the ligaments tear, and I ended up lying in the gutter gasping with the sudden pain. They carried me inside the Gàrda station where the officer, in his suspenders, looked at me in the light.

"You've gone a bit white," he said. "Have a sip of this while I look at your ankle." He handed me a bottle of John Powers whiskey and I took a large gulp. The ankle was already swelling rapidly. "Unfortunately, I haven't got my first aid kit," the policeman said.

Digby came to the rescue. He raised a baggy, tweed trouser leg, revealing a loosely wound, not very clean, elastic bandage. "It's for my varicose veins," he said with an air of martyrdom. "But you need it more than I do, just now."

So I thanked him and the Gàrda officer bound me up expertly. We all had a sip from his whiskey bottle and set off again on our rush through the night. I moved into the back seat, with my injured ankle propped up, feeling every jolt. Somehow the sense of adventure was leaking away.

Around 5 A.M. we got to Cork and found the docks. Improbably, we located and aroused a man with a fishing boat who agreed for £10 to take us to the rendezvous. The next step was to find a café for a heavy breakfast, because we hadn't eaten since the previous lunchtime. But the fisherman said we'd never make it by 8 A.M. if we didn't leave right away.

So, no breakfast. We unloaded the heavy camera gear down a steep, tide-exposed ladder into the boat, which was about twenty feet long and open, with only a small cuddy in the bow for shelter. The boat stank of fish, the worn planks of the decking were thick with scales. I wedged myself into a corner to protect my throbbing ankle and we set off, already in poor spirits.

Five minutes outside Cork Harbor, the seas became steep enough to make the old boat with its chugging engine labor up each wave as if it were a small hill, hover precariously at the crest, while the propeller roared out of the water, then sidle down into the trough. The wind came up and blew spray over us with each wave. After an hour we were soaked and miserable, beginning privately to curse Digby and his bloody radio. After two hours, we were feeling decidedly queasy and fed up and the cursing wasn't so private.

Finally the fisherman said we were ten miles out. We took his word for it because none of us wanted to go any farther and there was no way of knowing anyway. There was nothing in sight. Each time the boat lumbered to the crest of a wave, we got a glimpse of empty horizon. In all directions there was nothing but sea, except the gray smudge of land behind us.

We waited an hour, wallowing in that sea. The boatman seemed to think it was a perfectly natural thing to be doing. He kept cheerfully offering us swigs from his bottle of *poteen*, the white spirit illicitly distilled from potatoes. It went down like living fire but somehow subdued hunger, seasickness, and aching ankle.

Finally, we gave it up and turned back toward Cork, feeling foolish, angry, hungry, and frustrated. With the wind aft, the spray stopped, and when we dried, our heads, faces and clothing were caked white with salt.

Two hours later, we staggered back ashore intent on finding a café immediately. After more than five hours at sea we were so hungry that we were really getting foul-tempered with each other. Small mutinies kept erupting. But the minute we got into the car, we heard a news broadcast saying the survivors were just then being plucked off the freighter by helicopter and flown to a hospital in Kinsale. Damn! We got out the map. Kinsale was twenty miles away, over very narrow roads. Half an hour at least. The opposition would be there already. But we had to go. We stopped only for chocolate bars to keep the mutiny in check and set off, with Chris driving like a madman, swearing at Digby for sending us off on this crazy errand.

We pulled into the hospital the very moment the survivors arrived. We got our cameras set up with several competitors just in time to record the heartrending stories of the survivors.

One incident has stayed with me. A U.S. Army captain had survived but his wife had been lost. With his eyes full of tears, he described the last moments as the plane prepared to ditch at night in the open ocean. They sat in their Mae Wests.

"When the plane hit, we were catapulted forward in a bunch. The safety belts held but the seats broke loose. It was pitch dark and the water was pouring in. I didn't see my wife again after that." The captain faltered, tried to regain control, then broke down and wept. You could hear nothing but his sobs and the quiet whirr of several 16mm cameras.

We packed up our gear and prepared to race off to Shannon where we could ship the film to New York. Just as we were leaving, we saw the poor captain in the lobby. With him was an agitated British TV reporter, pleading: "I'm terribly sorry but I was late. I came in just as you were talking. I didn't have time to set up my camera. If we set up now, would you mind awfully just doing that bit again?"

The captain looked at him haggardly: "What bit?"

"That bit where you tell about your wife and then break down."

The captain turned contemptuously away. Suddenly, the agonizing sprain, the sleepless night, our salt-caked clothes, our empty stomachs, our bad temper, were all worth it. I thanked God I wasn't in the position of that reporter, feeling forced into such callousness because he didn't have "the bit" that everyone would carry that night, "the bit" the producers would jump on and run again and again in each newscast.

In most of the stories television cares to cover there is always "the right bit," the most violent, the most bloody, the most pathetic, the most tragic, the most wonderful, the most awful moment. Getting the effective "bit" is what television news is all about. It is the bit you always recognize when you've got it and which you will go through just about anything to get because it means success and missing it consistently means you'd better look for job other than a TV correspondent.

And to what purpose are thousands of men and women scrambling over the earth, sometimes at great risk, to get that bit? So that millions of people may be distracted for a moment from their own domestic concerns to witness another human being in great distress? To feel what? A moment of compassion? A second of titillation? A wisp of vicarious fear?

Does it not ultimately blunt and cheapen all those natural feelings to have them so often artificially stimulated? Does it not make human pity itself a banality? Does that not force competitive television producers to turn the screw a trifle harder each time to make the sensation fresher, to unbanalize it? Yes.

And what is the ultimate purpose of all this activity? The television journalists, like journalists everywhere, want to tell stories. The networks want to sell deodorant.

And that's the way it is.

If the craft teaches you automatically to jump on occasions like that, it also trains your ear to detect subtler stories. You develop a sense of what will work as a story, whether the ingredients are horror, adventure, nostalgia or humor. Some stories are worth pursuing even if you sense you're being fed a tall tale; and there is enough Celtic whimsy left in the British Isles to provide plenty of those.

One day in November 1961, I was walking in the West End of London with some time to kill. Near the end of Dover Street away from Piccadilly, I passed a barbershop or, as it called itself, a Gentlemen's Hairdresser. It was very old-fashioned, the windows half-curtained, displaying a few Kent brushes and combs and nothing else. Something about its serenity and seriousness appealed to me. I have never been quite sure that I was getting precisely the right haircut to suit whatever image of myself I was entertaining at any one time; not that I could have defined that very precisely. Whatever it was just then impelled me inside.

It was a very quiet, almost covert establishment. Facing the door was a row of cubicles, each with a curtain. One of them was drawn open and a chubby-faced, slightly balding man came out and ushered me into his chair. It was not a barber's chair but a wooden Windsor chair. I sat in it, he pulled the curtain behind us and began competently and conservatively working on my hair.

As he did, he began talking, with a slight Irish accent. He said his name was Paddy Demaine and told me something about himself; then he stopped, looked me carefully in the mirror, and said: "Can I tell you a very strange thing that has occurred?" Something in his tone as he stood there, in his gray cotton jacket, comb and scissors poised, gave me an odd feeling.

"Have you ever heard of Biddy Early?" and as he asked it was as though, on a movie soundtrack, an odd minor chord had crept in. I said I hadn't.

He began, with a storyteller's cadence: "Biddy Early was a witch. She lived about a hundred years ago in a village called Feakle in County Clare in the West of Ireland. She had red hair and tender eyes, as they said, and she outlived three husbands. She was known all over Ireland for her powers. People would drive all the way from Dublin in their carriages to see her, although the priests tried to prevent it by posting boys at the crossroads to misdirect them. She could heal people and foretell their futures." He said it as matter-of-factly as he might have said, "she could do fine needlework." He went on cutting my hair.

"Biddy Early's powers worked through a blue bottle. She kept it in a dresser in her cottage and when people came to see her, she took the bottle out, held it up and looked into it, then pronounced her cure. She was the most famous woman in Ireland and the most feared. They wrote songs about Biddy and printed engravings of her picture. Now, when she was old and ill and near dying she called the old women of the village to her bedside. She was holding the blue bottle. She told them to take it down the hill to a little lake and throw it in. She made them all swear, under terrible threats, not to try to fish it out again when she was dead.

"The old crones all swore themselves blue in the face and they carried the bottle down the hill and threw it into the lake. The minute Biddy died there they were, all scrambling down to the lake again trying to fish it out. But they couldn't find it. The bottle had disappeared. Some say that the priests took it away, because she took the faith just before she died, so she could be buried in hallowed ground. But I believe it disappeared into the lake," Demaine said, with a special emphasis that made me look at his eyes in the mirror. He was smiling at my skeptical look.

"You don't believe it?"

"Should I believe it?"

"Would you believe that I am Biddy Early's great-great-great-grandson?"

"How do you know that?"

"Because my mother told me, and her mother told her. And she told me something else. That a descendent of Biddy's would find the bottle again eighty years later. Eighty years later is this year."

"Has anyone found it?"

"Well, listen to me now and tell me if you believe it: I had been wanting to go back to Ireland for a long time and I finally went last summer. With my wife and small son we went over by the ferry and hired a car. I took her and the boy down to Tipperary to her family and early one morning I drove by the village of Feakle. It is a very simple place. They knew all about Biddy Early. A farmer called Jamsie Noonan showed me the remains of her cottage. It's just a ruin now on a little hill and there, down below, was the lake. We walked down the hill to the edge of the lake, all grown over with elder bushes and such. I pushed my way through the bushes to the edge of the water and there, God save me, a few yards out, was a blue bottle floating! I shouted out to Jamsie to come and see. We broke off a large branch and fetched the bottle into the shore and soon everybody in Feakle knew that Biddy Early's bottle had been found."

"What was it like?"

"It was a blue bottle, very old looking, about a foot long."

"What did you do with it?" I asked.

"I brought it back with me to London. And, you know? I can feel the power of it already."

"How?"

"My neuralgia. I always suffered terrible pains in my back. Nothing would make them go away, pills from the doctor, heating pads, mustard plasters, nothing. So, I sat down with the bottle in my hands one night, and I thought hard about it, and, suddenly, I knew for certain what the cure was. I should warm some newspaper with a hot iron, and then wrap it around my back. And it worked. The pain went away."

"Would you be willing to show me the bottle?" I asked.

"Of course," said Paddy Demaine. "And you could go to Feakle and ask them there." It was almost as though he could read my mind.

"Perhaps I will," I said.

In those days, late 1961, the NBC *Today Show* was on the lookout for light feature stories. I wrote immediately to John Chancellor, the *Today* host, proposing Biddy Early as a piece of whimsy too good to pass up. When the program agreed, I took off for Ireland with a film crew. We landed at Shannon Airport, stayed at the hotel there, and drove off to Feakle the next morning.

Dawn comes late on a mid-December morning. As the copper sun burns through the mist, its light makes strange magic of the winter country — the Celtic crosses, the lichened stone walls, the small trees, the dry brown grass, all rimed with frost, all shimmering in the golden sunlight. It could make you believe anything.

It was like that when we came into Feakle, a village so lost in other centuries that you felt that if you chanced to pass by five minutes later it might not be there at all.

We found Jamsie Noonan, with a lean, honest face, who abandoned his farmyard long enough to come down to the lake with us. We put up the camera and he told us how Demaine had indeed found the bottle. And something in his voice, and the meaning in his hands as he described holding the bottle, immediately revealed that Noonan believed. We went back into his snug kitchen to drink tea and get warm. He told us a story he had heard as a child.

In the time of the famine, farmers with cows guarded them because starving people tried to steal their milk. One moonlight night, a farmer came into his field and saw a rabbit drinking from his cow's udder. He shouted to chase it away and then fired his shotgun, wounding it in a hind leg. The rabbit kept bounding on, with the farmer chasing, till at last he saw it dart into Biddy Early's cottage. When the farmer went in, there was no sign of the rabbit, only Biddy Early herself, lying on the bed, panting and out of breath, with her skirt turned up on one ankle, showing a glimpse of bright red petticoat.

"You see, she had turned herself into a rabbit," Noonan said gravely. "Of course, they could do things like that in those days." And clustered around the kitchen table, his wife and wide-eyed children all nodded seriously.

One of Biddy's reported powers was to transfer illness from people to animals. "You will be well," she would say. "The cow will take your consumption."

Did the people of Feakle still believe in some eerie power from the lake? I walked around it looking for better camera angles and came upon the decomposed body of a dog, showing through the rotted sack it had been drowned in. Then, a short time later, another drowned dog. Then, for several yards, medicine and pill bottles of all shapes and colors. Were they just using the lake as a dumping ground? Or did they mean something else? No! Absurd! The atmosphere was affecting my judgment.

Everyone on the single, unpaved street of Feakle knew that

a man had found the bottle and you could have cast a John Ford movie from the faces and voices who told us so. We attracted a small crowd and they all began telling Biddy Early stories. Then one old man said, "I know where there's Biddy Early's dresser. It's in the old man's cottage in the woods."

They got out an ancient square black car to show us the way and we followed in ours. Halfway down a wooded lane, we had to stop because there were fallen trees blocking the road.

"I haven't been down here since the big storm. I wonder if he's still alive," the old man said.

Carrying the camera gear, we followed, climbing over tree trunks or around the torn-up roots, to a clearing with a beautifully built stone house in the middle. They called to the old man, but no one answered, so we all crowded in. There was only one large room, with a packed earth floor. Half of the room to the left of the doorway was filled with firewood, small twigs and sticks, piled haphazardly floor to ceiling.

At the other end was a huge fireplace with a mantel six feet high, large enough to walk into. In the center of the hearth, a very small fire of twigs was burning. Facing it on one side was a frail old man with a cloud of silky white hair, sitting upright in a ladderback chair inside the fireplace. Across the fire and sharing it with him was a small, white kitten.

The men from Feakle went up to him, shook his hand, and patted him on the back, delighted he was still alive. The old man looked bewildered, especially when we turned on very bright battery lights to film him and the dresser. Because, sure enough, against the wall near the fireplace, was a tall country kitchen dresser, with drawers and shelves above.

"It was in those drawers that she kept her bottle," one of the village men said. "It was a blue bottle."

"I know," I said.

"Wait!" he said dramatically. "You have to go and see old Bridget O'Malley down the road. She saw Biddy Early herself when she was a child. She was cured by her."

So we piled out of the cottage, leaving the old man and the kitten to their fire. I put a ten-shilling note into his hand but he stared at it as if he didn't know what it was.

Our cavalcade had picked up another old car and we rattled and bumped a couple of miles down the road to a farmyard. The farmhouse was of stone, L-shaped, enclosing the muddy yard. The local men ran ahead shouting importantly, "Bring out old Bridget. It's the television from America!"

The children stared at us but presently a very old lady came out wrapped in a shawl.

"No, no," the men protested, "*Old* Bridget, the *old* woman!"

The family clustered in the doorway.

"But she's in bed! It'll be the death of her out in this cold. She's ninety-seven," the women protested.

"Give her a drop of whiskey and wrap her up well. It's a warm day. She'll love it. It's for the television."

There was a lot of grumbling and scurrying inside, and eventually an even more ancient lady, smothered in shawls and wraps, came creeping out and sat down on the bench, in the winter sun which had indeed grown quite warm.

We turned on the camera. She scarcely needed any prompting from me. She must have been telling the story all her life, and was bright and hale enough to go on telling it for years after.

"When I was still a baby," she said, "I was very ill. My mother didn't know what to do. The priest had forbidden anyone to go to Biddy Early. They called her a witch. But my mother went by darkness, around by the fields so the priest wouldn't know. She came to Biddy's cottage at dawn with me in her arms. And Biddy Early took her blue bottle, and held it 'twixt her and the rising sun and she said, 'Woman, your child will live! Go home! Your child will live!' And my mother brought me home and I grew well and strong."

"What was the bottle like?" I asked. "What did it look like?"

"Oh, just like any old porter bottle," she said.

Back in London, Paddy Demaine showed us the bottle, but wouldn't let us touch it. It was blue and looked old and handmade, bulbous below the neck.

Millions of Americans saw it too when "The Story of Biddy Early" ran for twelve minutes on the *Today Show*. If anybody shared my suspicion that it looked like a Chianti bottle with the straw wrapping off, they never told me.

Feakle was real enough. Besides, I had learned another rule of journalism by then: you can kill some stories by asking too many questions.

Perhaps the hardest thing to learn, in refining my editorial judgment, was a sensivity to cliché. Journalism is cliché, after all. The more popular the journalism, the more blatant and unabashed is the resort to hackneyed situations and hackneyed responses, formula stories where you have merely to fill in the blanks to produce the professional effect.

If you aspire to be a notch more sophisticated, you are constantly on the lookout for the unique detail, a fresh human response to reilluminate the common experience that created the cliché in the first place. The dividing line between giving new life to a cliché and being trapped in one is sometimes very hard to find.

NBC, in the winter of 1961, asked all its bureaus to find comedians using John Kennedy material in their routines. I tracked one down playing the workingmen's clubs in the North of England. The clubs are a lucrative and exclusively British corner of show business and, for all their plebian atmosphere, are wealthy enough to afford top talent.

We had finished filming one of the stand-up comedians at a club in Manchester and he asked me and the cameraman, Adrian Console, to come back for a drink with him. The comedian was a well-known figure in British entertainment, a very engaging old trooper with wonderful stories to tell from his forty-five years in variety shows.

We drove to a pleasant house in a residential street and discovered a little party to celebrate the end of his tour; good drinks and food and half a dozen of his old friends. The hostess was a charming and handsome woman of about fifty-five, with a good figure and pretty face. She made us very welcome and we settled down around the glowing gas fire to drink and talk.

Presently, the old comic fell asleep in the middle of one of his stories. They all laughed, said the old boy couldn't hold his booze anymore; and the hostess and another guest carried him by his shoulders and feet up the stairs and tucked him into bed.

The other guests dwindled away but the hostess urged us not to go. We had been planning to drive back to London, but it was now one o'clock in the morning and too late to start out. "We'll have a drink," I said, "and then go and find a hotel."

In fact we stayed all night because I fell into a conversation with the lady that was so absorbing that I didn't notice the time. Adrian fell asleep on a sofa. Our hostess kept offering me drinks and later cups of tea.

She had a name like Brenda. She was very elegant in her tasteful white blouse and black skirt. She talked with the soft northern accent but very grammatically, like a school-teacher, sitting primly in her velvet armchair with its lace antimacassars on the arms, telling me about her life.

She had been a prostitute. It came out very matter-of-factly. She got "on the game" during World War II. She had married a private in the army, who had immediately gone over-seas, and was away for three and a half years. He seldom wrote, and her share of his pay was too little to keep her. A friend told her that if she was broke, the chemist down the road would give her "ten bob" for going into the back room with him. She did, and later moved on to picking up service-men and others downtown, finally, claiming her corner as a streetwalker. She had lived that way for twenty years but was now retired.

She wanted to talk about it. I asked almost no questions, merely nodded or mumbled sympathetically from time to time. There was not the slightest prurience in it: she was detached and clinical, but warm and amused at the same time. If you can imagine the present-day, somewhat matronly Ingrid Berg-man telling these stories, you get some of the contrast between the refinement of the teller and the nature of the content.

She was preoccupied with respectability and the hypocrisy that sustains it. Some of her oddest regular clients had been pillars of the community. Two of them stick in my memory because she described their foibles in such detail.

One was a Church of England clergyman, middle-aged, not married. He came to Brenda the same afternoon every week. His need was to be led around the floor, naked and on all fours, with a dog collar around his neck and another, tiny dog collar around his penis was attached to a leash, which Brenda held while she scolded him, saying: "Bad dog! bad dog!" until he was satisfied. He would then pack up his gear, resume his other "dog collar" and clergyman's attire, pay her, and leave.

The other unusual client was an older man whose identity she didn't know for a long time. He would pick her up from the street regularly in his posh car and drive to a secluded spot. From a suitcase, he would produce a rubber apron and rubber gloves which he had her put on while she performed on him. They were at this one night, when the car door on her side was suddenly wrenched open and a flashlight dazzled them. A policeman pulled her roughly out of the car and said to the man "Get out of here!" The man drove off in a hurry. The policeman said to Brenda, "Don't you know who that is?"

She said, "No."

"Haven't you been to magistrate's court recently?"

"No."

"Well the next time you go," the policeman said contemptuously, "you look up on the bench and that's who you'll see: your gentleman friend, Mr. Justice ———."

The policeman seemed so fatherly that she thought he was simply going to let her go. He did — after forcing her to have sex with him up against a wall.

She had many other stories, spanning the entire range of male sexual behavior. She recounted them quietly, with good humor, never really ridiculing the more pathetic of her clients, never denying their humanity.

Two things bothered her about her profession. One was the danger. How did a street girl size up a murderous or sadistic man in the brief exchange that led to a business transaction?

Brenda was never sure. She turned down many men who were probably safe because an irrational fear suggested that one had a funny look in his eyes and might have a knife. The fear got worse as she got older, and it finally convinced her to retire. She couldn't stand the anxiety any longer, and she believed that older prostitutes attracted such men.

The other thing that really bothered her was her daughter. The girl was grown and was about to be married. She had no known father and her mother had always fobbed her off with genteel lies about her way of life. Those stories were now getting a bit thin, but she was in some agony about what to tell the girl. Should she finally tell her everything? Was twenty old enough to understand? Should she never tell her? She was also worried about the proprieties in the wedding arrangements. She wanted everything to be right and, curiously, she knew very little about what was "proper" as she put it, and what was not.

She never lost her poise, or composure, but it was clear from her hesitations that the social problem gave her more anxiety than any in her professional life. It touched but also embarrassed me slightly to have her defer to my judgment, as though I somehow represented the "respectable" world in the sleeping houses outside the lace curtains of that room; the same respectability she could describe so scathingly in the other context.

What a book! I thought. If I could come back with a tape recorder and she told me all her stories, we could publish it under a pseudonym. I broached it to Brenda: she thought it was a splendid idea — as long as no real names were used. There were too many posh chaps still around who would be embarrassed, she said. Agreed. We would split the profits and make our fortunes. I took her phone number and address and left, promising to set up dates to return for the recording.

I never did. In the gray morning light, driving south to London, the project appeared very cheap and exploitive. I couldn't summon back the neat rationalizations that had occurred to me during the night.

And it gradually dawned on me that I had been wallowing

up to my neck in a pretty hackneyed literary convention: young man finds rapport with maternal and sensitive prostitute.

Another story broke somewhere, I got sent out of the country, and I never talked to Brenda again.

Curiously, I never felt any real anxiety about how she would sort it out with her daughter. There was something so reasonable and balanced about her that she could have made the Archbishop of Canterbury understand. Which reminds me of one of the last things she said:

"Wouldn't it be odd if the minister who married my daughter turned out to be the one with the little dog collars?"

One blessing of the kind of life I led as a general purpose NBC correspondent in London was that there was little time to brood over failures. There were plenty of stories which did not work or which slipped through my fingers; but the sea was so full of fish that I usually didn't pine for the ones that got away — with one exception.

It was June 1962. Charlie Chaplin, then seventy-three and living in Switzerland, was being given an honorary degree by Oxford University. I drove up from London with a film crew to record the event and with a remote hope that I might be able to corner him for an interview. Chaplin had never given a television interview; he had consistently refused to appear on television in any form.

He was staying overnight at Wadham College. The subwarden, Dr. John Thompson, said we could come round at breakfasttime the next morning. If Chaplin were willing, we could talk to him in the garden.

A reporter can get blasé about meeting and interviewing famous people. Most of them are political figures and, in the typical brief encounters of the news business, there is little transaction on the human level. So one's interest in them remains, with rare exceptions, as superficial and fleeting as the headlines that prompt the interviews.

Chaplin was different. I was far from blasé; in fact, I could hardly sleep all night for thinking about what to say to him.

We arrived at the warden's house while they were still at breakfast and were told we could set up the camera in the garden. The garden and the June morning might have been plucked from the pages of a book on the beauties of England. The garden wall was hundreds of years old, built of tawny Cotswold stone. The flower beds were planted as traditional English perennial borders — hollyhocks, lupins, foxglove, delphinium, sweet William, and the like. The sky was a pale unperturbed blue. The borders drenched the air with sweet odors. Heavy honeybees blundered in and out of the foxglove bells. On the smooth rolled lawn the charmed youth of Oxford had doubtless drunk tea, played croquet, composed verse, smoked cigars after dinner, eaten strawberries and cream, and whispered passionately to their ladies for countless years while the assorted terrors of the world created only vague murmurs outside. But of all the great men who might have used it, had that charmed garden ever seen the equal of the extraordinary fellow who now came prancing out into the sunny morning?

He was a very small, tidy, and elegant figure in a neat gray suit, his silver hair carefully combed, his tanned face consumed by the famous, toothy grin.

I introduced myself and the film crew.

"But there is a camera," Chaplin said, still smiling broadly. "There can't be a camera. I thought we were just going to chat for a little while."

I said I thought he had understood that we were from NBC News, and that it was a television interview.

"Oh," he said pleasantly, "I never do television interviews." I wasn't sure whether he was teasing. His manner was flirtatious, almost coquettish, as though further urging on my part, if delicately done, would win him over. He made it seem a game. His lustrous eyes sparkled with friendliness. He gave no sense of impatience, of being anxious to get away to something more important, none of the preoccupied body-language of the self-important. He looked as delighted to be with us as we were to be with him.

In twenty different ways I coaxed him and he found an equal number of graceful ways to refuse. This little quadrille of persistence and courtesy took the entire morning. But this was just the prologue to what turned out to be virtually a four-hour Chaplin performance. He could not talk without acting, could not tell anecdotes without impersonating the characters. So he did both.

I asked his reason for boycotting television, and his bitter answers to that flowered into a kind of animated Chaplin autobiography, backwards and forwards in time beginning with his persecution, as he saw it, in the McCarthy period up to his disgusted departure from the United States in 1952 and refusal to work there. He played all the parts, revolving around his own central and familiar persona, the winsome, persecuted Charlie.

Several times I begged him to let the camera run for a few minutes so that this shouldn't be lost. Each time he blithely sidled away from the question and continued his account. He danced a few steps to illustrate some story or sang snatches of a song all to elaborate his diatribe against the cowardice of Hollywood and the political sickness of the United States. It were as though he had been nursing this accumulated resentment a long time and it had merely needed someone to pull the plug for it all to flow out. Or perhaps it was in the front of his mind, because he was then halfway through his memoirs, which were published about a year later.

Clearly, also, he had nothing else to do that morning. He was glad of the company and the audience.

As I got more importunate, Chaplin began to drop little hints like, "Well, not this morning, but perhaps later."

As the morning wore on, he began to talk about perhaps being interviewed when his memoirs came out the following year.

Finally, he made me an offer I could not refuse: an exclusive hour-long interview, timed with the release of the memoirs.

To back this up, he wrote down the name, address, and phone number of his private secretary in Caux, Switzerland. There was no point trying the public route: there were too many solicitations; it might be overlooked. I should contact the private secretary. He would make the arrangements. Chaplin would speak to him about it as soon as he got home. It was certainly not a casual commitment.

Back in London, I cabled the private secretary. When there was no answer after two weeks, I cabled again. Still no response. I telephoned. He was not in. He did not return the calls. My Chaplin exclusive, which I had been privately building into the coup of my career, dissolved like a mirage.

The worst part was that because I had believed the little man, and fully expected to spend hours with him again recording every nuance, I made no notes. Because we did not want to trick him in the garden, we had not yielded to the temptation to run the tape recorder surreptitiously. It was galling to have been so close and to have come away with so little.

What I remember vividly is Chaplin's scorn for television. It had a political origin, but he professed to hate it as a medium. Television was "too hard . . . cruel . . . brutal . . . naked," he said. "Television has no poetry. It is too revealing."

He was undoubtedly right. Television would not have added to the luster of his name — only mine if I had bagged him. That was another lesson it took a long time to learn. Most television interviewing is done to show off the interviewer, not his subject.

There was one other figure alive in those days about whom I could not be blasé. He was Winston Churchill.

I remember the shock I felt the first time I saw him enter the House of Commons. I was sitting in the press gallery over the Speaker's chair. Coming to Parliament for a couple of hours in the afternoon had become a private hobby with me. If there was major debate scheduled I stayed on. Otherwise I came just for the fun of listening to Question Time and the interplay between the government and its backbenchers and the opposition. At that time Harold Macmillan was the Conservative prime minister, with Hugh Gaitskell (until he died), and then Harold Wilson, leader of the Labour opposition.

It was a quiet day with routine questions and I was only half paying attention, when I heard some members begin that loud murmur which means applause in the British House. They are actually saying individually, "Hear, hear," but in the mass it sounds like "Roar, roar" and it is used for all occasions to denote support. Sometimes it rises to deafening pitch, drowning out an unpopular speaker. Sometimes it is a low murmer. When I looked up to see what was causing it, there was Winston Churchill, a bent old man, leaning on his cane, creeping slowly up the center aisle of the House. Business stopped and the cheers continued until Churchill sat himself fragilely in his accustomed place — the first seat on the front bench below the gangway on the government side. Another senior Tory who was occupying it slid over and made way. Attention returned to the government minister who had been interrupted and business proceeded.

I couldn't take my eyes off Churchill. My reaction was, "So he really is alive, and he moves around London!"

I had seen his picture in the newspapers from time to time. And I suppose I knew that he came to Parliament now and then. But it was as startling to see him there as if Disraeli had suddenly walked in.

Winston Churchill had been a Member of Parliament since 1900 when his escapades as a soldier-journalist in the Boer War won him a seat. That made him a member of Queen Victoria's last Parliament. Thereafter, he served in Parliament and often in governments under five successive monarchs: Edward VII, George V, Edward VIII, George VI, and Elizabeth II. He changed parties; was adored, then reviled and ignored; and finally rose again to total mastery of the House of Commons and of the nation in World War Two.

He respected the House of Commons above all institutions. Although the British electorate sometimes treated him harshly, he never wished to remove his fate from their control. He refused titles that would have elevated him to the non-elected House of Lords. He was an obstinate Commoner.

The little thrill that went through the House when its greatest living member came and went was testimony to the living sense of that tradition. Watching him sitting there, the mystique of the place enveloped me.

He looked weakly around, his creased neck standing like an aged turtle's out of his collar, his eyes pale and blurred. It did not appear that he saw or heard very much. After a few moments, he subsided a little onto the bench, his cane between his legs, his chest collapsing gently onto the gray waistcoat covering his paunch, like an old gentleman having an after-lunch snooze.

It was impossible not to muse, as I watched him there, that out of that brain, from those lips had come some of the most stirring words ever uttered in this chamber; words that had galvanized not only his countrymen but the free world. The human flame, now almost extinguished in that old man, had burned with such fierce combustion that the force of the will it produced helped to turn the world around. That crumpled old man was living proof of the chemistry of leadership.

After an hour or so, he straightened up. They helped him to his feet and he crept out, remembering to turn at the door and bow faintly to the bewigged Speaker.

After that I saw him repeat the same performance five or six times, some days looking a little more vigorous, some more fragile. Each time that murmer of awareness that he was present swept the Members' benches and the visitors' galleries.

Recognizing his frailty, all British news media were alert for signs of an illness that might be his last.

There was a scare in June 1962. Churchill fell and broke his thigh in his hotel room while on holiday in Monte Carlo.

I flew down there to report for NBC as he underwent simple surgery to set the bone. The next day he was flown back to London for further treatment and I was outside the hospital as they brought him out. I leaned close to the ambulance window to see his face and judge how ill he was. Two feet away from me, the old boy opened his eyes and smiled. He raised his hand to me in the famous "V" for Victory sign of the war years. Evidently history couldn't claim him yet. But the incident debilitated him and, the following spring, he reluctantly resigned from Parliament.

When the end came in January 1965, I was in Europe, making feature stories for the *Huntley-Brinkley Report*. I had done reports from Gibraltar and Spain and was researching another in Brussels when news came that Churchill was very ill. London was no longer my beat (I was based in Washington) but I felt very proprietary about the Churchill story. Without asking anyone's approval, I went to London, assuming they would need extra help.

His life ebbed slowly. I spent several nights with the crowd of reporters and photographers huddled outside his home in Hyde Park Gate. It was a comfortless vigil. The weather was raw and damp but I felt, as the others did, that it was a privilege to be there to mark the passing of a great man.

On January 25 he died, and England prepared for the greatest state funeral ever afforded a commoner. I did many reports for NBC on his lying in state at Westminster Hall and preparations for the funeral. Two pieces of reporting gave me enormous satisfaction.

Churchill's underground war room was still intact, several stories beneath the Ministry of Defense on Parliament Square. I got permission to go there with my cameraman friend Chris Callery, and we were both awed by the experience. Three stories underground, time was frozen. Preserved exactly as it had been when the Battle of Britain ended was the Command Center complex, where Churchill directed the air battle that saved Britain. There were the maps where he watched the ebb and flow of battle on the Atlantic, North Africa, and the invasions of Europe, the pinholes tracking the movements of ships and armies still visible. There was the desk where he wrote the great speeches that rallied his countrymen, the microphone where he delivered them, the phone on which he talked almost daily to President Roosevelt. Churchill was so unaware of the time difference in Washington that they installed a third hand on the clock, so that he would not keep waking Roosevelt up.

The nerve center of that underground complex, safe from bombs and gas, had that quaint homemade look of the triumph of improvisation that kept Britain alive in those fateful years. The musty air, pumped down from the surface, breathed with the excitements of those times. On one pigeonholed box were little tags, written by hand and stuck with rusting thumb tacks, for routing Churchill's memos. They were marked "Top Secret," "Air Ministry," "The King." A pneumatic tube, like the ones that carried the money in old-fashioned department stores, was marked "Tube to GHQ Home Forces." War seemed a long time removed from today's electronic war rooms, with dark screens flashing illuminated information around the globe in a second by satellite, processed by computers calculating faster than the brightest man. This was the relic of a cozy-seeming, home-made war that used a technology the average man could understand.

These small rooms, shored up by heavy wood trusses and beams, gave me a strong feeling of intimacy with Churchill and his war. NBC ran our report three times.

I also drew the assignment of going to his birthplace, Blenheim Palace, and the adjoining village of Bladon, where he would be buried. His grave was beside those of his father, Lord Randolph Churchill, and his American-born mother, Jennie Jerome. The grave-digger who prepared her grave in 1921 said he had cut through the bones of soldiers killed in Cromwell's wars.

When we arrived, two old men were digging Churchill's grave. We filmed them from the top of the little church tower, a scene that might have come from any century of British history. The only noise, other than the pick and shovels, was the cawing of crows nesting in the nearby trees.

Looking for color, I called on the rector of the tiny church, and he produced a scrapbook kept by his predecessors for more than a century. I stayed for hours in his unheated parlor reading accounts of the village life. Churchill was born in 1874. In that year six village lads, all agricultural laborers, emigrated to the United States because of unemployment at home.

The women of Bladon were noted for making leather gloves which they sold for fivepence halfpenny (about eight cents) a pair at the turn of the century. The first airplane passed over the village in 1913. Electricity arrived in 1930, piped water in 1935. But the great preoccupation of Bladon for two hundred years was the palace and estate of Blenheim, a gift of Parliament to the Duke of Marlborough, one of Britain's great soldiers, and Churchill's ancestor. For generations the village lads carried the guns and flushed the game for the shoots on the estate and tended the vast ornamental and kitchen gardens. It was recorded in the scrapbook that older villagers remembered carrying ammunition for the young "Winston." They noted that in a day's shooting, he dropped many big cigar ends. They crept back later to pick them up. The village gave its name to the soft local sandstone used for its houses, the little church, the palace, and the medieval colleges at Oxford, a few miles away. Again, immersing myself personally in this detail added to that feeling of intimacy with the man to be buried there the next day.

Elie Abel, the London correspondent, and I jointly narrated the funeral coverage. Television logistics required that we do it from a remote truck parked at London Airport, so the tapes could be rapidly flown to the United States. That is one of the absurdities of modern communications. Provided you have the picture and know what you want to say, you could narrate such an event from Mars. You are so soon drawn into the spectacle that you forget where you are physically. It becomes immaterial.

I was very moved. Later in the day I wrote an impression for a radio special on the NBC network:

"It could have been, perhaps even should have been, anticlimactic. The old man had been waning for so long; the details of his illness, and his greatness, and the arrangements for the funeral so much gone over; the emotions of his genuinely devoted countrymen so long wrung by his slow death; that there was very little to say, or do, to honor him, or even to feel.

"The day could not have been more unfriendly unless the skies, as they did for the funeral of Lord Nelson one hundred and sixty years ago, had burst with hail. Dawn, that gray accident of light over wintertime London, happened as vaguely as usual, but even colder. The temperature was near freezing, but of that penetrating damp cold which finds its way inside all clothing. If Charles Dickens had wanted to open a novel upon an extreme note of gloom and discomfort he might have created such a day.

"But it was not an anticlimax and the weather did not spoil it. The sheer pageantry succeeded in wringing again from the frozen onlookers and the millions of TV watchers that ache of participation. People who lived through the war years here wept by the television sets to see the small, but apparently very heavy coffin (to judge by the efforts of the guardsmen who bore it) pass through the gray, frozen streets. Each landmark — Westminster, Whitehall, Downing Street, the Admiralty, St. Clement Dane's, the "Oranges and Lemons" church, the blitzed areas of the City — had associations with Churchill that were a cue for tears.

"The British are supposed to be a phlegmatic people, warm of heart but cold on the surface. The frozen face of the still-young Queen Elizabeth expressed this in St. Paul's Cathedral, when she deferred, as no other reigning British sovereign has ever done, to one of her subjects, technically a commoner. Those devices that are peculiarly British, the thin, sour sound of the bagpipes from massed highland bands playing a lament as the coffin passed from the shore to the launch to carry it up the windy Thames, the high wail of the bosuns' whistles that piped him aboard, were, for the unbending British, what tears and human wailing might be for others.

"Because there was no shock about the death, it could have been a day dry of emotion. But I imagine few Englishmen have had their hearts wrung by anything public as they had today by this cold, gray, impeccable spectacle."

TEN

Finland:
More Adventures in
the Cold War

THOSE YEARS WERE FULL of Cold War confrontations, some obvious, some subtle. I covered one skirmish that I had to score as a clear victory for the West.

No people, except perhaps the Berliners, lived with the Cold War as intimately as the Finns, the only independent nation on Russia's European borders. No people had such justification for fearing and hating the Russians; none were more devoted to the Western conception of freedom. The Finnish subtlety in accommodating this ambivalence and preserving their national independence, right on the Soviet borders, fascinated me. I made three trips there in 1962, visits to the front line of the Cold War, as it were, and came away each time with increased admiration for the Finnish people.

I was also very drawn to the country itself, resembling, as it did in climate and landscape, the severe beauties of Canada. The Finns share with Canadians the mystique of living in the presence of the North, in the way other peoples live with mountains or the sea, something always present even when they sleep.

The Finns possess a distinct linguistic strain with their own highly developed mythology. It was passed down orally for hundreds of years in rhythmic verses. In the mid nineteenth century these were collected by a Swedish doctor and published as the *Kalevala, the Land of Heroes*. It vividly personifies the terrible forces of the North and it tells the adventures of human heroes pitting themselves against these forces, like Greeks against the Homeric gods. What is so refreshing about the heroes of the *Kalevala* is that, faced with the implacable enemies of nature, infinitely more powerful than any men, the weapons they resort to are wit, humor, guile, and cunning. And that is how the modern Finns have survived as immediate neighbors of the Soviet Union.

The proximity was startling on my first visit in January 1962 to work on two documentaries for NBC. Every day a train, bearing a hammer and sickle emblem, puffed out of the Helsinki station for a run of only two hundred miles to Leningrad. Some Finns went there as casually as they went to Stockholm. Pan Am and Aeroflot jetliners shared the airport. *Pravda* and *Izvestia* were on sale alongside the Paris edition of the *Herald-Tribune* in the newspaper kiosks. Across the border river, near Imatra, you could see the grim watchtowers of the Soviet frontier rising from the winter forests.

Taking the train to Leningrad was the only way Finns could see their former province of Karelia, extorted from them by Moscow at the end of the Second World War. Karelia was the heartland of Finland, the source of its myths and legends. But the people stoically accepted its amputation, and quietly resettled the refugees — one fifth of the entire population.

I interviewed one of the refugees, a robust farmer's wife living on land that had been subdivided by law to make farms for the exiles. It made her weep to speak of her childhood in Karelia. It was a subject that could bring most Finns close to tears. One glory of Karelia was the ancient and highly cultured city of Viipuri (Vyborg). The Russians seized it, then let it decay. On the Leningrad train, the Soviet attendants pull down the blinds when they pass Viipuri to hide the shame of it. But, for the Finns Viipuri and Karelia may have been a small price to pay compared with the total subjection suffered by the other Baltic states, Estonia, Lithuania, and Latvia.

Stalin, nervous in 1939, attempted to swallow all four, Finland included, to expand his defense perimeter in the classic Russian manner. Three succumbed. Finland refused. Finland had been a duchy of Imperial Russia and had only wrested her independence after the Russian Revolution.

Stalin bombed Helsinki to make the Finns change their mind, but they didn't. Then, as winter came on, he sent several Soviet divisions to invade Finland through the forests of Karelia north of Lake Lagoda. The Finns fought back, while the world watched, and Western leaders argued about whether to help the vastly outnumbered Finnish ski troops who flitted through the dark forests of spruce and birch to hold off the Russian divisions for a hundred days. It was called the Winter War. It was elemental heroism; incalculable, individual heroism.

War cemeteries easily move me. But the way the Finns tend the dead of the Winter War is heartbreakingly touching. Each fallen soldier has his own granite plaque in the Helsinki cemetery. In the winter they are swept clear of snow. On National Day relatives come and light candles at each grave. Around each candle they build a small turret of snow to keep the wind from blowing it out. The candlelight shines through the thin snow walls and they glow, like flickering lanterns, hundreds and hundreds. At one end of the cemetery is the tomb of the soldier who led them, Marshal Mannerheim: the massive granite block flanked by two torches, their flames darting frenziedly in the night wind, while the hundreds of little candles burn serenely inside their snow walls. It is a scene to make your heart turn over.

The Finns wasted no sentimentality over the Russians. They developed the heavy industry necessary to fulfill the crippling Soviet reparations and they built a prosperous, Western economy. They sidestepped Soviet efforts to tie them into a common defense arrangement and they adroitly avoided the effort to pull them into Comecon, the Soviet Bloc economic system. The price for all this was a carefully nuanced neutrality, often exasperating to Cold Warriors in Washington, who worry when the Finns get too cozy with Moscow. But through the wily President Kekkonen, the Finns held their own, and they sometimes provided a useful channel for dialogue with Moscow. President Kennedy used it to warn the Kremlin of his seriousness about Berlin. But the Finns won the luxury of independence by accepting a subtle subservience on some matters. They went out of their way to avoid provoking Moscow pointlessly. All these strands were vividly illustrated by the arrival of the Eighth World Communist Youth Festival in Helsinki in July 1962.

These festivals constituted the major propaganda extravaganzas of the early Cold War years. They were designed to entrance the young of the world with the joy and fulfillment of Communist life. The Finnish government didn't want this kind of advertisement. It tainted Finland by association, making her look less neutral than she professed. It would draw welcome attention from the world's news media, but it suggested the wrong associations. To have refused, however, would have been too overtly negative for Finland's delicate neutralism, and the government agreed. What they did not count on was an aggressive attempt by Western groups, fronting for the CIA, to destroy the well-orchestrated harmony of the festival and create a confrontation.

One of the young people organizing this effort, though ignorant of its CIA inspiration, was Gloria Steinem. She and her colleagues were always remarkably well informed in advance about where "incidents" would take place; where, for example, a group of anti-Communist youths would stage a hostile demonstration on the route when all the national delegations marched to the grand opening in Helsinki's Olympic Stadium.

One of the chronic weaknesses of television journalism is its insatiable appetite for confrontation and violence. I practiced this craft enthusiastically for many years before realizing how often we were being manipulated. That hadn't dawned on me in 1962, and I accepted the information I was getting from the American counterfestival people as useful and legitimate. I entertained vague notions about their motivation and possible backing, but accepted them as part of the Cold War landscape. There was an unspoken convention among American reporters until the lid blew off in 1970 that when you stumbled on activity that smelled like CIA, you kept quiet about it. You might exchange worldly and knowing remarks in the bar with other reporters, but, on the record, the subject was taboo, and considered properly so.

The grand coup for the Westerners were the riots that developed around the festival. Wire services and newspapers are almost as susceptible as television to letting violence dictate their news judgment. The riots made the festival into a headline story around the world; people violently resisting anything Communist was news.

Rumors that there would be demonstrations in opposition to the festival had been circulated well in advance and probably influenced the decision of NBC New York to send me and a camera crew from London to cover it.

There were plenty of Finnish students ready to show their displeasure with the Soviet Union and tired of being constrained by the political anxieties of their elders. They were ripe for whatever infiltration and clandestine prompting they presumably received from what Moscow called "Western agitators and troublemakers."

The Finnish government was very anxious to have the festival pass off peacefully and get out of town with no damage done. Violent demonstrations were the last thing they wanted. They could have become the pretext for another of Moscow's periodic anxiety attacks about security and suggestions that Finland be enfolded into the Soviet defense system.

Rioting began the night before the festival opened. Several thousand students gathered on the street commemorating Marshal Mannerheim, shouting "Free Finland" and "Communists Go Home." They threw stones at festival buses and tore the festival neckscarves off delegates and burned them. Finnish police, obviously sympathetic to the demonstrators at first, received other orders and broke up the riots with repeated baton charges on horseback.

The demonstrators came back the next night in larger numbers, and the authorities resorted to tear gas. The mounted charges and tear-gas attacks were the most severe measures ever used to control crowds in Finland. Reporters were asking, What next? Thousands of rioters were taking over the center of the city each evening. The story going out to the world was one of rampant anti-Communism and generational revolt — all nicely suiting the aims of the CIA, but deeply embarrassing to the Finnish government. It became very exhausting for us, up most of the night covering the riots, then all day and evening covering the events of the festival.

One night got particularly nasty. I was again with Chris Callery and soundman Digby Jones. It now seems stupid that we went on filming riots night after night, but it didn't then. If we hadn't, and CBS or ABC News had shown a violent episode we didn't have, we would have been thought to be not covering the story.

We were using a portable, battery-powered Frezzolite, which I was carrying, filming in a small pocket in the center of the dense mass of demonstrators, when a small object soared through the air and landed at my feet. I shone the light on it and, because the police hadn't used any tear gas until then, it took a few seconds to recognize the white smoke beginning to squirt out of the grenade. I turned to shout "Tear gas!" to Digby and Chris, then turned back, meaning to take one breath of clean air and run for it. But the wind must have changed because I turned and sucked in a lungful of tear gas. I felt instantly paralyzed and fainted.

When I came to, I don't know how many moments later, I found myself alone in the street, lying across some streetcar tracks. The demonstration had scattered temporarily. I shone the Frezzolite into the air and Callery appeared but not Digby. We looked in doorways, alleyways in all the adjoining streets, even under cars, where he might have taken refuge, but no sign of him. Chris and I began to worry. Digby was old. He suffered from numerous ailments, from varicose veins to asthma, and he sometimes talked about his heart. Could the poor fellow be lying somewhere, stricken with a heart attack? We redoubled our search efforts, fanning out to other streets. The riot swirled back and we got caught up in filming that again. Now the chief of police was riding around personally tossing tear-gas grenades out of his car windows to force the demonstrators to go home.

I had to go to the radio studio to broadcast a report to New

York, while Chris went to the airport to ship film. When we met again we decided to have a drink before going out to search again. We went to the bar at the top of the Vaakuna Hotel and there was Digby, looking as usual like a rumpled absentminded professor. He was sitting at a table, with his Nagra tape recorder in front of him, a big snifter of brandy on top of the Nagra, and, across the table from him, a very pretty girl.

"Aha! So there you are!" Digby said, his glasses slipping down his nose. "Let me introduce this young lady. She is a nurse. We have just rescued each other from the riots. Haven't we, my dear?"

The riots probably expressed the views of ninety percent of the Finnish people, but the government could not say so. President Kekkonen had ostentatiously stayed clear of all festival activities. But after three nights of rioting he made a public statement condemning "irresponsible youths" and announcing that he would spend a week's fall vacation with Soviet Premier Khrushchev. That underscored the price of maintaining Finland's independence and made some Finns believe the whole exercise had gone too far.

Such CIA meddling is not now condoned in the political climate created by revelations about the agency's excesses. And I certainly don't dispute that there must be some curb on foreign policy by clandestine dirty tricks, like the efforts to overthrow Allende in Chile. But as one who saw it all in Helsinki, including both the Communist side of it and the Finnish, it was probably one of the neatest and most successful operations they ever pulled.

The festival was carefully engineered by its Communist planners. I went to the harbor the day the Soviet cruise ship *Gruzia* brought the Soviet youth contingent by sea from Leningrad, her decks ablaze with peace and friendship. These carefully schooled youths were regimented by their particular skill, uniformed in national costume or sports clothes or carefully informal. They gathered in their sections at the rail. All smiled broad white smiles, waved vigorously, and, the moment the gangways came down, skipped onto the jetty and began instant, impromptu performances of folk dances, songs, and gymnastics. It was as contrived and rehearsed a performance as I have ever seen. Every girl was pretty, every boy handsome. These were the cheerleaders of world Communism, thorough-bred delegates, as disciplined and regimented a cadre of Soviet society as the Bolshoi Ballet or the Red Army; fitted with matched blazers and instructed to travel abroad like an animated trade exhibit. It was transparently false, too polished, too artificial.

The Western response was a little bit of what the Soviets were masters of themselves, and used to call "agitprop" or agitation-propaganda. Was it healthier for the competition of ideas, that the world, especially the nonaligned nations, saw the festival as a sunny celebration of Soviet life; or that a lot of other young people violently disapproved of that way of life?

On the first night of the riots, the Soviet poet Yevgeny Yevtushenko, a hero to both Eastern and Western youth, wandered unnoticed in the crowds. A Finnish friend told me the demonstration appalled Yevtushenko. He said it was the first anti-Communist demonstration he had ever witnessed. He could see it was not organized and was profoundly disturbed by it.

For a time, Yevtushenko, with Khrushchev's blessing, had enjoyed extraordinary freedom to write and publish. He was now struggling to retain that freedom. Somehow, he was prevailed upon to come up with an instant poem condemning the demonstrations. He called it: "I have seen fascism in the streets of Helsinki" and I ran into Yevtushenko just as he was about to read it live on Moscow television. There was a section for foreign television in the vast stadium and Chris put our NBC camera right beside Soviet television. I got into conversation with Yevtushenko, whose poems like *Babi Yar* I had greatly admired, and asked him if he would read his poem to our camera for Americans before he read it to Russia.

He pulled me aside, with a funny smile on his face, looked around to see who was listening, and said, "You do not want. Is just propaganda."

Then he got his cue from Moscow television, so we filmed

him reading it to them, declaiming it in his long-voweled style.

It was *all* propaganda and, without trying to be too objective about it, I preferred Gloria Steinem's style to the plastic sent by Moscow.

The Communists were so tawdry in their deceptions. The festival was full of petty trickery, of sordid little machinations, so blatantly performed that I wondered for whose benefit they were taking the trouble.

In addition to inflating the number of delegates attending by one-third, they wanted to name as many countries as possible. So they included the Philippines. But the only Filipino present was a journalist. They simply used his name as leader of the Filipino delegation — which did not exist. Other delegations were packed — on paper — by naming fictitious organizations in such countries as Mexico and India. Even more blatant, because more supposedly impressionable delegates could see it, was the steering of discussion groups and seminars. When one debate got out of hand, two busloads of Russians and Poles were sent to the scene to sway the audience.

Everybody saw through all this. It was a theater of the absurd with no audience, or an audience that was all part of the action. That should have amused Berthold Brecht's Berliner Ensemble, whose presence was a highlight of the festival.

It made me think that the stone-faced people committing these absurdities were merely frightened little bureaucrats creating a record for their bosses back home. And men have been doing that from the Roman Empire to the farther reaches of the American corporation. In a perverse way, it made the Soviets seem human and vulnerable.

ELEVEN

A Guest of
Fidel Castro

A FEW MONTHS LATER I ran into Yevtushenko again in decidedly different circumstances. It was three in the morning in a seedy nightclub in Havana and the world was reeling from the shock of the Cuban missile crisis. It was the most dangerous moment of the Cold War. For days the United States and the Soviet Union were on the brink of war, and I spent part of that time locked up in Havana. It came about through another of those accidents that have often put me where things were happening.

In October 1962, NBC recalled me to New York to discuss some personal business. I happened to arrive on the twenty-first, the night that Kennedy revealed the missile crisis to the American people. In the late afternoon I checked in at the NBC newsroom in Rockefeller Center, planning merely to give them the number of my hotel and then go out to dinner. But I ran into Ed Newman, who was a friend from his days in the Paris bureau, and he said, "You might want to stick around. The president is making a special television address at seven o'clock. We think it's about Cuba."

As I had been flying all day from London, I hadn't seen the ominous Washington lead in that morning's *New York Times*, talking of an "air of crisis in the capital" and "speculation that there has been a new development in Cuba."

A lot of people at NBC decided to stick around that night instead of catching their trains to the suburbs. By 7 P.M. there was a considerable crowd of news executives, writers, and producers gathered around the television monitors in the fourth-floor newsroom as Kennedy's grave face appeared.

My first reaction was one very common in Europe over the next few days, that Kennedy was rashly risking World War III over Cuba. Up to then, the British and other European allies considered Cuba a slightly dotty American obsession. The missile flap of that autumn seemed an episode cooked up by the Republicans to make Kennedy look bad for the midterm elections. Everyone recognized that Kennedy was particularly sensitive because of the Bay of Pigs debacle of the year before. Until this speech, it looked from London as though the president were wisely refusing to be panicked by Republican charges that the Soviets were secretly installing intermediate range ballistic missiles which could carry nuclear warheads far into the United States. Now he was saying there was "unmistakable evidence" that they were. It was a condition Europeans had lived with since the Cold War began. It took them some days to see it as Kennedy put it that night — as a "deliberately provocative and unjustified change in the status quo which cannot be accepted by this country, if our courage and our commitments are ever to be trusted again by either friend or foe."

I remained skeptical that extreme measures like the naval blockade Kennedy announced were justified. But my private feelings were irrelevant. I was quickly snatched up by the assignment editor as NBC News began deploying its worldwide resources to cover the greatest crisis for America since Pearl Harbor.

Instead of drifting off to dinner with some New York friends, I was sent to Washington on the next shuttle flight. It was my first time there and I drove through the strange, darkened streets to my hotel trying to imagine the feverish crisis activity that must be going on that night in the White House, the Pentagon, and the State Department.

I got my first real taste the next morning. I was assigned to the Pentagon to help out the resident correspondent, Peter

Hackes. There, at the nerve center of America's vast military complex, the sense of excitement and foreboding was very real. It had jumped instantly to a warlike footing. In the center of the Pentagon, where thousands of employees gather at lunchtime, they had set up a booth with continuous showings of a propaganda film on Cuba. It showed atrocities, executions, haranguing speeches by Castro, and evidence of the increasing Soviet connection. The tone and style sounded calculated to convince Pentagon personnel, military or civilian, that Castro was the enemy and to create a warlike attitude.

That was scarcely necessary. All around me people were really scared. My NBC colleague Sander Vanocur told me that he and his wife, Edith, went into their small sons' bedroom and stood for a long time looking at the sleeping children, wondering if they would be alive to see them the next morning. Another correspondent, Herb Kaplow, was with me at the Pentagon. Kaplow is a sane and levelheaded guy with a wonderful sense of humor. In the press room, I overheard him call his wife on the second day of the crisis when the talk of nuclear war was mounting. They discussed a plan to put the kids in the car with some bedding and clothing as well as bottles filled with fresh water. When the right moment came she would drive to her parents' home in South Dakota. They never implemented the plan but it was extraordinary to me that, with access to the same information, he had so much starker a sense of what might be about to happen than I.

I knew that a confrontation was approaching hourly, when the first Soviet ship would meet the U.S. Navy's blockade. That Tuesday evening the wires reported a Soviet general telling an embassy reception that the Soviet ships had orders not to stop. If one were sunk, how would the mercurial Nikita Khrushchev, the Soviet party chairman, respond? By firing one of the Cuban-based missiles? President Kennedy had said that any nuclear missile launched from Cuba would bring full U.S. retaliation against the Soviet Union. Or would Kennedy himself lose his patience and bomb the missile sites first? And what Kremlin response would that invite? As the hours went by and each successive briefing seemed to tune the strings tighter, these were the possibilities on everyone's lips. Yet in my own private emotions I could not convince myself that it would come to such a catastrophic end. It was unthinkable.

On Wednesday, I was moved to the State Department to help out with the reporting there. The day began with a statement from Khrushchev: if the United States carried out the "piratical actions," as he called the blockade, "we shall have to resort to means of defense against the aggressor to defend our rights." But it ended with a Pentagon announcement that twelve of the twenty-five Soviet ships bound for Cuba and the blockade line appeared to have altered course. It was the first faint public clue that Khrushchev might be backing down.

On Thursday, as U.N. Secretary-General U Thant begged Moscow and Washington to avoid a confrontation at sea, and as the United Nations Security Council met in an atmosphere of imminent war, NBC suggested that, with my Canadian passport, I try to get into Cuba.

A few phone calls showed there was no way to get a visa in the United States, so I packed up and flew to Mexico City on Friday morning. As I left, the White House was announcing that work was continuing rapidly on the Cuban missile sites and U.S. officials were beginning to talk of bombing to remove them.

The Cuban embassy in Mexico City refused me a visa but someone suggested that Cuban Airlines might sell me a ticket without one. They did, and on Saturday, October 27, I was flying to Havana. Checking with New York by phone before boarding the plane, I found the news exceedingly grim. It was the darkest day of the crisis. A Soviet surface-to-air missile had shot down one of the U-2 spy planes photographing the big missile sites. Khrushchev had not backed down and was sending conflicting signals to Washington. President Kennedy had repeated his insistence that the missiles must go. Len Allen, the foreign editor, told me to "be careful."

The plane to Havana was almost empty. It had piston engines and the flight took hours; time to discover that several other foreign journalists were aboard, all safely provided with visas. I was the only one working for an American organization. I went back to my seat and thought: "This may be a very dodgy business. Perhaps I'd better not be an NBC correspondent, at least right away." My Canadian passport described me as a journalist, but I felt I could do without a lot of things identifying me with the "U.S. imperialist aggressors," in case the first Cubans I encountered were a little hysterical. So I took any papers associating me with NBC, tore them up, and stuffed them surreptitiously under the removable ashtray in the armrest. All this clandestine activity made me feel a little silly, but I was worried that the others had visas and I did not.

I half-expected our plane to be buzzed by U.S. or Cuban jets, but we saw no other aircraft.

We landed in Havana after dark. The airport ramp was brightly lit up. Over the terminal building was a giant poster dramatically announcing that Cuba was *"en pié de guerra"* (on a war footing). The terminal was swarming with men in fatigues and camouflage battle dress, carrying large pistols or machine guns.

When it came my turn, I gave my passport nervously to the immigration officer. He looked a bit surprised and motioned me into another room, where I was soon joined by the other journalists. Apparently having a visa made no difference. After about half an hour, a couple of soldiers with machine guns came in and ordered us outside with our luggage. They directed us to climb into the back of a military truck with a canvas top. We were a little nervous but we joked along the way and observed as much as we could from the truck as it drove through Havana. It was a very hot night, the air humid with the smell of the tropic sea, the streets sticky with the exhaust from badly refined gasoline, making the tires sizzle on the pavements.

We were driven to a modern hotel, the Capri, where the officer in charge of us talked to the manager and informed us politely that we were going to be "the guests of the Cuban government." I said I didn't want to be their guest; I would make my own arrangements. The officer repeated firmly: "You are going to be the guest of the Cuban government." We were given room keys and escorted to the ninth floor by armed soldiers.

The Capri was a tall hotel block in the middle of Havana, overlooking the harbor on one side. We were each given rooms at the end of a corridor, thus forming a little enclave of five rooms.

Outside, to confine us, they posted two soldiers with machine guns. They gave them chairs to sit on and they became permanent guards.

I looked around my room. It could have been any Holiday Inn in the United States, except that the mass-produced American motel furniture looked a little shabby. I tried my telephone but found it disconnected. I looked out my window at the lights of the harbor where some of the Soviet ships permitted through the blockade might now be docking. Finally, I went to bed wondering if I would wake up in the middle of an American air raid. But all was quiet and I slept soundly until I heard someone putting a breakfast tray outside my door — coffee, toast, and fruit juice. As I picked up the tray I noticed a new pair of guards on duty.

The night before, my fellow prisoners and I had scarcely noticed each other. Now we opened our doors and started getting acquainted. Next door to me was Gordion Troeller, a Luxemburger, and his Belgian wife, Marie Claude. They worked as a photojournalist team for the German newsmagazine *Der Stern*. Across the hall was Atsuhiro Horikawa, a tall, friendly Japanese, who was the Washington correspondent for *Yomiuri Shimbun,* one of the largest Tokyo dailies. The other two were young freelancers, an Englishman, Alan Oxley, and a Canadian, Don North.

Horikawa had a Zenith Transoceanic radio and we spent a lot of that first day, Sunday, listening to news broadcasts from the United States. Khrushchev had retreated. Moscow radio broadcast a long letter to Kennedy agreeing to remove the missiles under U.N. inspection. In return, Kennedy pledged no U.S. invasion of Cuba. The crisis between the superpowers was abating. The world pulled gratefully back from the nuclear abyss. But the settlement enraged Fidel Castro, who felt betrayed by his Soviet friends. He issued a long statement totally rejecting any U.N. inspectors on Cuban soil.

For Castro the crisis continued and we were his enforced

guests with no way of telling anyone where we were. Late in the day, we picked up the NBC station in Miami carrying the *News on the Hour* from New York. One news item reported that I had gone to Havana and had not been heard from. They repeated the item several times Sunday evening and by Monday were saying I was "missing." While I felt intrigued — like Tom Sawyer listening to his own funeral — it was worrying because I had left my family in England thinking I was in the United States.

Monday passed and no one came to see us. The guards were uncommunicative. They actually carried little Marxist-Leninist textbooks propped on the machine guns across their laps, and read them assiduously when they weren't eyeing our movements.

We settled into a routine. I kept a very detailed diary, unfortunately later taken by the Cuban secret police. I read all the books on Cuba I brought with me and made thorough notes. All that was later confiscated as well. I did an hour's exercises every morning. I hadn't been reading adventure stories since boyhood for nothing; I knew how imprisonment could debilitate a man.

We were fed well, if monotonously. Meals were sent up from the hotel kitchen. It was usually *arroz con pollo,* chicken with rice. The Cuban chicken was fine. The rice, presumably from a fraternal East Bloc partner, was of poor quality. Then, we found that we could wash it down very agreeably with strong Bulgarian red wine, at five dollars a bottle, from the hotel cellar. Our evening meals became quite festive as the days wore on. As we examined our "prison" more closely, we began to see just how dependent Castro was. By 1962, there had been only two years of East Bloc penetration of the Cuban economy. But an inventory limited to the hotel room showed Soviet light bulbs, Polish cutlery, Czech pencils, Rumanian glasses (and the wine to fill them), and Chinese cups and saucers.

We spent a lot of time trying to be reporters, gleaning any other political information we could from staring for hours out the hotel windows. On the harbor side we could see a lot of ships, but not closely enough to identify them.

There was plenty of crisis activity to watch in the town. They had frequent alerts. American reconnaissance planes flew in very low, under the weather ceiling. There was an anti-aircraft battery of what looked like World War II vintage near the hotel. Cuban soldiers would jump on it and wheel the guns around feverishly, but too slowly for the speed of the jets that had just screamed overhead.

Platoons of *milicianos*, civilians on military duty, men and women, would march very smartly through the streets, sometimes at the double. We could sense a lot of bustle and feel the tension from the Cuban radio. It broke into the hotel Musak every few minutes with stentorian announcements, slogans, news bulletins, and pieces of speeches by Fidel. The country sounded very charged up indeed. Cubans fully expected, or were being told repeatedly that they expected, an imminent invasion by the United States.

Yet there were contrary signs. We could also see a lot of relaxed, very normal behavior. The people of Havana were of a gay, extroverted disposition. From our ninth-floor windows we could look down on the pretty girls off work, setting out for the evening in their best clothes; couples embracing or holding hands; people laughing and drinking at outdoor bars; a young woman, hanging out of an apartment window, looking dreamily at the evening sky.

There was a limit to what we could see and hear, and more and more our attention turned to ourselves: how we were going to let the outside world know where we were and how we were going to get out of there. We were not mistreated in any way. We were simply being held incommunicado. In the politest way, we had been kidnapped.

From the first day we began devising ways to get the word out.

The British reporter had lived in Havana and knew that the Associated Press office was just along the street from the hotel. If we wrote a letter saying, "Help, we all are here," typed "Associated Press" on the envelope, and dropped it out the window, he thought, somebody might think it was a misplaced letter and take it to the AP. So, we wrote the letter, giving all the information, put it in an envelope, and typed the address. To make it fall better, we slipped in two big English pennies that I had brought from London.

There were no windows you could simply open. Our windows had louvers and you can't really throw anything through them. As best we could, we tossed the letter through the slot between the louvers but the pennies slid out. The letter began to waft down like a dry leaf. It came to rest on the roof of a little guardpost usually occupied by two Cuban soldiers.

That seemed to be the end of it until Oxley noticed two men drinking at an outdoor café. He recognized them as Canadian pilots who flew regular cargo flights into Havana.

After a great deal of shouting through the louvers from the ninth floor of the hotel, the pilots finally recognized him and came bounding across the street. Oxley told them to get the letter when the guards moved away. But the pilots were drunk. Paying no attention to the guards, they climbed up on the top of the guardpost and they grabbed the letter; whereupon the guards grabbed them and marched them off at gunpoint. Their rooms in the hotel were searched, and we heard they were sent to prison for smuggling currency.

The next day, I was again in Oxley's room, when he suddenly said, "My God!" Right across the street from the hotel, about two stories down, sunning herself in a bikini on the balcony of an apartment building was a girl he knew. She was the friend of a woman with whom he had lived and who had a child. He shouted, and the girl looked up. We soon realized that shouting wasn't the best way of sending a real message. So I took the cardboards out of my clean shirts, cut them in quarters, and, with a felt-tipped pen, made large alphabet cards.

We devised a message and Oxley held up the cards while I arranged the words behind him. He asked her to tell his former girlfriend to bring the child to see him at the hotel. The next day they actually arrived and the guards let them in. He had a long meeting with his former girlfriend and the little baby. Just before they left, we slipped a typewritten message folded very small inside the knitted bootee of the baby. Unfortunately, the baby was searched on the way out and they found the message.

After that, the guards came in and closed all the glass louvers. They confiscated the small window handless — except mine, which I hid. They told us very sternly not to try to send messages out. The guards looked at us more sharply upon learning that they had some hardened criminals to watch. They read for hours on end their small Marxist-Leninist textbooks even more avidly as they sat in the corridor with their machine guns on their laps.

The idea that really worked — and worked brilliantly — was that of Horikawa, the Japanese. The phones in our rooms were all dead — shut off at the switchboard. He noticed that the modern American construction of the building meant that there were conduits rising in the walls of the hotel with branches out serving pairs of rooms all the way up. We posted Oxley as a lookout and went into my room. We pulled the bed away from the wall, unscrewed the terminal plate, and pulled out a fistful of multicolored little telephone wires. We disconnected my phone and, with the corner of a razor blade, gently slit each of the wires in turn and inserted the little terminal connections. We figured that by trial and error we would eventually hit another pair and another dial tone. The call would appear to come from another room.

I listened on the receiver while the Japanese and the Luxemburger made the incisions and inserted the little terminal into the wires. We intercepted many phone calls in Chinese, Russian, Spanish, German, and God knows what else. If we had been really smart we might have picked up a lot of information, but we were simply anxious to get a message out before we were caught.

Finally we got a dial tone and excitedly dialed the number for the Reuters bureau. They answered and we told them who we were, who we worked for, how we got there, and asked that they notify our respective embassies and employers. Then we pulled the terminals out of the little wires, reconnected my telephone, shoved all the other wires back into the wall, replaced the plate, put the bed back in position, and relieved Oxley, who'd been watching outside.

About twenty minutes later we were strolling up and down the corridor, which the guards now let us do, when the elevator door opened. A woman got out and talked excitedly to the guards. Gordion Troeller, who spoke good Spanish, said she was the telephone operator and she was saying, "Somebody has been phoning from the empty room."

Farther down the corridor there were several empty rooms, apparently reserved as honeymoon suites for deserving Cuban newlyweds, people who had overfulfilled their patriotic norms in one way or another. Indeed there had been, we knew, a honeymoon couple in one of the rooms, but they had left and the room was empty. One of our guards went downstairs with the telephone operator. About fifteen minutes later they came back with a whole squad of soldiers. They went down the hall and lined up on either side of the door of the empty room, with their guns pointing to the door. The officer pounded on the door and said, "Open up or we'll break the door down." Since the room was empty, nobody replied. Then he stepped back and made the dramatic gesture of throwing his shoulder against the door. But it was very tough and didn't break. Then he rather meekly turned the handle with the key and the door opened easily. They all rushed in and a moment or two later came out again, obviously having found nothing. After some whispered consultations and glances at us they went downstairs.

We listened to the radio. A short time after our phone call, the NBC *News on the Hour* broadcast our story from Reuters. Some days later representatives of our various embassies were allowed to see us and began trying to secure our release.

When we weren't up to such amusing occupations or devising impractical escape plots, we spent a lot of time playing games. That sounds silly but we had really begun feeling like prisoners. Time passed very slowly. One of the games we played endlessly was "Battleship," where you use folded squared paper, hiding ships in some of the squares. By calling out coordinates you "drop bombs" on the other person's piece of paper. If you keep on long enough, one or other gets his battleships sunk and the other wins.

I introduced them to "Shove Ha'penny" which I had been playing in the pubs in London. Since we were not feeling very charitable toward the Cubans, we scored the top of the cheap dresser in my room to make the lines for a "Shove Ha'penny" board. We didn't have ha'pennies (or halfpennies) but I did have five more full-sized English pennies. Rubbing one side of them on the stone windowsill smoothed them down, and they worked very well. To play "Shove Ha'penny," each of the people playing has a turn and five coins. By hitting them with the base of the thumb, you send them spinning between the lines and, if they come to rest without crossing any lines, you score. When you have scored three times in each row you fill the next row and so on. The first person to fill all the rows wins the game. It is a very good game, involving a lot of skill. You can become very adept at spinning the coins so that they stop just where you want them to.

We played for many hours and it was Horikawa who rapidly became very good at it. But he hated to lose. Any time his coin spun where he didn't want it, he would suck in his breath and make terrible noises of self-recrimination. But he satisfied the honor of Japan because eventually he beat us all.

On our fourth day of confinement, October 30, we heard on the radio that Castro had rejected the settlement. U Thant flew in to Havana to persuade him and failed. Peking was egging Castro on in his resistance to both Moscow and Washington. Three days later, on November 2, the Soviets sent their veteran negotiator, Anastas Mikoyan, to reason with Castro. Mikoyan was still in Havana when we were suddenly released on Sunday, November 4. We had been confined for nine days.

A young representative of the Foreign Ministry came and announced that we were free. We could go where we wanted and report as we liked. He hoped we would forgive his government for having detained us. We should understand that the crisis made it necessary.

There was a slight catch. We couldn't file any copy overseas until we had press credentials from the Foreign Ministry. We could do that on Monday.

So we celebrated that evening by going to the thriving nightclub in the Capri Hotel. Adjoining it was the Salon Rojo, the famous gambling casino once run by Americans, still with its red damask wallpaper and rectangular chandeliers marking the roulette tables that had been purged as pre-revolutionary decadence. It now served as a bar, a bizarre cultural crossroads, with a small combo playing "Midnight in Moscow" and a black girl who sounded like Ella Fitzgerald singing "The Man I Love." At small tables, Western and Communist businessmen mingled with girls and others with something to sell or buy— black-market stockings or dollars, information or warnings. It had all the paraphernalia of paperback thrillers brought uncomfortably alive by the occasional glimpse of the butt of an automatic pistol in someone's belt or the fact that no one's eyes ever stopped restlessly moving.

The big hotels like the Capri still mounted lavish floor shows, typical of pre-revolutionary Havana. The show that night at the Capri Casino was as exotic in girls and costumes as Hollywood's idea of a New York nightclub: Cuban girls, Czech costumes. The tables were crowded with well-dressed couples. Each had an ice bucket containing a bottle of Russian vodka ($15) or Cuban rum ($20). They iced the bottle instead of the drink, we were told, because the ice was dirty. And the air was rich with Havana cigars.

We wasted a lot of Monday at the Foreign Ministry discovering that they would not give us press credentials. I took off into Havana to soak up as much color and information as I could; walking the streets, talking with Communist and Western diplomats, going to restaurants, shops, and nightclubs.

The old city, with its palm trees, tiled roofs, and shady stone arcades, still had its casual tropical charm, if gone slightly seedy. The Floradita, the bar Hemingway frequented, and where they claimed to have invented the daiquiri, still flourished. The bullfight mural behind the bar had been painted over with some crude socialist realism depicting Fidel wading ashore before the revolution. Hemingway's bust was in the corner, and many of the individuals hanging over the bar looked like permanent fittings.

Like the mural dominating the Floradita, crude revolutionary propaganda was dominant in Havana. There were posters, flags, and banners everywhere — on walls, windows, lampposts, fences, store windows, in elevators, restaurants and government offices—exhortations to work harder and fulfill norms, to remember the Bay of Pigs and never to forget the menace of America. Everywhere were posters showing Fidel in heroic pose, knapsack on shoulder, rifle in hand, on a cliff in the Sierra Maestra mountains, contemplating the land he was about to liberate. Ironically, in view of his anger at Khrushchev's capitulation, there was a ubiquitous poster showing a Cuban soldier holding up his hand like a traffic cop saying: "Stop, Mr. Kennedy. Cuba is not alone." Behind him was the shadowy figure of a Russian soldier.

Everywhere was the slogan "On a War Footing," and on a high building a huge neon sign flashed over Havana at night: "Patria O Muerte" (Homeland or Death) and "Venceremos" (We Shall Conquer). The switchboard operator answering the phone at the hotel said it as a rapid salutation: "Buenos Dias, Patria O Muerte. Venceremos. Hotel Capri." The slogan was printed on every kind of document, even the hotel stationery. And in the toilet in the Foreign Ministry I noticed some tiny graffiti at the bottom of the door. It read, "Patria O Meurte/Venceremos."

The impact was as if the most garish stretch of outdoor advertising in an American town were all devoted to one product.

In the middle of one night, I found myself in a bar where the entertainers from the other Havana clubs went when their acts were finished. It was smoky and noisy and very animated, with a band, a rhumba dancer, and drums. Sitting at a table, looking very morose, was Yevgeny Yevtushenko. Trading on our brief meeting in Helsinki, I sat down at the table. He was drinking beer and smoking Agrarios, Cuban cigarettes with a tractor on the package. He spoke very little English and I no Russian, but we pieced together a kind of conversation.

During the height of the crisis he had produced (whether enthusiastically or obediently, I couldn't tell) another of his made-to-order editorial poems which was published in *Pravda*, rather mechanically romanticizing Cuba's resistance. Now he appeared totally irritated by the Havana experience and bored with the young Cuban aficionados surrounding him. The talk, in bits of several languages, was stilted. The noise made it almost impossible to hear and I have forgotten most of what was said. But I remember the atmosphere. Just finding myself sitting there talking to Yevtushenko, on a tropical night, in what had once been a capital of Western decadence and which had just nearly tripped us into a nuclear war, was a surreal experience, full of incongruities. Not the least of them was the growing ennui and world-weariness apparent in the young Soviet poet. His sharp lyric realism, his uncompromising voice had made him a hero with the literate youth of the world. Now he had been forced to turn that voice to the hack work of the state. I could see that he knew it; the adventure and the humor had gone out of him.

On the fourth day of freedom I was having dinner in a restaurant with a Canadian diplomat. There was a screech of brakes outside and several armed soldiers came running into the restaurant. Having identified me, they ordered me to go out, leaving the diplomat at the table. They made me get into a truck and I wondered what the hell was going to happen this time. I was driven at high speed through the streets of Havana and down into the old part of town near the harbor. We finally stopped in front of a small jail used for immigration cases in years gone by. I was joined there soon afterwards by the very distressed Horikawa and by Don North, the Canadian. All three of us were put into a cell at the back. We had no luggage and no clothing except what we were wearing. The next morning they let us out into an exercise area separated by a wall of bars from the front of the building where the policemen had desks. That opened into the narrow street. For breakfast we got food by bargaining with small boys and women who were allowed into the jail. They took money in any currency and brought back delicious coffee and rolls. The food for lunch and supper was nauseating — a vegetable soup gone sour. So we ate mostly coffee rolls and coffee whenever we could get the people along the street to fetch them.

The guards spent most of their time sitting with their boots up on their desks, leaning back in their chairs watching television. The television set was high up on the wall, and the highlight on each of the three evenings we were there was a Cuban television serialization of Hemingway's *For Whom the Bell Tolls.* I clearly remember an interminable sequence where Robert Jordan, the hero, and his Spanish guide survey the bridge that he's come to blow up. The scenery was very crude, the acting amateurish, but Hemingway was still very popular in Cuba and the guards were utterly engrossed in *For Whom the Bell Tolls.*

The other memory I keep from the jail, apart from the squalor of the cell, was when they got Don North to shave off his beard. It was on the third morning. Ever since we had been locked up in the Capri Hotel, nearly three weeks before, North had stopped shaving and he had quite a respectable beard. The guards told him to shave it off. And he said, "No, I don't want to." They said, "In Cuba only Fidelistas have beards; you're going to shave it off." He said, "I haven't got a razor," and they gave him an old Gillette with no shaving soap. Then they stood there with a gun in his back while he stood up against the sink and shaved off his beard.

Later that morning they came and dumped our luggage and told us to look at it. We did. My camera had been emptied of film, all my notes had been taken, and all my private papers had been gone through by the Cuban security police. I knew that because they had obligingly left, pinned to each of them, little notes with their Spanish translations of the contents, written on the notepaper of the Cuban security police. So painstaking were they that they even scrutinized some papers I had in my briefcase involving a nursery school that my three-year-old son was about to enter in London. Somebody had spent hours translating it all and had actually attached one of their little notes saying, "These documents concern the admission of a child to a nursery school in London."

Shortly after the luggage came back, we were signed out of the jail, bundled into a car, driven to the airport, and deported.

Back in New York NBC made a nice fuss over me. The press department interviewed me and put out stories about my experiences. I was interviewed on several NBC programs, including the *Today Show.* In each of these experiences I felt a certain ambivalence. It is very satisfying to the vanity to be treated like a hero, however minor. And in the television world publicity is a valued commodity. I enjoyed being the focus of so much attention. Yet I was bothered by the hyping that went with it. The press department stories were factually accurate but they sounded sensational and overplayed. On the *Today Show*, it was clear that Hugh Downs was prepared for me to relate horror stories of my experience or of life in Cuba. What I felt justified in describing sounded, even as I said it, flat and disappointing, well beneath their expectations.

Television deals routinely in such hyperbole — the most amazing escapes, the most barbaric treatment, tortures, whatever — that it creates a psychological context in which the unsensational sounds out of place. I felt slightly embarrassed to be taking up their time.

The most practical result of my Cuban experience was probably the box of Havana cigars I smuggled back for Sander Vanocur to give to Pierre Salinger to give to John F. Kennedy.

TWELVE

The Long,
Hot Summer of 1963

IN MARCH 1963, when I moved from London, Washington, D.C. seemed as exotic and different to me as any foreign capital. I had spent only a few bewildering days there during the Cuban missile crisis the previous autumn, seeing nothing but the insides of the Pentagon and the State Department. I knew less than many of the tourists descending on Washington that spring. It was a foreign country for me, to be learned, and to be learned in a hurry because I ran the risk of making a fool of myself and showing my ignorance every time I went on the air.

For safety's sake NBC parked me at the State Department for the first few weeks, no doubt assuming I couldn't do much harm covering foreign affairs. So I spent the early spring of 1963 in effect back on the Cold War beat, reporting on the aftermath of Cuba, as the Republicans nagged Kennedy about proof of the Soviet withdrawal; and all the negotiations leading up to another Cold War climax, the nuclear test ban treaty.

To someone used to northern climates, the spring in Washington is unbelievably profuse: rivers of daffodils in Rock Creek Park; startling clumps of white, pink, and champagne dogwood glimmering through the other bare trees; the blaze of cherry blossom around the tidal basin; banks of fluorescent azalea and rhododendron and the magnolias.

The sweetness of that advancing spring was mingled with my feelings about the political atmosphere in Washington. The impressions that had filtered abroad about the Kennedy aura did not exaggerate the lightness of spirit it gave the city. It was a pleasure to go to the State Department auditorium to cover his press conferences. Of course they made news, but they were captivating in themselves. To my ears, stuffed with the stale rhetoric of Cold War, it was enormously refreshing to hear Kennedy redefining that rhetoric; to hear him schooling Americans not to assume that war was inevitable and peace impossible, or that Cold War was permanent. It was liberating to my spirit at any rate to listen to a man with the long sweep of history in his grasp and the confidence to look beyond the immediately fearful. "Across the gulfs and barriers that now divide us, we must remember that there are no permanent enemies. Hostility today is a fact, but it is not a ruling law. The supreme reality of our time is our indivisibility as children of God and our common vulnerability on this planet," he told the Irish Parliament.

And when Kennedy finally brought off the test ban treaty with Khrushchev, I thought my personal optimism about the triumph of rationalism was being vindicated. Kennedy was no Aneurin Bevan, but there he was, using language that would not have sounded odd on Bevan's lips: "I am haunted by the feeling that by 1970, unless we are successful, there may be ten nuclear powers instead of four, and by 1975 fifteen or twenty. . . . I see the possibility in the 1970s of the President of the United States having to face a world in which fifteen or twenty nations may have these weapons. I regard that as the greatest possible danger."

Yet this shining Athens of the West, casting its beams of rationality out to the world, tolerated, like ancient Athens, gross human injustices. Another assignment had brought me into intimate contact with the blacks in the District of Columbia, and as the civil rights summer of 1963 advanced I found myself covering them more and more. Yet I was also assigned to help cover the White House. So, it developed into a summer of startling contrasts: the sweat and drama of the civil rights struggle in the streets, interspersed with gilded days in the White House and unreal weekends covering Kennedy on Cape Cod. It was so kaleidoscopic a summer, and the contrasts so vivid, that it's all a bit jumbled up in my memory.

Because assignments kept shifting so rapidly, I never quite got over the feeling that I was a foreign correspondent, just in from abroad for the quick once-over. The real difference was that I was broadcasting to the people of the country I was covering. That took some mental gear-shifting to get used to, with imperceptible slidings from "they" to "we."

The foreign-correspondent feeling was particularly acute when I found myself in Washington's black ghetto, east of 14th Street, N.W. NBC's local station, WRC-TV, asked me to narrate a documentary on the racial situation in the District, which many considered ready to explode. In fact probably only the distractions of the enormous publicity given to the civil rights struggle in Birmingham, Alabama, and elsewhere that year kept Washington cool. When it did blow in 1968 after the murder of Martin Luther King, it blew appallingly.

Unbelievable as it seems now, Washington was still a segregated city until the 1954 Supreme Court decision on school desegregation brought swift change. The new tolerance and the lure of federal jobs attracted a huge migration of poor Southern blacks. By 1963, Washington, D.C., was the first major American city with a majority of black residents, and Southern migrants were still trickling in through the bus terminals that summer. But black unemployment was three times that of white and there was rampant discrimination in housing and employment. The city was seething. In the fall of 1962 a high school football game erupted into a race riot. Five hundred and twelve people, mostly white, were cut, bruised, or stabbed when a mob of black youths raced through the crowd, lashing out at men, women, and children with fists, umbrellas, stones, bottles, and knives.

We decided we had to show the living conditions that lay behind this great anger. I had never seen anything like it in a developed country. Within a few blocks of the White House, I talked to a Mrs. Taylor living with eight children and other relatives in rooms that would have been squalid in a Dostoevsky novel about nineteenth-century Moscow. A large piece of the kitchen ceiling had fallen in, leaving a hole with the rafters open. While I looked, several large rats came to the edge and stared brazenly down. Mrs. Taylor would not let her children come into that room. Her conditions were repeated endlessly in the nearby streets.

The more radical black leaders, so considered because they didn't go along with gradualism, laid responsibility at the doors of a "willful group of white racists." They meant Southern congressmen controlling the House committee that was still the real power in the District's affairs. In the minds of the blacks, those men were trying to make integration fail.

It was interesting to experience the tension this subject produced at NBC. On one side the network news director, Bill Monroe, was pushing for a tough, provocative piece of reporting. On the other, the local station with its ties into the business community wanted no feathers ruffled in the Establishment. That made for extreme editorial caution. But it made me understand something I had never had to face as a journalist: for the first time in my career what I said on the air could have a direct impact on the community I was broadcasting to. At its most extreme, it could have incited people to riot. It made me pay very careful attention not only to the effectiveness of what I said (the usual devices to keep people awake and listening) but also to the weight of my statements. The experience constipated my thinking and resulted in conclusions that were unnecessarily tame. I was newly arrived and too eager to please.

President Kennedy agreed with the arguments for D.C. Home Rule. That was a relatively mild and innocuous gesture compared to the activist role he was being forced into by events, particularly in Birmingham.

In April, Martin Luther King's demonstrations to end

segregation in Birmingham were met by the police chief, "Bull" Connor, with police dogs and fire hoses. Pictures of those atrocious scenes flashed around the world in newspapers and on television. The president and the attorney general, Robert Kennedy, intervened to help create a dialogue with the white community. When Alabama Governor George Wallace tried to prevent the integration of the University of Alabama at Tuscaloosa by "standing in the school house door," the Kennedys sent federal marshals to prevent it. That night on national television John Kennedy made the strongest presidential address on racial equality since Lincoln's Emancipation Proclamation. The next week he sent the first civil rights bill since Reconstruction to Congress — a bill passed only after his death.

I spent several days in Birmingham in late May, my first time in the Deep South, my first experience of the stunning impact racial segregation makes on the white conscience that has not been exposed to it before; the deep humiliation of it, and the immediate guilt. I also experienced for the first time the fear created by maddened whites, seeing their society torn asunder, giving vent to their own anger and anxiety.

I saw a lot more in another town ignited by the Birmingham example, Cambridge, Maryland. That racial battleground became my beat for half of the summer; it was the civil rights revolution in miniature. It even had a main thoroughfare called Race Street.

Cambridge was a small city on the Eastern Shore of Chesapeake Bay, an area culturally remote from the rest of the East Coast. An old reporter for the *Baltimore Sun*, Charles Whiteford, told me the first story he covered for the paper in the 1940s was the lynching of a black man by a mob on the Eastern Shore. The whites were a tough, independent breed, hardened by generations as watermen toiling out the Chesapeake's famous soft-shell crabs, oysters, and clams.

Even in 1963, it felt remote. I remember driving down from Washington one morning in mid-July, just before dawn. A band of mist hung over the roads and lush cornfields. As I drove toward Cambridge, disturbing the mist at the edges of the road, it was like gently ripping open a cocoon. And Cambridge itself seemed wrapped, cocoonlike, in its traditional insularity, tucked away from the fast movements of the twentieth century.

It had burst or been ripped out of that cocoon by the civil rights revolution and the town frightened itself with the viciousness which erupted when the old patterns of segregation appeared to have been seriously interfered with.

Compared to other trouble spots I had covered around the world, the violence in Cambridge was modest, but it always looked ready to burst into open racial warfare. I was sent there first, in the middle of a June night, because two people had been wounded by shotgun blasts. Black demonstrators, emulating those in Birmingham, had marched through the town demanding integration of the schools, restaurants, bowling alleys, and movie theaters. White onlookers assaulted the demonstrators. Several people of both races were injured by stones. Then someone fired a shotgun, wounding two whites. Blacks appealed to Robert Kennedy, and the governor of Maryland sent in two hundred National Guardsmen to keep things cool. For twenty-five days Cambridge was under a form of martial law and there was a large press contingent in town. As usual, they made the situation sound about 300 percent more dire than it actually was, and I did my share of it. But there was no exaggerating the viciousness of the emotions that surfaced. Racial hatred and fear are surprising emotions to someone who has never felt them.

I was standing with a young black man called Freddie one evening while the leaders decided whether to start a march in defiance of the National Guard orders. A group of whites were standing across the road, cheering and cursing. Freddie pointed to one of them. "You see that Hank over there? I grew up with him. He ate as much as I did off my table. My mom wiped his nose. He wore my clothes and he screwed my cousin and when I walked up there today, you know what he said to me? 'You black son of a bitch.' "

Another night, there was a fracas outside the courthouse. The police arrested one of the tough oystermen who was making trouble. The white mob threatened to storm the court-house to get him out. At the height of the agitation one of the whites screamed: "If you walk away now and leave him in there, we're lost. We'll be scrubbing niggers' floors!"

Another time, the Guardsmen, with fixed bayonets and gas-masks on, were lined up shoulder to shoulder to stop a march by a sullen group of blacks. I heard one of the young Guardsmen say to the soldier beside him: "All I want is to get a crack at one of them."

Their presence and the virtual martial law made Cambridge different from many other cities with civil rights explosions that summer. So did the leader of the demonstrations.

A slim, rather pale-skinned woman of forty-one, named Gloria Richardson, the granddaughter of the first black town councillor of Cambridge, she was a tall, delicately boned woman, who you thought could have been blown down by a strong man's breath. But she was very determined and to me she exhibited a lot of charisma. At one point Marlon Brando offered to come to help her.

Gloria Richardson turned the white power structure of Cambridge upside down by simply following Martin Luther King's example: she organized a successful boycott of white stores and she kept on parading with men, women, and children. They were spat upon by whites, stoned, beaten up, and taunted with the vilest abuse, but they kept marching and singing. The more they marched, the more furious and frustrated the whites became. And when the National Guard stopped them from marching, they filled the AME Zion and other churches to hear powerful speeches and to sing to get their courage back.

I spent many evenings that summer sweltering in those churches; the temperature well over a hundred degrees, the only breeze coming from the cardboard fans (compliments of the local black funeral director) waving in all the pews; everyone swaying to the beat of "I woke up this morning with my mind set on freedom," or "And before I'll be a slave I'll be buried in my grave and go home to my Lord and be free," or the anthem of that summer: "We shall overcome."

I'm a little disappointed when I hear that sung now for effect by antinuclear demonstrators, or environmental protestors. I feel they are using something that isn't theirs, that they didn't earn. You needed to be in some of the places that was sung in in the summer of 1963, when the singers were so scared their voices trembled; when they held on to each other and swayed with the hymn, they were often desperate for the physical comfort of the others, as they wondered what lay waiting for them in the dark night outside the church when they finally had to go home.

I moved around, spending time at Gloria Richardson's comfortable frame house filled with antiques, listening to them plot strategy. Some evenings I'd go and drink bourbon with the boyish-looking National Guard commander, General George Gelston, a wry, civilized Baltimore lawyer when he was not playing soldier. And still other times I hung around trying to find out how the whites were adjusting. In the bars you could meet and chat with the colorful watermen and their friends. As all such social disruption does, it brought out and briefly legitimized the riffraff in both races.

I was in a bar one night with George Sozio, the NBC cameraman working with me, and he fell into conversation with a youngish man with a beer belly and a squint. After several beers, he told George that he was planning to bomb one of the black churches. Sozio told me and we encouraged the man to talk. He was half-drunk but comprehensible, and his conversation was the vicious antiblack litany that was becoming familiar to me. The more impotent or defeated by life a poor white felt, the more abusive he grew about blacks. This fellow was like that: a sorry, bewildered man, very tedious to listen to. But he said he was going to put a bomb under a church, and talked gleefully of the number of black people it would kill. That was his plan. That would show those goddamed, motherfuckin' sons of bitches, including the Kennedys, in Washington.

If he was serious, we had to keep tabs on him and decide whether to alert the police. He would not tell us which church or when. He just drank beer and rambled on. Finally he said he would only tell us the rest in his own place. We had to go and have something to eat with him. It was about 1 A.M. and the bar was closing, so we followed him home, his beaten-up car weaving drunkenly along the road.

He lived in an apartment over a gas station and we climbed the stairs behind him. It was a wretched place, with shabby, broken furniture. He called to wake his wife up and told her to cook us some breakfast. But when he turned on the living room light, there she was, with a boy of nine or ten, asleep fully dressed on a battered velvet sofa with their arms around each other. The boy crept off to bed. The wife got up, a pathetic, overweight girl with unwashed, straggly blond hair. When she protested that she was tired, he shoved her viciously into the kitchen. She whined but obeyed him. She acted dim-witted.

Disconcerted, George and I began saying, "Oh, don't bother. It's very late. We aren't really hungry." But he turned on us angrily.

"What is it? My place and my food aren't good enough for the likes of you? Maybe you think I haven't got any eggs and bacon. Is that what you think? Well, look."

He opened a tall refrigerator with a flourish and I looked at it astonished. It was filled, crammed actually, with just that, eggs and bacon. There must have been at least two dozen cartons of eggs.

"You see? No need to worry about whether I got food. C'mon there," he shouted to his wife who was falling asleep again, leaning against the door. "Get the goddamned pan on. We're hungry. And cook some scrapple too!"

Scrapple is a kind of country sausage, very highly spiced. It usually comes in blocks, and to fry it, you cut off slices. Soon the dirty kitchen was filled with the smell of bacon, eggs, and scrapple, cooked by this slatternly, half-awake woman barely able to keep her hair out of it. The smell became discouraging.

"Don't worry about me," I said, "I'm not very hungry. I'll just sit here while you eat."

And Sozio said, "No, I'm not hungry either. You eat and we'll talk."

Our friend lashed out again. There was a crazy streak in

him. He reached behind me where there were two shotguns in the corner. He grabbed one and cracked it to make sure there were shells in both barrels.

"Now you're going to eat my goddamned scrapple and eggs whether you like it or not. You get them plates on the table."

His wife slouched over to the table and put plates in front of Sozio and me and stood back. Her husband raised his shotgun at us and said, "Now you eat every bit of it."

Naturally, we started to eat and he stood there laughing his head off. Satisfied that we really were eating, he sat down and began attacking his own plate, the shotgun leaning against the table beside him.

The scrapple was very strong and the eggs thick with grease.

He still wouldn't talk any more about the bomb, muttering about "tomorrow." We finally got out of there, leaving him sitting at the table with his dirty plates and his shotgun. It was difficult to imagine what went on there normally.

I thought he was quite capable of bombing a church. He was a social inadequate, his self-esteem very precariously maintained; perhaps seeking an identity in the shreds of prejudice shared by the other whites. Perhaps he found that in the crisis atmosphere, with their known world threatened by frightening change, talking tough about "niggers" made people listen to him who normally didn't. What else might he do to be noticed and applauded? We told the police on the way home. They took the information carefully. As far as we could tell, the incident died there.

The crisis liberated some whites from their fear, and Cambridge produced one of the most uplifting stories that summer.

Faced with irresistible pressure from the black demonstrators and from Robert Kennedy's Justice Department, the city council began discussing integration of public accommodation. But each time they took a step forward, the anger of the white community drove them half a step back. Instead of simply passing a public accommodation ordinance, as neighboring towns had done, the Cambridge council chose to amend the city charter. That opened the public accommodation question to challenge by petition. A restaurant owner named Robert Fehsenfeldt set out to organize the petition to defeat the ordinance.

But Gloria Richardson and the blacks weren't waiting. As soon as the National Guard left, they marched downtown and staged a sit-in at Fehsenfeldt's restaurant. Helped by several whites, he threw them out bodily into the street. When some refused to move, Fehsenfeldt gleefully broke eggs over their heads. All of the proceedings were filmed for television.

The scene was shown on the news that evening. Fehsenfeldt saw it and made a public apology. He said that seeing himself doing that to the blacks made him ashamed and he regretted what he had done.

Slowly and painfully, Cambridge whites accepted the inevitable; some never quite understood what had turned quiet Gloria Richardson from Muir Street so "uppity" or why ever she got invited to the White House. Some continued to blame the whole affair on the national press.

The cameramen felt the white community's wrath more than we reporters did because they were more visible. George Sozio got attacked one night by an angry crowd and had to use his Filmo, a very sturdy 16mm camera, as a weapon. A shot of him about to club someone with it went out across the country on the wire services. That made Sozio feel it would be healthier for him to get out of town. On his last night there we gave him a present.

Sozio was a nut about antiques, which he defined pretty broadly. The roadways of the Eastern Shore were littered with so-called antique stores and it was hard to get Sozio past them without stopping.

On Sunday I was with another reporter, Rene Airth of Reuters, and we passed a church rummage sale. It was a picturesque setting on the lawn in front of an old white church, under huge elm trees. Standing in the middle was an old potbellied cast-iron stove, which made me think instantly of Sozio. I bought it for two dollars and Airth and I, using all our strength, got it into the trunk of the car. It was so heavy it lowered the back bumper of the car almost to the ground.

Back at the motel where all the press stayed, I got the key to Sozio's room. We had to take the iron monster apart to get it upstairs, but in about two hours we had it bolted back together, standing between the twin beds in his room. In the dark it could have looked like a person.

We took Sozio out to dinner that night and made sure he didn't come back too sober. When he went up to his motel room, we all waited down below. It was very gratifying. He let out a yell and came running out shouting there was someone in his room. We all had our laugh and went to bed, happily imagining Sozio trying to dispose of the stove.

But he fell in love with it. The next day other newsmen told George that a bunch of whites in town now had his name and were looking for him. He had to leave. Sozio wouldn't go without the stove and insisted on taking it apart and putting every bit of it in his car. He got out of town safely and the stove ended up in his den in Washington — installed and working.

After Cambridge, it was the White House of "Camelot," of the "Thousand Days," suffused with the mystique and charisma of John F. Kennedy. And it gave me a problem.

I don't carry around a lot of theoretical baggage as a reporter and I did not imbibe serious Fourth Estate notions with my mother's milk. In place of that quasi-constitutional defensiveness bred into American reporters, I have my own instinctive aversion to being snowed. The more I hear everyone telling me that some public person is wonderful, the more I tend to ask myself, Can he really be all that wonderful? Conversely, I never believe anyone can be quite as consistently terrible as his reputation.

I had the distinct feeling of being snowed about Kennedy; not snowed *by* him, but by the breeze of favorable publicity that always seemed to blow about his name. It was as though Kennedy created his own climate, his own high-pressure area, whose influence prevailed over anything else.

The press has a barometer for each politician. The readings go up or down as journalists collectively sense the accumulation of positives or negatives around the man. For example, Senator Edward Kennedy's barometer read very high as he prepared to challenge President Carter for the Democratic nomination in 1979; it dropped into a low-pressure spell through the early primaries; but gradually rose again through the summer of 1980 as the press considered his campaigning chivalrous and brave.

With Jack Kennedy there never seemed to be any low-pressure areas. His barometer always read high, in the heroic range. So all his defeats appeared graceful and his victories magnanimous. Kennedy had plenty of critics, some in the White House press corps, but it was virtually impossible to be objective about this man. News tumbled out of his White House days in such profusion that reporters were constantly rushing to report it, or rushing with him somewhere in the world to make it. In making news JFK displayed the personal qualities universally admired: he appeared brave, handsome, confident, eloquent, intelligent, witty, virile; all packaged with the glint of sardonic humor and a faint wash of Celtic melancholy.

Faced with all this, it seemed churlish to carp at his weaknesses, even if you were sure they *were* weaknesses; for example, his apparent caution on civil rights.

It is the popular wisdom now that Kennedy virtually led the civil rights movement, that he was out there with Martin Luther King, holding the torch of liberty. I arrived at the White House in July 1963, fresh from three months' contact with black Americans who had a very different view of it. They thought Kennedy was dragging his feet, that he had been pushed to act only by the violence in Birmingham and its visibility on national television. In August, when they were planning the historic March on Washington, black leaders thought the president was too cautious. The White House said he did not want blacks to antagonize the Congress just as it began considering his civil rights bill. Blacks thought Kennedy feared that civil rights advocacy might defeat him in 1964.

I was in the White House all day during the March on Washington, watching on television and waiting for Kennedy's reaction. Many other White House reporters were gathered around the sets. As the day unfolded and the huge mass of marchers behaved in a manner dignified and moving beyond description, we kept saying to each other, "Why doesn't he go over there? Why doesn't he go and make a speech to show the nation and the Congress that he really cares?" We knew that Kennedy was watching in the Oval Office and we were amazed at his coolness.

We felt it even more strongly when Martin Luther King delivered his incredibly moving "I have a Dream" speech, standing in front of Lincoln's statue, one hundred years after the Emancipation Proclamation. It was the most exciting political speech I have ever heard. Merely re-reading it now, I can feel the hairs rise on the back of my neck. Part of it sounded like a direct reproach to the president:

"We have also come to this hallowed spot to remind America of the fierce urgency of *now*. This is no time to engage in the luxury of cooling off or to take the tranquilizing drug of gradualism. *Now* is the time to make real the promises of Democracy. *Now* is the time to rise from the dark and desolate valley of segregation to the sunlit path of racial justice. *Now* is the time to open the doors of opportunity; to all of God's children. *Now* is the time to lift our nation from the quicksands of racial injustice to the solid rock of brotherhood."

The president partially dispelled the impression of caution by receiving Martin Luther King and the other march leaders and giving them coffee and sandwiches in the cabinet room. Two decades later, his caution appears politically reasonable, given the opposition that faced his civil rights bill. But one grabbed at reeds like that to avoid being swept along by the current of approbation.

There was seldom time for such reflections. Even the extraordinary reality of the march was swept aside by other events. That same night, the president signed legislation averting a nationwide rail strike, to many a more important story than a quarter of a million blacks demanding their rights.

In any case, broadcast reporters did not deal much in nuance on the White House beat. The fierce competition made us errand boys, dashing from briefing to microphone with scribbled notes for fifty-second spots on the hourly news. When I look at some of my scripts now I am amazed I could read them on the air, they had been so sketchily prepared. We were seldom analysts. When we were not rushing into the little booths to broadcast, we were pestering White House officials for advance information, for access for camera crews, or passes for VIP tours of the White House.

I have never been sure whether my reservations about Kennedy were personal or professional. Did I even feel reservations or merely experience the need to entertain some? It puzzled me a lot. Was I reacting emotionally to the fact that I was a very late comer? Most of the reporters at the White House by midsummer 1963 had been with Kennedy since the campaign. They were familiars at court. When I got to Camelot, the legend was made; the epic poems were already written; the knights all had their places at the Round Table.

My copy from that time doesn't reveal anything negative. If anything, it is a bit too "gee whizz" and breathless. When you are running around saying, "The president did this to-day . . . did that . . . ordered this . . . proposed that . . . ," you are feeding not only the nation's sense of presidential importance but your own. He did it: it must be important. The president acts: I report it, therefore I am.

Whatever was eating me made the assignment exciting but uncomfortable. I felt an outsider, not of the club, and it got in the way. It created a psychological barrier that only the assassination broke down.

The first time I asked President Kennedy a question, I found myself blushing like a choirboy and shaky with stage fright. Would he think my question too stupid to answer? No other public figure ever intimidated me like that.

That incident occurred at an impromptu press conference called during one of the weekends at Hyannis. The press secretary, Pierre Salinger, shepherded us over to Kennedy's house on Squaw Island to make some news. There was JFK with that sardonic, half-amused look on his face, as though he were a trifle embarrassed at the event, so patently stage-managed to create a Sunday headline. The evidence for that was very subtle, perhaps only my imagination, but it made me think, If he doesn't take this little staging seriously, why should I? Something rebelled in me.

The very appropriateness of his sports clothes, casual and unstudied, was intimidating to one from elsewhere, not quite sure he was wearing the right thing. The man's assurance was so colossal, so all-encompassing, that the effect on me must have been what kings were able to do to their subjects. Reading Theodore White's *Making of the President 1960*, I could sympathize with Hubert Humphrey, Richard Nixon, and other opponents. How put-down they must have felt, confronted with all that social and sartorial assurance, not even considering all the other Kennedy assets.

Some years later, Harold Macmillan got very upset with the idea that I was trying to "denigrate" Kennedy. It was in London at the BBC just as we were about to tape a program on the Cuban missile crisis. As prime minister and as a friend, Macmillan had been very close to Kennedy during the crisis, frequently on the transatlantic phone to him and to his ambassador in Washington, David Ormsby-Gore (now Lord Harlech), who was also to be on the program. The occasion was the posthumous publication in Britain of Bobby Kennedy's book, *Thirteen Days*.

The BBC gave a small lunch for Macmillan and Lord Harlech before the taping and the former prime minister, who is one of the world's great raconteurs, was regaling us with candid stories about Winston Churchill.

Before leaving to prepare for the taping, I took Macmillan through the list of points I wanted to cover. One of them was a recently published article by Dean Acheson in *Esquire*, accusing Kennedy of having won out in the missile crisis through "dumb luck." When I said that, Macmillan got very upset and red in the face.

He pointed his finger at me across the table and said: "You are all the same, you journalists. You're nothing but denigrators. You just want to tear down great men."

Tears rolled down Macmillan's cheeks, as he said: "Jack Kennedy was my friend. He was a great man. I will not hear him denigrated."

Before I could say anything, Lord Harlech said quickly, "No, no, Harold, you missed the point. MacNeil wasn't saying that. He was quoting Dean Acheson."

The name Acheson set Macmillan off again, but eventually he calmed down. When I left the room, he apologized generously to me and later the taping went very well.

But Macmillan was right. As journalists we are often the denigrators. It is not that we set out to destroy people, to "tear down great men," as he put it; it is the amount of time and energy we spend looking for the negatives. With John Kennedy, in my brief exposure to him, I was very conscious of looking for negatives, as a kind of self-protection.

It was hard to be blasé about those Hyannis trips. Virtually the entire White House press corps decamped and followed when Kenndy went there for the weekend, some joined by their families. On the Cape, we virtually took over the Yatchsman Motor Inn. Everyone donned the current mode in sport shirts, wash pants, and boating shoes, ate seafood, played tennis, attended press briefings, and filed copy to show they were actually working.

Several moments from those trips stick in my memory. One was at Otis Air Force Base in Massachusetts where the president transferred from Air Force One to a Marine helicopter. Caroline and John came to meet him. Caroline ran to him and caught his hand and pressed it to her face. The gesture touched a paternal chord in me at the time. It was only months later, after the assassination, that I recognized the moment in what is now one of the classic Kennedy photographs.

One weekend I was a member of the "pool," the group of four reporters representing the wire services, newspapers, magazines, and networks, who travel with the president and share anything they consider significant with the full press corps at the other end.

We left from the South Lawn of the White House, the helicopter rotors blowing leaves off the trees, distorting the fountains, and bewildering the small flowers. At Andrews Air Force Base, we boarded Air Force One and sat in a rather luxurious press section up front. Robert Kennedy came up to chat with us. It was the first time I had met him and I was disconcerted by the strength of his handshake. He talked mainly about the christening of his eighth child, which we witnessed later that day.

(I am writing about dead men. I was the commentator for the BBC broadcast of Bobby Kennedy's funeral in 1968, hours of it: the service in St. Patrick's where Teddy's voice broke; the slow train ride to Washington; the nighttime burial at Arlington. In April I had done the same for Martin Luther King. The BBC has a tradition of letting one person describe such events, in their entirety. It gives the commentator a chance to prepare well, then shape the commentary, weaving it in and out of the events, complementing the picture, creating an aesthetic whole. Doing it left me with a deep feeling of intimacy with these men.)

At Otis AFB we switched to another helicopter which soon arrived at the Kennedy compound at Hyannis. We got out and stood to one side to watch the president's helicopter land.

It is an odd convention the American press has with the president, compared with the practice in other countries. It witnesses episodes in the president's life that elsewhere would be considered private and none of anyone's business. Since it was my first time, I felt how odd it was that I was using a lot of government machinery, being plopped down in front of the president's father's house, for the privilege of seeing him land and go into it. We could as easily have left him at Otis and simply taken Salinger's word that JFK was going to the compound and not slipping away to do anything else. Judging by the amount of "slipping away" that has since come to light, we might have been brought along more as witnesses to normalcy than we suspected. Whatever the rationale was, I'm glad of it because the scene that day was so extraordinary.

It was a brilliant late afternoon in July, the light yellow from the lowering sun. The white shingled houses faced the sea across a stretch of lawn that ended in thick sea grass and then merged into dunes and the beach. The bay to our right was a brilliant blue, with moored sailboats riding in it, like a Dufy painting. On the verandah of the senior Kennedy's house was a mess of weatherblown young mothers, children, and dogs.

The president's helicopter blew in, as it seemed, scattering the sunlight with its rotor blades, flattening the glossy sea grass on the dunes, tormenting the hair of Jackie who came out, sunburned and very pregnant in a flowered shift. She was followed by a parade of Pucci worn by Ethel Kennedy, Eunice Shriver, and Pat Lawford, all bronzed, athletic, and salty looking. A late Friday afternoon in summer: the commuting of the rich: cold gin and tonic and the promise of tanned limbs in seablown bedrooms. Whose nose was not pressed against that candy store window?

I used to wonder why my eyes were not scarred by these contrasts. Two days before I had been watching poor blacks in Cambridge testing their courage for the right to have a glimpse of the American Dream. Here was the American Dream so dazzlingly achieved that it was painful to look upon.

We drove to St. Francis Xavier Church for the christening of Christopher George Kennedy, fifteen days old. We crowded into the small sacristy with photographers and Kennedys — mostly children — and Archbishop (later Cardinal) Cushing. We sweated almost audibly while the archbishop's Boston voice rasped through the long version of the baptism service in Latin. Some fifteen Kennedy children, including Caroline and John John, jammed around the font, talking freely among themselves about the proceedings.

The baby slept, the perspiring archbishop clowned, and the Robert Kennedys laughed. Ethel, the mother, came into the church bareheaded and hastily whipped out a piece of white lace and donned it just as the service began. The only one fairly calm and apparently not sweating in the terrible heat was the president.

Some Kennedy child, a little girl of about three, was being crotchety and held by a black nurse. As her eyes were turned away from the christening, she was looking at me and kept trying to grab my notebook out of my hand. Another Kennedy trying to manage the press.

Ten years later, in October 1973, I went back to Hyannis to interview Rose Kennedy for a BBC documentary called *Rose Kennedy Remembers.* It was a mild autumn day and there was a great quiet and emptiness. That is common on the New England coast in the fall, but it seemed particularly silent in the Kennedy compound. The helicopters and wives and children and dogs had all gone away. When I walked to the end of the lawn by the sea grass, to the spot where I had watched the president's helicopter land, there was no sound but the waves on the beach.

The camera crew were affected by the atmosphere, and were unusually quiet as they set up in the living room overlooking the sea, a room whose walls and tables were covered with photographs of smiling, dead Kennedys.

There was an imperious call from upstairs: "Where's the one who is going to ask the questions? Send him up." For Rose Kennedy television interviewers ranked with other workmen like rug layers and men who delivered flowers for a party.

I went upstairs and into her bedroom, where a professional makeup artist was just beginning his work. Mrs. Kennedy was eighty-three, a very old lady, gaunt and pale, with large age freckles. She sat in a straight chair facing a wall of wardrobes with mirrored doors. She wore a slip, an old housecoat, and black lace-up shoes like a nun's. As I came in, the makeup man was just attaching false eyelashes. On the four-poster lay a new blue woolen dress by Cardin, to be worn the first time in this interview.

Gradually as we talked, I saw her transformed from a sagging, depleted old lady into a much younger woman. And it was not all makeup and externals. She gradually came alive. The strength acquired by years of her strict regimen, swimming, walking, dieting, became apparent. Her own spirit radiated energy and youth. She was like an aged actress in her dressing room, gradually working herself into her part. By the time she sat dressed, made up, her hair arranged, in a wing chair downstairs and the assistant cameraman snapped the slate board, "Rose Kennedy, Scene One, Take One," she came alive, as if awakening from a dream of old age. If you deliberately blurred your vision, and looked at Rose as at an Impressionist painting, she could have passed for forty. Remarkable.

Also disconcerting. If there was a strong suggestion of Tallulah Bankhead in her dressing room, there was an equal flavor of dowager queen.

"Is this one who will be asking the questions?" she asked without turning her head. Her secretary introduced me.

Rose did not say, "How do you do?" She said, "I have dictated what I want to say in the interview. It's been typed up. You'll find it there on the bed. Bring it over here and sit down and we'll go through it."

I sat on the small stool she indicated beside her chair, feeling like the man brought upstairs to polish her shoes.

It took about an hour gently to dissuade her from filling the interview with rehearsed speeches about how wonderful she thought Queen Elizabeth, the queen mother, whom she had known when Joe Kennedy was ambassador to Britain.

"They never could have found her equal, I don't think, had they searched the whole world, because she was so charming and gracious on every occasion," Rose said. "I think it's a terrific responsibility to have that honor from the time you're born. If you're in politics, you can relax for a few years and pick and choose; but to be *always* on time, to be *always* ready to meet people from different countries; to do it day after day and weekend after weekend!" That was almost equally a description of Rose's life, a life of fulfillment found in duty and a sense of responsibility seldom relaxed.

I wanted her to talk about more mundane things — what the children were like when they were young — and eventually she did, showing me the card index by which she kept straight the multitudinous health problems of nine children, and the dental care needed to produce all those Kennedy smiles.

And then the assassinations. Very few women have lived through what she has, at least on so prominent and public a level. She was a woman who could identify, not unreasonably, with the burdens of queenship and the torments of the Virgin Mary. "I think I've had great tragedies," she told me, "and I think of the Blessed Mother when she watched her son being crucified and reviled and she still trusted in God and she bore everything patiently; and I thought of her so often at the Crucifixion when I saw Jack [lying in state] in Washington in the Rotunda and Bobby again in New York."

Her throat closed around her voice as if she were going to break down, but as I listened, very moved, she suddenly straightened her back, cocked her head defiantly on one side, and laughed: "And I'm not going to be vanquished either — so I'm going to carry on. I think God intends us to be happy. We must live for the living."

We filmed several hours of interview in Hyannis, then more that winter at her home in Palm Beach. But it is in Hyannis that my emotional memory places her, on the day of the president's assassination. In her own words from her book, *Times To Remember*: "At that time of year on Cape Cod, there is a special quality to the light. . . . It is golden, pure. And as that afternoon wore on, I spent much time on our beach, and walked and walked and walked, and prayed and prayed and prayed, and wondered why it had happened to Jack."

THIRTEEN

Did I Really
Meet Lee Harvey Oswald?

WE ALL WEAR A protective covering, like a membrane, around our subjective lives. Few outside events ever penetrate it; but the killing of John F. Kennedy was one that did and did so universally. I have never run into anyone, in any country, who does not remember precisely where he was when he heard the news.

It happened that I was in Dallas, traveling with Kennedy, another of those professional accidents. Sander Vanocur was the chief White House correspondent for NBC and since midsummer 1963 I had been number two. Because Sandy had decided to follow Dean Rusk and other cabinet members to Honolulu for a meeting on the Vietnam war, Dallas fell to me. It was my first big presidential trip, the first time with my name on a White House manifest and linen labels saying "Trip of the President" on my luggage.

November 21: We got to Fort Worth late in the evening. Through San Antonio in the afternoon and Houston in the evening, the crowds had been more effusive than anyone expected, and indications of hostility negligible. From the Kennedys' point of view the trip was a success.

The press plane landed at Fort Worth after the Kennedys'. The night was clear and warm. All the main buildings downtown were outlined with strings of yellow lights, so it looked from a distance like a black sheet with buildings drawn in bright beads. We filed our stories, got our bags, and headed for our preassigned rooms in the Texas Hotel, where the president and Mrs. Kennedy were also staying. I got involved in a long discussion as to which sound camera should be sent on to Dallas for the luncheon speech the next day and which should stay behind to cover the two breakfasttime speeches in Fort Worth. I was so tired that I did not unpack even my pajamas, just fell into bed at 2:30 A.M. with a call for 6:00.

November 22. Until it happened the day was interesting but mundane. I often thought about this afterward. The difference between life and literature is that in literature the sense of foreboding is cultivated. As Sartre said, the end is present at the beginning. In classic drama you know what will happen and the dramatist plays on that knowledge, thickening the meaning with ironic comments. On November 22, obviously, we did not know what would happen. I describe it now, as nearly as I can, as it seemed then, before we knew.

It was chilly, dark and drizzling at 6 A.M. I checked out of my room, leaving my bag outside my door for the White House luggage people to pick up, and went to the press room. The Chamber of Commerce had laid on a breakfast of coffee, orange juice, and rolls.

Most of the reporters and White House staffers were talking about the night they had spent, first at the Fort Worth Press Club, then at some grimy nightclub where things got pretty wild. I was glad that I had been too tired to go. Everyone looked washed out. I heard someone say that several of the Secret Servicemen had been in the group.

We drank our coffee beside our typewriters and studied advance copies of the speech JFK was to deliver at the lunch in Dallas. It was a spirited attack on his conservative critics.

"In a world of complex and continuing problems, in a world full of frustrations and irritations, America's leadership must be guided by the lights of learning and reason; or else those who confuse rhetoric with reality and the plausible with the possible will gain the popular ascendancy, with their seemingly swift and simple solutions to every world problem. There will always be dissident voices raised. . . . But today other voices are heard in the land . . . voices preaching doctrines wholly unrelated to reality, wholly unsuited to the Sixties, doctrines which apparently assure that words will suffice without weapons, that vituperation is as good as victory, and that peace is a sign of weakness. . . .

"We cannot hope that everyone, to use the phrase of a decade ago, will 'talk sense to the American people.' But we can hope that fewer people will listen to nonsense."

As I have mentioned, since coming to the White House in the summer, I had maintained a certain skepticism about Kennedy; perhaps just in self-protection against the terrible weight of the man's gifts and accomplishments. But on reading this speech, I felt a surge of the intellectual power and rational force that he represented. I felt warmed by it and was looking forward to the moment when he would loose his barrage on the citizenry of Dallas.

One by one as reporters came in and glanced at the text, they brightened up and said: "It's a good speech," or "It's a hell of a good speech" — remarks they don't often make. Their pleasure, like mine, was in large measure divorced from any political approval of the speech; newsmen sense instantly what will make good copy, and this would.

It was significant that Kennedy had chosen to attack the spirit that had made Dallas seem such a nest of extremists. Right-wing demonstrators had assaulted fellow Texan Lyndon Johnson during the 1960 campaign. Just a few weeks before the Kennedy visit, United Nations Ambassador Adlai Stevenson had been spat upon and struck with posters. Dallas city officials were determined there would be no repetition of such incidents. Dallas police had mounted the biggest security operation in the city's history. That was the atmosphere, we all knew, that awaited Kennedy, and in which he would deliver these provocative remarks.

I finished marking the text, then checked the crowd which had gathered before dawn on a parking lot across from the hotel. Through the windows you could already hear the hubbub of several thousand people waiting. I had put on a summer suit because I had been too hot the day before, but found

I had left the belt for it in Washington. At 8:30 I went across the street to a men's store and bought a belt. I then edged through the crowd to be near the rostrum when Kennedy came to speak. Frank Cormier of the AP and I found ourselves right beside the stage.

At 8:45 JFK came out looking very rested and tanned, his hair still damp from the shower. With him were Governor John Connally, Vice-President Lyndon Johnson, Senator Ralph Yarborough, and the local congressman, Jim Wright. When they all lined up, flanking Kennedy, they looked a little like guilty schoolboys made to stand together after being caught fighting, which is what they had been doing. The feuding between the liberal Yarborough and the conservative Connally — and the efforts to cover it up — had been preoccupations of the trip. So far Connally had managed to prevent Yarborough from ever riding in the limousine with the president.

There was just a taste of rain in the air when Kennedy spoke. He said: "You'll have to excuse my wife for not being here. She's still organizing herself — but that's because she looks better than we do." The wide grin and sparkle in his eye at this remark, his way of beginning to laugh at his own joke before he quite finished delivering it, triggered a warm ovation from the crowd. They listened to a few more minutes of vigorous politicking: a thrusting sermon on the effort the nation was making to stay great and how vital a role was played by the city of Fort Worth.

I had never seen him in better form — brisk, energetic, warm, with a perfect sense of timing, as though he were sucking some delicious nourishment from this contact with the people. From the platform he went into the crowd. He passed within a few inches of where I was standing and his eyes rested on mine for a second. They were quite cold, as usual. The warmth in his face came from his smile and from the crinkles it made, but not from the eyes.

I followed him inside the ring of Secret Servicemen in their plastic raincoats, anxiously trying to form a shield around him as he moved. He shook hands all the way around the ecstatic, screaming crowd, then walked back into the hotel. Walking just to one side of him, I was surprised again to notice how coolly he emerged from the explosion of emotion that had surrounded him a moment before. He was wiping his right hand on a folded white handkerchief, making it quite dirty, and saying very casually to Jim Wright, "Well, that was quite good." It was as though he had hastily retreated to a safe point in his personality. Many people had commented on his tendency to be more shy with one person than with a hundred.

The marquee in front of the Texas Hotel read: "Welcome to Fort Worth, where the West begins." Four sheriff's deputies, dressed in the best movie-style Western outfits, were sitting on their horses in the middle of the street. JFK reached up and shook their hands.

There was a large crowd in the hotel lobby, held back by a rope, leaving a path to the elevator. Again the president shook hands and when a woman cried out that she had been missed, Congressman Wright touched her with one hand and, reaching as far as he could stretch, touched JFK with the other. The lady was satisfied. Merriman Smith of the UPI found an opening under the rope through the crowd on the stairs and we got into the Chamber of Commerce breakfast.

It looked like any political banquet, a long head table with lines of other tables leading away from it. There was a band in one corner, scarcely heard above the roar of conversation, the clinking of cutlery, and the grunting of waiters under trays of dishes.

The band managed a ragged "Hail to the Chief" as Kennedy came in. The entire Chamber of Commerce, it seemed, was introduced. A local boys' choir sang "The Yellow Rose of Texas." There was only one seat vacant at the head table and the entire room began twisting and muttering, "Where's Jackie?" Then Bob Kahn of USIS pointed to the kitchen door. I went over and saw Jackie wearing a broad mischievous smile waiting outside with the Secret Servicemen. Everyone by the door thought that was very funny. There were a lot of remarks (well out of her hearing) like, "Wait till Lady Bird sees this entrance," or "You're going to see a lot more like this next year" (meaning in the '64 election).

The preliminary speeches finally ended and Jackie was announced. The band struck up, the cameras whirred and followed her through the crowd until she emerged in the lights at the end of the head table, resplendent in a suit the color of strawberry ice cream, with a pill box hat and a dark blouse. She caused a sensation. She was cheered all the way to her seat. And in the back of the room the reporters laughed and wondered how they could describe so blatant a bit of staging without going too far. Kennedy's Air Force aide, Godfrey McHugh, was standing beside me with a big smile. "What kind of an entrance do you call that?" I asked. "Tactical," he replied.

The speaking went on. The gay mood struck outside in the parking lot grew warmer. Capitalizing on his wife's new verve and zest for politics, JFK began his speech, 'Two years ago, I introduced myself in Paris by saying that I was the man who had accompanied Mrs. Kennedy to Paris. I am getting somewhat the same sensation" (he began to laugh himself and the crowd laughed too) "as I travel around Texas. Nobody wonders what Lyndon and I wear!" That brought the roof down. It was a full minute before the crowd was composed enough for Kennedy to go on with the main point of his speech — a defense of the TFX fighter plane which would be made in Fort Worth and bring much benefit to the town when Congress approved it.

When he finished, they were given cowboy hats and boots in a series of presentations that began to sound like a string of commercials for local stores.

The locally based cameraman, Moe Levy, turned up and we discussed what parts of the sound film he should take back to NBC's Fort Worth station to pre-edit for the *Huntley-Brinkley Report* story I was to fly back from Dallas to do that evening. I remember saying to Moe: "Well, even if nothing else happens, we've got a story with Jackie."

From the breakfast, we grabbed our typewriters and were shepherded by Mac Kilduff, the assistant White House press secretary, down the hall to a press conference called by Governor Conally. Everyone was in high spirits and not feeling overly respectful toward Connally, who obviously wanted to repair some of the damage caused by stories about the splits among Texas Democrats which Kennedy's visit seemed to have exacerbated, not healed.

The governor spent fifteen minutes assuring members of the national press, to whom he was so delighted to have an opportunity to talk, that there were no difficulties among Texas Democrats that really mattered. It was like the governor of Maine calling a press conference the morning after a blizzard to tell you it didn't snow. Connally's information was greeted appropriately.

By the time we got outside and into the press bus, there was bright sunshine, a sparkling day getting quite warm. As we waited for the motorcade to begin, several reporters, including Marianne Means of the Hearst papers, argued about how to describe the color of Jackie's suit. They settled on pink. Most reporters don't like to be caught too far away from the pack on details like that; fearing to sound affected for knowing too much or of sounding dead ignorant for knowing too little, they prefer a consensus. Pink was the consensus.

The motorcade moved off through the main streets of Fort Worth. The crowds were thick. Every high school on the route to the airport had its costumed band and cheerleaders performing mightily as the president swept by. Some people downtown threw torn-up paper.

We were seven minutes behind schedule leaving for Dallas. Our press bus ran straight up to the press plane, a Pan Am Boeing 707. We raced aboard and immediately taxied out for the takeoff. As soon as the doors were closed the stewardesses began dispensing the Bloody Marys that are traditional on press planes. The flight lasted eight minutes.

I felt a little lightheaded after my insignificant breakfast and the Bloody Mary. As we landed at Dallas, I was still draining the glass, with the ice cubes and lemon wedge bumping my nose. There was the usual applause for the pilot on landing (another press plane tradition) then a rush for the door with typewriter, briefcase, and raincoat.

It was even sunnier in Dallas, so bright that my eyes ached. We dumped our things in the press bus, then found the enclosure where we could see the Kennedys come out of Air

Force One. In the center of the big crowd were Confederate and Texas flags, blowing out firmly in the brisk wind.

Air Force One landed and taxied in with the usual ear-splitting whine.

I don't know whether hindsight makes me remember the next moments extra vividly, or whether — as I think was true — the image of the Kennedys framed in the doorway of the plane was thrust into my consciousness with more than usual force. As the sunlight hit Mrs. Kennedy's pink suit, it was like a blow between the eyes. As they descended the ramp, they seemed enveloped in an aura of extra light. At the foot of the stairs, someone gave Jackie a huge bunch of deep red roses and the effect of those, almost blood red against the pink suit, was electrifying. Her hair was glossy in the clear light. Her brown eyes gleamed luminously and I saw clearly for the first time that what had looked like a dark blouse inside was the navy blue lining from her jacket, with the lapels turned out.

She bent to shake hands with an old lady in a wheelchair. Someone in the welcoming committee insisted on introducing a great many more people than JFK expected to meet, and his smile grew less and less cordial. Eventually they both came over to the wire fence which bulged with the enthusiastic crowd pressing on it. I was close enough to touch them both as they progressed through a storm of hands, one of which I glimpsed for a second plucking the head off one of Jackie's roses.

At the corner in the fence one of the boys holding the Confederate and Texan flags let them droop so that Secret Servicemen had to hold them up like a canopy over Mrs. Kennedy's head.

Finally they settled themselves in the Lincoln convertible, JFK in the right rear seat, Mrs. Kennedy beside him; Governor and Mrs. Connally on the jump seats in front of them.

We ran for the press buses. I got into the first one but discovered that my typewriter and so forth were in the bus behind. In order to have a better view of the motorcade, I decided to worry about that later. I was sitting at the right front on the side-facing bench seat, able to get a clear view out the front window. In front of me, Bob Manning of the

White House staff was standing in the door well. Although we were higher up in the bus, there were two cars of photographers and camermen ahead of us and they were sitting up on the backs of the seats. We could just see the presidential limousine, which was seven cars ahead.

The crowds were sparse on the outskirts of Dallas and only one or two deep in the suburbs. We were all watching for some kind of demonstration but didn't know quite what to expect. The route was thick with policemen. But indications of opposition were pretty innocuous, a few Goldwater signs, perhaps half a dozen all the way in. One man held up a poster reading: "I hold you JFK and your blind socialism in complete contempt." To the right of the roadway three windows in a small office building were completely blocked with the letters "B-A-H." But the crowds were very friendly. A couple of times people swarmed out onto the roadway and motorcade slowed down.

We did not talk very much except to point out the various signs and make notes. The sun remained bright. The crowds gradually grew thicker. As we came through a prosperous suburb of big houses separated by trees and lawns, someone said, "This is called Walker Avenue. He lives somewhere up here," referring to retired Major General Edwin N. Walker, leader of one of the right-wing political groups in Dallas.

It began to get monotonous and I was a little drowsy from the heat, the lack of sleep, and the Bloody Mary. All the faces and clapping hands that slid past the windows looked the same. My eyes grew tired from searching ahead for something to happen.

I don't remember at just what stage it happened, but during this half-drowsy phase I found myself wondering what I would do if someone shot him. How would I get to a phone? A reporter is constantly forcing himself to think ahead, not only about what the story may be, but how he can cover it and how to communicate it back to his office. It becomes a habit. But it surprised me to come out of a daydream with the thought of someone shooting Kennedy actually in my head. Where had it come from? Even with our premonitions about Dallas, such an explicit idea had never occurred to me. And it had suddenly appeared in a reverie. The idea was so outlandish, so preposterous that I dismissed it.

Along Main Street the crowd was so thick that it overflowed the sidewalks. From the bus you could look down the length of the street, which was in shadow, and see a twisting, sinuous canal left by swarming people held back by police down the center of the street. For a few moments it would look too narrow for the motorcade, then it would widen to let it pass.

Just as we turned the corner onto Houston Street, I looked at my watch. I know it was roughly five minutes fast and it said something like 12:36. I began to go over my personal schedule; to figure when to write a one-minute radio spot based on the text JFK would deliver at 2 P.M., in time to phone it to NBC in New York for the *News on the Hour*. I had just decided, "Well, I won't worry about it till we get there," when we heard what sounded almost like a shot. The bus was still on Houston Street.

I said, "Was that a shot?"

Several people said, "No, no," and others said, "I don't know."

That reaction took a few seconds, then there were two more explosions, very distinct to me. I jumped up and said, "They *were* shots! They were shots! Stop the bus! Stop the bus!"

The driver opened the door and I jumped out, just as the bus was turning the corner of Elm Street. I couldn't see the president's car but I really started to believe there was shooting because on the grass on both sides of the roadway people were throwing themselves down and covering their children with their bodies. The air was filled with screaming, a high unison soprano wail. The sun was intensely bright. I saw several people running up the grassy hill beside the road. I thought they were chasing whoever had done the shooting and I ran after them. I had to run around some people lying on the grass. It did not enter my head at that moment that Kennedy had been hit. I was thinking, It must have been some crazy right-wing nut trying to make a demonstration by firing a gun off. He couldn't have been trying to hit Kennedy.

With several policemen I climbed a wooden fence at the top of the grassy slope. Over the fence was a large stretch of railroad tracks. Uniformed police and plainclothesmen fanned out to search the tracks and two trains parked with their ornate observation cars facing us. I was level with the first of the policemen and figured they knew what they were chasing. It soon became clear they didn't, and I thought I had better look for a telephone.

I ran to the right and into the first building I came to that looked as though it might have a phone. It was the Texas Book Depository. As I ran up the steps and through the door, a young man in shirt sleeves was coming out. In great agitation I asked him where there was a phone. He pointed inside to an open space where another man was talking on a phone situated near a pillar and said, "Better ask him." I ran inside and asked the second man, who pointed to an office at one side. I found a telephone on the desk. Two of the four Lucite call buttons were lit up. I pushed another, got long distance, and was through to the NBC Radio news desk in about ten seconds.

One of the editors picked up the phone, said, "Wait just a minute," and put the receiver down. I could hear much talking in the background. Thinking it was David Lent, I screamed over the phone for about thirty seconds, "David, David, David." Finally Jim Holton answered. I said: "This is Mac-Neil in Dallas. Someone has shot at the president." He was very cool, got the tape running, and I recorded a bulletin ad lib of all I could safely say at that point:

"Shots were fired as President Kennedy's motorcade passed through downtown Dallas. People screamed and lay down on the grass as three shots rang out. Police chased an unknown gunman up a grassy hill. It is *not* known if the shots were directed at the president. Repeat. It is *not* known if the shots were directed at the president. This is Robert MacNeil, NBC News in Dallas."

I told Holton I had left the motorcade and was going with the police. A small crowd had begun to gather outside the Book Depository. A little black boy of about eight was telling a policeman, "Mister, I saw a man with a gun up there in that window," pointing above our heads. Another man corroborated that. It was the first I knew that the Book Depository had any connection with the shooting. And I still did not realize that the president had been hit. Just then a woman ran up crying hysterically. Seeing my White House press badge, she asked dementedly, "Was he hit? Was he hit?" I said: "No, I'm sure he wasn't." And then it began to dawn on me that what I thought so impossible could have happened. I rushed over to a policeman who was listening intently to his motorcycle radio. "Was he hit?"

"Yeah. Hit in the head. They're taking him to Parkland Hospital."

That put me in a frenzy. The president had been hit and I was now separated from the story! I had to get to the hospital. I ran out into the middle of the street but it was jammed with vehicles in all directions. Police cars with sirens wailing were rushing up to the Book Depository, bouncing over curbs, across grass and through flower beds. There was no taxi in sight, and the traffic was seized up on Elm Street. Frantic to get to the hospital, I ran across Dealey Plaza to Main Street and dashed in front of the first car that came along. He stopped and I opened the door.

"This is a terrible emergency. The president's been shot. I'll give you five dollars to take me to Parkland Hospital."

He was about thirty, not very bright. With a smile, he said, "Okay," and moved off. His car was filled with cardboard packages like cakeboxes.

He said: "Yeah. I heard something about that on the radio a coupla minutes ago."

"Where's the radio?"

"I put it in the back seat."

I was stunned. He had been listening to the radio. He had heard about the shooting, perhaps he had even heard my bulletin, and had calmly shut off his small transistor and put it in the back seat. It was there now. I grabbed for it and he turned it on and held it out the driver's window as he drove.

The traffic was infuriatingly jammed up. I kept urging the young man on, telling him to go any speed, take any risks, go through red lights. I would pay any fines. Besides, what could the police care right now? In fact, police cars were still racing by us going the other way.

I got him to stop at a gas station while I phoned New York again, to give them another spot, quoting the policeman about the president being hit and going to Parkland Hospital and the eyewitnesses who had seen a gunman in the Texas Book Depository. New York told me I had been ahead of the AP and the UPI with my first bulletin but it had taken them five minutes to get it on the air. I told them I was on my way to the hospital.

I dashed out of the gas station, kicking over a watering can as I ran between the gas pumps. I forced the young man to drive faster, taking the inside lane to pass. Eventually — it seemed like half an hour but was only a few minutes — we got to the hospital. I gave him his five dollars and ran around the grounds to the emergency section.

I got there just after the second part of the motorcade with the pool press and camera cars. The bus I had left was just arriving. So I was still competitive. There was a cluster of reporters around Senator Yarborough, who said the president was "gravely wounded." I looked into the limousine. The roses from Mrs. Kennedy's bouquet were scattered in the bloody back seat. In the corridor inside the emergency section, I got more details from Bob Clark of ABC, who had been in the pool car. He had seen the president carried in on a stretcher, bleeding and apparently unconscious. Connally had been hit too.

The corridor was jammed with reporters, Secret Servicemen, and White House staffers, and the hospital personnel were trying to clear it. Merriman Smith of UPI, who won a Pulitzer for his reporting that day, was dictating from a phone at the nurses' station. The nurse in charge kept saying, "You have to leave this phone. You can't use this phone," but Smitty went right on dictating. Seeing that was hopeless, I opened the door of a small waiting room. Behind the door were three pay phones no one had noticed. I grabbed the one nearest the door and never gave it up for the rest of the afternoon.

I got through to New York, while the *News on the Hour* was on the air. They told me to stand by for a cue then "talk as long as you like." I got a switch from Peter Hackes in Washington and told them what I had to that point. From then on

I kept the line open to New York. I was vastly relieved to be back in the right place to be covering the story. Without very good fortune I might still be back in that traffic jam. As it was, by getting out of the bus, I was the only reporter in the White House press corps who knew where the shooting came from and I filled the others in.

The emergency section corridor was dimly lit. At the far end were two wooden swinging doors, through which they had taken him. I got a hospital intern to hold the phone open for me periodically while I went down the corridor to talk to the FBI, Secret Servicemen, or White House staffers who stood around with ghastly, expressionless faces. Then I would go back to the phone.

Now Frank McGee was on the other end and we were patched live into the television network. Through some difficulty in switching the telephone line right away, I had to say everything in phrases which McGee repeated. It gave me a little more time to think. I left the phone again when Lady Bird Johnson came down the corridor looking very unsteady. She would only say: "Lyndon is all right." She wouldn't comment on Kennedy.

A priest, Father Huber, came out and said he had delivered the last rites to the president. Bob Pierrepoint of CBS and I talked to him together. We both understood him to say, under our repeated questions, that the president was not dead when he administered the rites. Pierrepoint told me that someone on CBS was saying the president was dead. Pierrepoint pleaded with them to wait for an official announcement.

I played it very carefully with NBC, cautioning them not to say more than we knew, putting in phrases like "we do not know the exact extent of his injuries." It seemed to me totally irresponsible to say that the president of the United States was dead unless you knew it for certain.

Another dash from the phone when Lyndon Johnson and a circle of worried Secret Servicemen came barging through the swinging doors. The FBI had cleared the area but had missed Pierrepoint and me behind the doors of the waiting room. I stepped in front of the vice-president to ask, "Is the president dead?" LBJ stared at me, his face white with shock, and said nothing, practically bowling me over as he walked out. He entered his limousine and was driven off at great speed.

Mac Kilduff saw us and told us to follow him. There was going to be a briefing. We followed Mac around the outside of the whole Parkland complex, up several slopes of grass, under fences, Pierrepoint and I panting after him, shouting, "Tell us, Mac, for God's sake. What is it? Is he dead? Tell us!" He wouldn't. We entered a nurses' classroom where a press room had been set up. It was full. Kilduff stood behind a wooden desk on a small platform. The cameras were switched on. His face was very white and he kept twisting it to avoid crying, but his cheeks were shining with tears. His hands were shaking and he tried to steady them by pressing down firmly with his fingers on the desk. With great difficulty in controlling his voice, Kilduff said: "President John F. Kennedy —"

Someone said, "Wait, what time is it?"

Someone else: "One thirty."

"That'll be it then." Again, reporters wanting a consensus.

Then Kilduff: "President John F. Kennedy died at approximately one o'clock Central Standard Time of a gunshot wound in the brain."

Bob Pierrepoint broke for the door and I followed. We raced all the way back around the outside of the building to the emergency section. I was gasping for breath as I grabbed the phone receiver and did the announcement that Kennedy was officially dead.

Then the coffin came out on an undertaker's cart, Jackie walking with one hand on it, possessively, her pink suit still spattered with the darker spots of her husband's blood.

There was a great quiet when they drove off. We heard that Lyndon Johnson had been sworn in and that Air Force One had taken off for Washington. I waited for further instructions from New York, about whether to stay in Dallas or go to Fort Worth to the NBC affiliate to start preparing a report.

It was then that I heard on television that a young man called Oswald, arrested for the shooting, worked at the Texas Book Depository and had left by the front door immediately afterwards. Isn't that strange, I told myself. He must have been leaving just about the time I was running in. But I had no memory of a face. My attention had been focused solely on finding a telephone, and the Book Depository had no other significance for me at that point. When Lee Harvey Oswald's picture appeared shortly afterwards, there was no leap of instant recognition.

It was about a year and a half later that I got a call in New York from William Manchester, who was writing *The Death of a President*. He said he had gone carefully over the ground to find out who had been in the Book Depository before and right after the shooting. He had seen a statement I had made to the FBI. He had traced my call through the telephone company to 12:34, four minutes after the shooting, and he was convinced that I had spoken to Lee Harvey Oswald. Could I tell him any more about it? I couldn't; it was possible, but I had no way of confirming that either of the young men I had spoken to was Oswald.

Then Manchester asked if I knew about the statement Oswald had made to the Secret Service. Oswald had told them that as he left the Book Depository, a young Secret Serviceman with a blond crewcut had rushed up the steps and asked him for a phone. Since no Secret Serviceman had entered the building, Manchester concluded that Oswald had mistaken me for one. I could say only that it was possible. I am blond. My hair was very short then and I was wearing a White House press badge he might have mistaken for Secret Service ID. But I had no way of proving it.

"Well," Manchester said, "I'm ninety-five percent convinced that it was you and I'm going to do some more checking."

Evidently he overcame his five percent of doubt because he states flatly in *The Death of a President* that at 12:33 P.M. Oswald "leaves Depository by front entrance, pausing to tell NBC's Robert MacNeil he can find a phone inside; thinks MacNeil is a Secret Service man."

It is titillating but it doesn't matter very much.

Far more important to me as a reporter was why I had not had the wit to stop and talk to the people lying on the grassy knoll. They had seen the whole thing. I later heard several of their eyewitness accounts. They are the most graphic descriptions of that terrible moment. And I had run right by these people, fixated as I was about chasing a gunman, because I didn't believe Kennedy had been shot. However much violence I had witnessed around the world in those years, it was still inconceivable to me that this could happen to Kennedy. I suppose unconsciously I thought him invulnerable.

There is no time to think in such situations. You follow your instincts and mine led me up the grassy knoll. It is one of the personal reasons I have for paying serious attention to those who claim there were shots from there as well as from the Book Depository.

Tom Pettit arrived that evening to share the Dallas reporting duties, notably at the police station where Oswald was being interrogated. I saw him once that evening, on one of the occasions when he was led through, that strange, frightened smirk on his face, and a bad bruise. I spent all of Saturday and most of Sunday with a film crew, retracing Oswald's steps back from the movie theater where they arrested him, to where he shot police officer Tippit, to his rooming house, to the Book Depository. I interviewed every eyewitness of his movements I could find. NBC put the twenty-minute film report on the air Sunday evening immediately before the district attorney, Henry Wade, gave a televised press conference to outline the evidence they had against Oswald. I had more eyewitnesses than he did.

I was still editing that report at the station in Fort Worth when Oswald was shot by Jack Ruby. Pettit was on the scene and NBC switched to him live just at the moment of the shooting. Pettit's "He's been shot!" became part of the history of that weekend. NBC sent me back to Dallas from Fort Worth and for the second time in forty-eight hours I entered the emergency section at Parkland Hospital and attended a briefing in the same nurses' classroom when Oswald's death became official.

I was shown a photograph of his body after the autopsy, the abdominal incision pulled roughly together with crude basting stitches.

It was not until Monday, three days after the shooting, that my private emotions caught up with the professional drive that had preoccupied me. From the moment the shots were fired and I got out of the press bus, I was thinking, What a story, what an incredible story. How do I cover this? Where should I be? — as though I were a reporting machine with no emotions. Actually, I think I was so stunned by the improbability of what happened that I was emotionally anaesthetized. Part of my brain went to sleep in disbelief. My thoughts came in slow motion, like tired legs dragging up too many stairs. Uttering the sentences I did to NBC from Parkland Hospital was like squeezing toothpaste out of a tube that has hardened; the normal, relatively facile flow of words was cut off. Something was blocked.

I decided on Monday, the day of the funeral, to do a piece for the *Huntley-Brinkley Report* back at the grassy knoll. People had come and put flowers there, small bouquets and big wreaths, some with notes attached:

"To my friend, J. F. Kennedy," in a child's scrawl.

"God forgive us all."

"Please God help us to gain from our great loss."

"I'm sorry, Caroline and John John."

These floral tributes had become in themselves a shrine to visit — the only tangible sign that anything unusual had happened there. From the evening of the assassination, there was a constant slow swishing of cars down the inclined road while people stared and took pictures.

On Monday, many people got out of their cars and walked over the grass to look at the flowers and read the notes. We put our camera with a long lens at the top of the hill to capture their reactions. Some of them had their hair in curlers and were chewing gum. I later wrote a radio commentary about how difficult it was to read grief, or anything else, into the face of someone chewing gum.

While we were filming, an old man sat down near us and turned on his transistor radio. Over it came the broadcast of the president's funeral in Washington. It was when I heard the lament played by the bagpipes of the Black Watch Regiment, marching in the funeral procession, that I really understood, with my feelings, what had happened. I sat there in the sunshine with the tears running out of my eyes; aware of how much the salt in them burned because crying was such an unaccustomed thing to do.

Two weeks earlier I had watched those same pipers playing on the South Lawn of the White House. It was a glorious autumn day, with President and Mrs. Kennedy, watching from the balcony, with Caroline and John John.

My own two children, a girl and a boy, were their same ages.

FOURTEEN

Travels with Barry
and Lyndon

BEFORE THE KENNEDY ASSASSINATION I had spent six weeks traveling with Barry Goldwater as he assessed his presidential chances. In January 1964 Goldwater became my full-time job until the November election, except for a few weeks with President Johnson's campaign in the fall. I covered about a hundred thousand miles with Goldwater, a lot of it in the same seat in his campaign plane. In that seat, I ate my meals, wrote stories, and often slept, drank about as much as the other reporters, helped to compose satirical songs about the campaign, and incidentally visited every state in the union except Hawaii and Alaska.

A presidential campaign is the best reporting assignment the United States can offer. It is exhausting and mind-numbing; the accumulated lack of sleep gives reality a surreal cast; the geography is a blur; the repetitive speeches become a kind of stale verbal wallpaper. But, provided you have a prominent candidate, he will always make news, your stories will always get used, and, if he goes far enough, it will help your career. Those are the practical reasons. The real reason reporters like campaigning so much is that it is fun, boyish, sometimes rollicking, good fun, in which all the domestic imperatives can justifiably be left behind, as in wartime. There is the exhilaration of travel in the most congenial company — the other reporters. If the campaign is efficiently run, you are cosseted like a small child; campaign aides will do everything to make your life uncluttered — except undress you and put you to bed, and even that service is not unheard of. Reporters return to the mundane world of neglected wives, estranged children, unpaid bills, and uncut grass with considerable culture shock. Many can't wait for the next campaign; and most of us nurse an affectionate nostalgia for those we've covered.

Covering Barry Goldwater was an added pleasure because he was such a courteous and decent man, whose personal manner often belied the strident rhetoric required by the movement he led, or which propelled him as its willing vessel into the presidential nomination. For all his public exposure, the senator remained shy and private, reluctant to see himself as something extraordinary, irritated by his own popularity when he wasn't in the mood. He disliked unscheduled crowds. He did not draw the nourishment many politicians do from popular acclaim in the flesh.

Late one night, his plane taxied into an airport where an unexpected crowd had gathered. "Who's responsible for this?" Goldwater barked and refused to get off the plane. Finally his campaign director, Denison Kitchel, went back and said, "Dammit, Barry, you're a national figure!" The reluctant national figure finally got off and made the right noises to the crowd.

Goldwater was also very funny, with a nice, self-deprecating humor, like his joke about having been born to a Jewish father but brought up Episcopalian. He told of going to a golf club which did not admit Jews and saying, "But I'm only half Jewish; can I play nine holes?"

The campaign produced a lot of unconscious humor, some of it created by the paranoia in some of his followers. In a suburb of Los Angeles, the senator was making a speech, when a man motioned a Goldwater aide outside and whispered: "There is something you should know about. There are men in there with notebooks and they're writing down every word the senator says."

Writing down every word was not always a kindness to Goldwater. There was the much-quoted plea from one of his staff, "Don't report what he says. Report what he means!" Verbal precision was not one of Barry's strengths.

But the substance of the Goldwater campaign has all been well documented. What I like to remember from it are some of the unusual adventures I had in the process of covering him, and the feel I developed for Arizona in all seasons through frequent trips whenever he went home.

In the early days, when only four reporters were covering him regularly, he invited us to fly down with him to Nogales, Mexico, for an evening. Nogales was one of the haunts of his youth and this was a sentimental "evening off." We flew down in his plane, a twin-engined Bonanza. Goldwater, a major-general in the Air Force, flew everything they would let him. That included a hair-raising spell at the controls of the campaign airliner leased from American Airlines, a new 727, which the senator threw into a turn like a jet fighter, giving a planeload of sedentary reporters enough G-forces to qualify them as astronauts, or convert them to conservatism.

The flight from Phoenix to Nogales that evening was very sedate. The Mexicans heard he was coming and laid on a lavish welcome. The Goldwaters took us to a restaurant where they knew him and made a fuss, and there was much mariachi music and consumption of tequila.

Back in Phoenix much later, standing under the wing of his plane, passing a tequila bottle for a nightcap, Goldwater said: "You guys really should go down when there's a bullfight."

We all said, "Sure, great" but it wasn't until six months later, in September, just as the fall campaign began in earnest, that it became possible. It had nothing to do with the campaign, but if it hadn't been for Goldwater I would not have had the experience.

The Senator himself did not feel like going, but his children all did, Barry Jr., now a congressman, and his two sisters and brother. They laid on three small planes and made the other arrangements.

The Mexicans thought the senator himself was coming and

we were met by a full-scale motorcade which conveyed us with great flamboyance — sirens and flashing lights — to the bull-ring. I had never been nearer to a bullfight than Hemingway's *Death in the Afternoon.*

We equipped ourselves with wineskins and paper plates of tacos and enchiladas, and climbed to the top tier of the small, intimate bullring. It was about half-full, mostly with Americans.

The Mexican mariachi band of violins, trumpets, and guitars struck up the proper march for the corrida and there was an impressive entry by all the finely costumed gentlemen. Then the trumpet laid a syrupy call on the air and in came the first bull, very young and very strong. He galloped in and immediately jumped the rail into the narrow corridor that runs around the ring at ground level. They teased him out and the picadors, riding padded horses, came on. They had just enough time to tickle the bull with a spike when he suddenly overturned one of the horses, got under the padding, and gored it badly. By this time a lot of American women were crying and wishing they had never come to the fight.

Suddenly the sky grew very dark and there was a loud explosion of thunder. They got the horse back on his feet with much excited shouting and prodding and pulling of its tail, while scared novice bullfighters kept the bull on the other side of the ring. After the bandillero had placed the two barbed sticks in the muscle of the bull's back, the young matador strutted around and began making his passes. The crowd was not enthusiastic. The matador got booed for appearing to sidestep almost every pass.

And then it began to rain. It was like a monsoon. At one moment it was all quite dry and then we were soaked through by great, splashing drops. Paper plates with soggy tacos floated by on the cement tiers. But the fight went on.

The bullring quickly collected several inches of water. There were drains ending in ornate stone spouts, which were gushing with water like firehoses filling a circular swimming pool. The bull didn't mind the rain at all, but the matador and his helpers kept wiping their faces on their soggy arms of sequined velvet. The bull continued charging and the matador sloshed after him. It was raining so hard you could scarcely see the other side of the ring.

When they decided it was time to make the kill, the ring looked like a shallow wading pool.

The bull had his head up and looked quite alert. When he charged, the matador aimed his sword but it buckled and went twanging away off the bull's back. While the animal was wheeling for another charge, the matador was fishing around for the sword in the bloody water at his feet. He tried again, and missed; and yet again, and missed.

Thinking about it afterwards, trying to put my afternoon to account, I was tempted to find a metaphor in all this for the doomed Goldwater campaign. Was this absurd ritual a symbol for the hopelessness of the conservative cause that year? Was this blundering matador a burlesque of the vain but chivalrous efforts of Barry Goldwater? That was reaching a little far.

On the level above me, Goldwater's sons and daughters were huddled with the mariachi players under an edge of roof. They were all laughing.

It got worse before it ended.

The bull broke away and jumped the barrier, but he got stuck halfway, balancing on his stomach with his legs hanging down on either side. Four or five Mexicans were pulling his tail while an equal number were twisting his horns to make him come forward. Eventually, the bull got off the fence, the matador retrieved his sword, wiped the rain off his face with his shoulder, and faced him. The crowd jeered and the bull charged. The sword went in about nine inches, but the bull galloped away with it whipping back and forth out of his neck until it jerked out. The bull came to rest and several assistant matadors commenced to stick swords into his neck.

Finally, with much grace, the bull knelt down and it seemed his decision, not the result of a defeated spirit. A team of horses was brought in to tow him away by the horns. A wake of blood and water and sand was created behind him.

Even Ernest Hemmingway would have needed a few drinks after that, so we all repaired to a tequila bar, bought a bottle, and consumed it with a lot of lemon and salt. Michael Goldwater went to a shop and bought loose Mexican dresses for his sisters, who were soaked to the skin.

When we were dry we went back to the airport and took off for Phoenix. The rain had stopped, but the air over the mountains was heavy with dry electrical storms. Senator Goldwater knew about the weather and was worried. We could hear him calling the planes on the radio from his house to check that we were all right. I was sitting on a side-facing seat holding a paper cup of tequila, when suddenly our plane was thrown violently half upside down for a moment, then flipped back upright. The lights went out in the cabin and for a few seconds it was very panicky. My seat belt held me in place but the drinks went everywhere. Barry Jr., who was flying, came out of it quite unruffled.

We made it to Phoenix and the Goldwater boys thought we all needed feeding so we went to a Mexican restaurant that had a band, and I don't remember how, but when we left, the band came with us. We drove to the senator's house in Paradise Valley, near Scottsdale, in an open truck, on which journey I found myself playing the bass fiddle. The senator had gone to bed but the party continued until several of us slunk away to our hotel to recover.

Things were not always so boisterous. Gradually I absorbed from Goldwater a strong sense of what he loved about Arizona. He was torn between Rotary Club pride about its rapid development and nostalgia for the purity of its landscape before the boom began — before Phoenix, for example, had a smog problem.

He told us of the days before air conditioning, when the dry heat reached 115 degrees. To get the boys to sleep, their mother wrapped them in soaking sheets; by the time they were asleep, the sheets would be dry.

His mother, known to the family as Jo Jo, had come to Arizona as a young woman with tuberculosis, expecting to die. Instead, she developed into a frontier character who slept with a pistol under her pillow and took her sons on desert camping trips.

Barry loved the desert. When he built his very modern house on a hill near Camelback Mountain, he was careful that its profile did not obtrude. He planted the hillside around with every variety of cactus and desert plants. On election day 1964, Goldwater calmed his nerves by transplanting cactus for several hours, alone.

He was a first-class photographer and had produced remarkable photographs of the Arizona landscape. He was fascinated by Arizona's Hopi Indians and was admitted as an intimate to their ceremonies. He was proud of a tattoo of dots on one thumb that showed his initiation. He made the first collection of their arresting art form, the cochina dolls, used in religious ceremonies to depict aspects of human and animal characteristics.

He was also an insatiable gadgeteer. He installed an elaborate intercom system between all the rooms in the house. To help him go to sleep in the quiet desert night, he built a little waterfall in the garden, and piped the soothing sound into the bedroom. And lest his patriotism ever be caught napping, his Stars and Stripes rose and fell automatically on the flagpole outside when a photoelectric cell detected the dawn's early light and the twilight's last gleaming.

All of us who saw him almost daily for a year speculated endlessly about how much he really wanted to run for president, how much his heart was in it. He had such a diffident, laid-back manner; he read woodenly the harshly worded speeches prepared for him, as though his attention were elsewhere; he constantly allowed his own altruism to get in the way of efficient campaigning, like spending half an hour in a New Hampshire high school auditorium telling fifth-graders about the Indians of Arizona, while his campaign aides gnashed their teeth over the wasted time.

One trip he made in that spirit was typical. The California primary was crucial to him and Nelson Rockefeller was mounting a strong challenge. The Goldwater campaign needed to strain every nerve to hang on. But two weeks before the election, Goldwater insisted on taking off to visit a small town in northern Arizona because he had promised to go to the high school graduation. The town was Fredonia and it had a special meaning for Goldwater.

It lay in the plateau country of northern Arizona. It was

late spring and tall new grass was bursting out of the rather barren-looking earth to feed the cattle and sheep. The air was so clear that you felt you could see a hundred miles as you looked out between the sandstone buttes and mesas that mark the area of the Grand Canyon. Fredonia was nestled in the shadow of these weird rock shapes, almost on the Utah border.

The town had only six hundred people, so small that it didn't have a recognizable main street. It made a living with a saw mill and by taking a little money from the tourists driving down from Utah or over from California to see the Grand Canyon.

The saw mill had caught fire one night in the 1950s when Goldwater was in town making a not very incendiary speech during his first campaign for the Senate.

He won that election and Fredonia became a talisman; he went back there every campaign for good luck. That was why he was flying over the mountains from California in a small plane, like an ancient Greek coming to consult his oracle.

It was the kind of dreamy late afternoon reserved for very small towns. The two-car motorcade ambled up to the mayor's house for doughnuts and lemonade, then around the corner to the pastel-painted high school. There were clusters of people waiting outside. From open windows in the warm air came the sound of the school orchestra rehearsing Handel's "Largo" with a beguiling predominance of reedy wind sounds.

Girls to be maids of honor to the graduates came from all directions, shy but happy in long evening dresses held carefully off the sidewalks. A knot of boys near the school self-consciously ignored them.

The sun, now low in the west but still strong, cast a golden light over the lilac trees and the school lawn. From down the road some Chinese elm trees delivered into the faint breeze the golden petals of their flowers. They drifted with the sunlight shining through them like a golden snow across the scene.

We went into the auditorium. There were only six graduates. Goldwater's oracle turned out to be a tall, nervous girl in a white gown and motorboard, the valedictorian. She said in her address: "If you would like to win, but think you can't, you'll lose."

We flew back across the mountains to Los Angeles pondering that, and grateful to Goldwater for such a poetic interlude.

Whether Goldwater actually did think all that year that he couldn't win, he certainly remained ambivalent about the exercise. He was very candid with me in one conversation in his Senate office shortly before the Republican convention gave him the nomination. He said: "I just finally said to myself, 'You've got to do it.' I realized that I had a responsibility to Conservatism and to the young people who had become interested in it. I felt, too, that if I didn't do it, that those young people who were voting, many of them for the first time, might drift away. I had a question in my mind all the time, all through the year, whether or not this was the right time for a conservative candidate to offer himself. . . . And I wasn't convinced, frankly, at the time I made the decision, that this *was* the year."

The Kennedy assassination created the doubts. It sickened him and it removed the pleasurable anticipation of running against Kennedy. "I lost all interest in it," he told me. "It was about four or five days after the assassination, I told my wife, 'To heck with the presidential thing!' "

He remembered a visit to the Oval Office the day of the ruinous Bay of Pigs invasion attempt. Kennedy had called Goldwater to come over.

"I went down and he was out of his office. But his girl said, 'Go in and sit down.' So I went in. I sat in his rocker. And I was giving it a good test because we both used the same [back] doctor, and she was trying to get me to get one of them but I didn't want one. And he came in smoking that little cigar and he looked at me and said, 'Do you want this job?' " (For the record Goldwater deleted Kennedy's expletives.)

"I said, 'No, not in my right mind.'

" 'Well,' he said, 'I thought I had a good thing going until this morning.'

"Whenever we'd see each other, he'd ask me how I was doing, and I think he kind of looked forward to it, too."

After November 22, "all the anticipation, all the — I don't like to say, to use the word 'fun'; but all the desire left me because I couldn't see Johnson able to draw the fine line."

Goldwater was right about it being the wrong year.

I carried away an emotional hangover from that campaign. I liked the man enormously. His private persona was so different from the belligerent, combative image he projected to the world. Yet, I was convinced from the beginning that he would not make a good president. Apart from his political ideology, he seemed too casual in his judgments, too careless about words and facts, too indifferent to complexity, a man of too little intellectual discipline.

But as the turmoil of the later '60s engulfed the country, with the Johnson White House paralyzed by self-deception over Vietnam, I often wondered if Goldwater's qualities might not have served the nation better; whether his decency and common sense had not been undervalued and his belligerent rhetoric taken too literally.

There were grounds for ironic comment. By 1965 some Republicans were joking ruefully: "They told me if I voted for Goldwater we'd be mining Haiphong Harbor and defoliating the jungle — and I did — and we have!"

Right after the Republican Convention I had a ten-day holiday in Trinidad. One evening we drove to San Fernando, the island's second city, to attend a political meeting where a friend was speaking. It turned out to be a group of comically conspiratorial Trinidadian Marxists, like characters from a V. S. Naipaul novel, who were having a good time whipping things up against the United States. One of their themes was the recently passed Gulf of Tonkin Resolution. Their version was that it was concocted by the Johnson administration as a pretext for enlarging the war in Vietnam. The argument continued on the two-hour drive back to Port of Spain because we found ourselves in the same car with two of the young speakers.

I listened to them for a long time and finally decided to set them straight. I said I had just come from Washington. I was very current on the thinking there and they were wrong about Johnson. Here was a man, I said, able to seize the historical moment to complete the unfinished social agenda of his great mentor and idol, Franklin Roosevelt. With a compliant Congress, Johnson could use his great political skill and his compassion for the poor to force through a revolution in medical care, education, and civil rights. Why would he want to see this chance of greatness dribbled away in a war in Southeast Asia which interested him very little? No, I assured them; when Lyndon Johnson says he does not want a wider war, he means it. And those polite Trinidadian intellectuals bowed to the authority I carried as a journalist in contact with the highest sources on Washington.

The only problem with all that, as I reflected about a year later, was that they were right about Johnson and the Gulf of Tonkin and I was dead wrong.

After Labor Day, NBC assigned me to the Johnson campaign for a few weeks for perspective. It was overwhelming, not the panoply of White House power but the human force of the man himself. Everyone who went anywhere near Lyndon Johnson came away staggered, like someone who has just had a tornado pass by. The adjective that most commonly came to mind for Goldwater — diffident — would have been ludicrous applied to Johnson. He was the most undiffident man I ever met.

One busy campaign day, I found myself in the "pool" aboard Air Force One. It was a day of dashing across the entire United States from Indiana to Texas to California with stops in each for motorcades and speeches. On the long leg to Texas, Johnson asked me and Frank Cormier of the AP to come back to the bedroom at the rear of the aircraft; he wanted to talk to us. When we got there, Lyndon was still sweating profusely from the exertions of the last stop, where it had been very hot. He told us to sit down on the twin beds in the cabin and launched into a political monologue. I took in very little of what he was saying because he immediately began taking off all his clothes, down to his shorts. He took his time about it, pausing to gulp down large glasses of Fresca — replenished by a steward — interrupting himself to warn us not to report that he was drinking bourbon. He continued talking about the campaign, toweled himself dry, and slowly redressed in a clean shirt, tie and suit.

There were plenty of stories about Lyndon talking to people half naked. I heard of one reporter who was called over to the White House one night and had Johnson bend his ear while he was having a massage. When the masseur finished the president stood up quite naked, bent over a drawer, and came back with an LBJ tie clip which he fixed on the reporter's tie, all the while behaving as if he were fully dressed.

I remember very well what Johnson said when he was dressed again. He sat down beside me on one of the beds and as he talked for an hour or so, he emphasized his points by tapping me on the leg. Johnson was a big man and his tap for emphasis was like a heavy jab. For a couple of weeks after that conversation I walked around with a bruise on the lower thigh.

The gist of that monologue was that if Cormier and I trusted him, Lyndon could really put us right with our bosses. And it went something like this:

"Cormier — " (he drawled it out, Corm-ear) "you don't want to be White House correspondent for the Associated Press all your life. You want to be one of those big fancy editors the AP has up there in New York." And turned to me. "And MacNeil, you don't want to be just a correspondent for NBC News. You want to be a guy making the big money like Huntley and Brinkley. Well, here's how you go about it." And he leaned over and got very intimate, as though he was drawing us into a real conspiracy.

"Now what impresses your bosses up there in the Associated Press and NBC? Is it you guys reporting what everyone else reports? President Johnson did this? President Johnson did that? Anyone can do *that*. No. What really makes them pay attention is when you have something the other reporters don't have. When you have inside information. When you know about a story before anyone else does. When you have a scoop. Now you fellas are good reporters and you're smart. You play it straight with me and I'll see that both of you get lots of little bits of information, special information. That'll make those guys up in New York think you're the smartest sons of bitches they've ever seen.

"Now, I have ideas for this country that no one knows about yet. I'll tell you one of them. If you look down there, you can see there's an awful lot of these United States that is dry. There's very little water. Water could become the greatest problem, the greatest crisis, this country ever has to face. But I'm determined to do something about it. We can beat it with technology. If those Israelis can desalinate salt water, make fresh water out of it, so can we. We got all the oceans out there. I want to step up research to find the scientific breakthrough in getting fresh water from the sea. Right now it's too expensive. It uses too much energy. You'd end up paying as much for water as you do for whiskey. But the time will come when it will be cheap, and I want to get us there."

Most of my other memories of my two weeks on the road with Johnson's campaign involve his comments on my work. What got on the network nightly news programs each night was of vital importance to the momentum of the campaign. NBC guaranteed me a piece on the *Huntley-Brinkley Report* each evening, and since I was the newcomer LBJ thought I could use a working over. His working over took several forms. Often the message was transmitted through Bill Moyers, his press secretary. Moyers would find me late at night and say in his sincere way, "The president really admired your report tonight. He just wanted you to know." Or, "The president saw your story tonight and he was awfully disappointed with the angle you took." And Moyers looked like a kindly, earnest teacher who had been let down by a star pupil. Back in Washington after one swing, I did a *Huntley-Brinkley* piece pulling together my impression of the themes Johnson was stressing. When I came out of the studio into the NBC newsroom they said, "The White House is on the phone."

It was Moyers who said: "The president thought that was one of the finest pieces of reporting he has ever seen" and carried on in that vein for a while. I wasn't so blasé that I could go out to dinner indifferent to that kind of attention.

The president's flattery became outrageous one day in

Indianapolis. The press corps was waiting in a roped-off enclosure on the tarmac when the president's plane rolled in. Johnson came out the door the minute the ramp was rolled up. He stormed down the steps, ignored all the dignitaries lined up along the red carpet with their hands outstretched, and strode straight over to the press enclosure. He climbed the rope barrier and shouldered his way through the other reporters to me. He clamped his arm around my shoulders and bellowed to everyone, "I just want to point out to all of you a fine example of a good reporter. His reporting of this campaign on NBC ought to be an example to everyone." Then he slapped me on the back, climbed out of the press enclosure, and went back to the red carpet to greet the governor and other pols. All the other reporters laughed cynically, as I did. It took me a while to figure out why he took the trouble to do it. I didn't believe what he said about my reporting and he probably didn't expect me to. But he expected me not to be totally indifferent to the attention and he was right: I wasn't. In fact, for all the embarrassment I was privately quite puffed up. He had shrewdly found his way to a pressure point for my vanity and pushed it, as he had done to tens of thousands of people he felt he needed in his career.

I never totally believed Johnson, or I believed the politics and doubted the man. It was partly cultural. Something in his Texas accent when he was being his most sincere made it sound theatrical and false to me. I could be very moved by him: I was by several speeches in that campaign. But I was impressed by their effectiveness with the crowd, not whether I believed he was sincere. Something in his manner, some faint echo of Uriah Heep, some suspicion that I was hearing the insincere preacher give me the smarmy bit at a funeral, always left me a fraction skeptical about LBJ. It is not that I thought he was lying. What made me suspicious was that he was working too hard to make it seem he was telling the truth. But I have a low tolerance for preachers of any stripe — the air of moral certainty offends me — and Lyndon had a strong dose of preacher in him. And I say all that remembering that I was privately very certain that he should be president of the United States and Barry Goldwater should not.

At the end of that election year, Goldwater gave me his picture inscribed with the words, "To a fair and objective man." I took it as sincere. If LBJ had written the same words, I would not have believed them. From Johnson I got a gold tie clip with his initials and a relief of Air Force One.

Nineteen sixty-four was my first presidential election campaign and the only one in which I followed one candidate all the way. I have covered all the campaigns since in some part for the BBC or PBS. What amazes me now, as I look back on them, is how network reporters manage to invest their coverage with any editorial coherence, because the logistics are so overwhelming and distracting. Considering that it may be the only objective information the mass electorate receives about the campaign, the correspondent's responsibility is enormous.

Through the primaries in 1964, I covered Goldwater for all NBC programs, television and radio. But in the fall campaign, those programs wanted stories every day, in the case of radio, every hour. Other reporters were assigned to do radio and to cover television for the *Today Show*. That left me clear to do one piece a day for the *Huntley-Brinkley Report*. Even that was very complicated, and NBC assigned a coordinating producer to handle the logistics.

In a typical campaign day, we would study the candidate's schedule very early in the morning. There would usually be stops in three or four cities, sometimes many hundreds of miles apart, with an hour or two of jet travel between each. First we would look for the point in the day when I could drop off; leave the candidate's entourage with the film we had shot so far, to go to the nearest city with an NBC affiliate station, and feed my piece to New York. Choosing the drop-off point, usually in midafternoon, meant what *Huntley-Brinkley* viewers saw that night would be the candidate's action up till then. By 1964, campaign managers were learning to schedule at least one important event early enough in the day to make the network evening news programs.

Since each of the three programs reaches some twenty million Americans, the "bite" each network selects to run is considered vital to the success of the candidate. That puts a heavy responsibility on the correspondent, who chooses each day what to emphasize.

I tried not merely to report each day that the candidate went here and said this, but to weave those events into a wider narrative stretching over the weeks, so that, if read together afterwards, they would make a coherent whole. Constantly breaking away and rejoining the candidate made that very difficult.

The correspondent is also trying to think like a television producer. Each day he is making a tiny documentary of two or three minutes. Ideally, it should have a beginning, a middle, and an end. It should convey flavor and atmosphere, and make editorial sense.

Finally, the correspondent is aware of the need to expose himself. Getting his face and voice on the screen are as important to his career as the newspaperman's byline. So, within the other structures, he must contrive to think of something reasonably trenchant to say and find an opportunity to say it to camera in the midst of all the other hectic goings on.

Advancing technology has made some of this easier. Portable electronic cameras and cassette recorders have made it possible to shoot events later in the day and give a wider range of origination points. In 1964, we were still using 16mm black and white film for news. Different NBC affiliates had different equipment. Our camera crews had to carry different film stock because some stations could run only "A" wind film and some 'B" wind. Some could handle only film with the magnetic soundtrack attached to it, or "striped"; others could take a separate soundtrack or "double system."

The coordinating producer, Don Roberts, had the nightmarish job of choosing an NBC station I could get to from the drop-off point; determining what film system it could handle; then ensuring that our crew used that type of film for only those parts of the campaign events that would go into that report. When he had figured that out, people in New York would work on how to get me there.

Usually, an NBC messenger would meet me at the drop-off point with a car or motorcycle. Clutching my film, I would ride to the nearest airport, jump into a small chartered plane, fly to the originating city, and take a taxi to the TV station. In the plane I had worked out what pieces to cut for the report and had drafted out my script. While the film was being developed I would call the *Huntley-Brinkley* executive producer in New York, discuss my piece with him, and agree on how much time I could have for it, two minutes, two and three-quarters, or three.

With the film out of the processing, I would sit down with the local film editor. Usually there wasn't time to screen several rolls of rushes. We would fast-wind through to the pieces I wanted, look at them, time them, and hang them up so the editor could splice them together. Then with the exact times, I would find a typewriter and bash out the short pieces of script to narrate the film. With luck, we were finished in time for a run-through, projecting the film through their system and reading my copy at the right places to make sure it fitted. Often there was no rehearsal time. We would be right up against the deadline for transmitting the piece to New York, where they would put it on videotape. Obviously, because of the different time zones, the farther west we were, the earlier in the day we would have to feed to meet the *Huntley-Brinkley* air time, 6:30 P.M. EST. From California, for example, we had to have the whole process finished by 3 P.M.

After the feed to New York, I would get a cab back to the local airport, get into the chartered plane, and fly, not to where I had left the campaign, but where it would now be, five hours later. Often that meant several hours flying, getting me back to the campaign just as they were finishing the evening event.

I would join my friends among the print reporters, find out what had happened, locate the room the campaign had allotted me for the night, hoping that my suitcase had been delivered, and crash into bed till 5 or 6 A.M., when it was time to start the process again.

Occasionally, things went wrong. One day in the New Hampshire primary, Goldwater told a press conference that NATO field commanders should be able to decide to fire small tactical atomic weapons. That was already ringing bulletin bells on the news agencies when I got a taxi to Pease Air Force Base to board a chartered plane. It began to snow as we took off and it was snowing heavily when we reached the New York area. For nearly an hour our tiny plane was stacked up over La Guardia, circling blind with scores of commercial airliners. Finally we got clearance to land. At the end of the runway is a large pile of rocks where it has been extended out into the water. A sudden down draft caught us and pushed the plane down below the rocks. Instantly the pilot pulled back his wheel and looped the aircraft up over the rocks and down onto the runway.

Still shaky from that experience, with three cans of film under my arm, I mounted the pillion seat of an NBC motorcycle which zoomed off through the blinding snow, weaving crazily in and out of the traffic into Manhattan and Rockefeller Plaza. The film was rushed up to processing and I sat down in the *Huntley-Brinkley* office to catch my breath. Half an hour later, the editors called down to ask "Where's the soundtrack?"

"It's on the film," I said.

"But there's nothing recorded on it," they replied. The sound equipment had misfunctioned. There was about fifteen minutes to airtime.

We had three rolls of film, totaling half an hour of Barry Goldwater talking soundlessly. And I had made that hare-brained dash through a snowstorm to get it there. But the story was important, so the producer decided to run the film silent while I reported what Goldwater had said. We were so late that they had to change the running order of the program three times, pushing me lower and lower down the half-hour to give us time to finish. The piece went on half-scripted and I provided a rather messy ad lib commentary for the rest.

David Brinkley had an even better example. On September 29, 1964, he closed the *Huntley-Brinkley Report* like this:

"Finally, Associate Producer Bill Corrigan wants us to explain why we have no film of Senator Goldwater's whistle stops in Athens, Marietta, and Chillicothe, Ohio.

"It seems, says Corrigan, that our chartered plane could not land in Athens, Ohio, to pick up the film because of the weather. The plane went to Zanesville. Our courier on the plane hired a car and went to Athens but missed the train.

"Corrigan, who had gotten off the train to make a phone call in Athens, also missed the train when the engineer blew a three-minute warning whistle and departed less than a minute later.

"Our other courier, on the moving train, jumped off with the film and took a cab back to Athens. But he didn't know the plane was in Zanesville and Corrigan had already rented a car and left for Chillicothe.

"So, as best we can make out tonight . . . Corrigan is in Cincinnati.

"The film is somewhere in Ohio.

"Two couriers are lost.

"The candidate is in Cincinnati.

"And one of our aircraft is missing.

"Good night for NBC News."

FIFTEEN

Vietnam Metaphors

FOR A LONG TIME the image of the hearse encountered on the way to a picnic on Jones Beach haunted me. It became my private symbol for how I saw the Johnson administration sweeping the Vietnam war under the rug. It reminded me that the war, which so often seemed a distant abstraction, was having real consequences and that television was not adequately reporting them.

Television's priorities seemed what LBJ would have wanted them to be: U.S. initiatives in battle and the yardsticks used to convey progress — body counts, kill ratios, hills captured, villages pacified, and the tonnage of bombs dropped.

In retrospect, that moment in 1966 became a turning point. Until then I had privately deplored Vietnam. I considered it a stupid waste of American energies and a tragic drain on American idealism. But I entertained those attitudes coolly, surveying the distant folly with detachment. Now the horror of it crept into my personal emotions; the official rhetoric sounded hollower and more self-deluding as the administration found it impossible to explain satisfactorily why it was sending young men to be slaughtered in a war they could not win in any recognizable way.

Now I can see that it was also a turning point professionally. Twice I rationalized myself out of actually going to Vietnam. The first was a suggestion from the local station, WNBC, that I go to interview New York–area soldiers for a Christmas special. At the time that seemed so mawkish that I refused. Years later I realized it would have been sensible to go. Vietnam was unreal to me. I needed to go and get a sense of it myself; and I could have made a lot more out of Christmas interviews than greetings to mom and pop.

In January 1967 the network suggested I go for a six-month spell as a correspondent. This time I refused because my wife was expecting a baby any day and because it appeared that the network was being rather cavalier with my budding career as a famous anchorman. If they could casually ship me off for six months, that meant, in career terms, a demotion. It also meant a considerable drop in income, since I would have lost the extra fees paid for the various television and radio programs I was doing in New York. Perhaps I was also a bit nervous about getting killed, although that had not given me much anxiety elsewhere.

So I nursed my conflicts in private and in the one journalistic outlet where a point of view was permitted. NBC Radio broadcast a regular feature called *Emphasis*, a three-minute commentary, forty times a week. Three minutes is a comfortable length, about 450 words, roughly equivalent to a newspaper column — room to develop an idea. NBC encouraged good writing and did not discourage analysis that spilled over into editorializing. Radio was something of a backwater in the '60s, and there was an editorial freedom in radio unthinkable on television. My three *Emphasis* spots each week let me play at being a commentator, able now and then to question the growing contradictions in Vietnam: for example the absurdity of American men dying to protect democracy in a land whose government trampled on democratic freedoms. Or the repeated spectacle of high U.S. officials rushing off to Saigon on new fact-finding missions, only to come back saying once again: "We have turned the corner," or, "There is light at the end of the tunnel." I said in one broadcast that the U.S. Army must have had optimism packaged in aerosol cans because every official who went out there full of doubts appeared to have been sprayed with optimism before he came home.

All around me on American radio and television, with a few exceptions, correspondents were happily chirping away about body counts, kill ratios, and American casualties. Television news was dominated by the action story. To my ears the coverage had that tone of breezy meaninglessness that passes for professional delivery by many American announcers; occasionally pulling out the husky stop for an obviously emotional sentence. The business-as-usual tone of voice was putting the war into too ordinary a context.

Vietnam was creating a national emergency but on most nights it was just another story. There was little differentiation. To be sure, there were attempts at weekly specials in 1967, but they were buried in low-viewing weekend hours and discontinued when they found no commercial favor.

Contrast the treatment with that of the Iran hostage crisis in 1979–1981. From the moment the embassy was seized by Iranian terrorists, ABC News broadcast a nightly half-hour special. On CBS, Walter Cronkite made a daily litany of the mounting days of the hostages' captivity. There may be substance to the speculation that President Carter was, in part, made a hostage of the crisis himself because of the intensity of television's attention. Certainly, U.S. television provided an instant world stage for the political theater being so cruelly mounted in Teheran. But as a crisis for this country, Iran was never in the same league as the Vietnam war. For several years, hundreds of Americans were dying every month; the war machine was distorting the world's most powerful economy, engineering a global inflation. Yet most of the time it was just another story.

The correspondents and crews in the field were brave beyond any public's right to expect. The anchormen, writers, editors, and executives at home were decent and concerned. Yet the values applied to the coverage of Vietnam were in part amoral, empty of values. Television simply ate up its first accessible picture war. The words and talk needed to consider its purposes deeply and critically received very secondary treatment. Television was bound to give absolute priority to action pictures, and Vietnam produced them abundantly. Political questions did not produce action pictures, only "talking heads," which news producers always subordinated to action. So pictures of the fighting dominated our screens — the same pictures almost every night. For a long time, that made the other war, the growing doubts at home, relatively invisible. I believe it helped to postpone the day when the American people discovered that the emperor had no clothes.

In the end, the turmoil at home came to be the more important war. Long after the fighting stopped in Vietnam, America still feels the pain of it. Vietnam undid this country. The trust that binds a society together is a fabric of infinite complexity, woven of many strands painfully accumulated over generations. Vietnam cut across the American fabric like a razor slash. And that is what television did not tell us until long afterwards.

My puzzlement over this paradox, my growing conviction that, despite the coverage, the meaning of the war was being hidden from the people, gradually made me look more closely at the kind of journalism that was evolving on television and becoming *the* mass journalism of our time. I slowly became aware of its frequent triviality, its distorting brevity, its obsession with action and movement, its infantile attention span, and its profound lack of thoughtful analysis.

When I left NBC in 1967 to join the BBC in London, I was able to write a book about some of the things that worried me about network news. Much later, in 1975, I was able to put some of my own ideas into practice in the *MacNeil/Lehrer Report*. In all this awakening, my frustration over what to say as a journalist about Vietnam acted as a catalyst. Vietnam helped to open my eyes professionally.

For a long time I carried, obsessively perhaps, the image of bodies being quietly shipped home while the rest of America went to the beach. I wanted to know more about the story television was not covering — what Vietnam was doing to America at home.

That obsession took me naturally to New Hampshire in 1968. The presidential primary had become almost a referendum on the war, and what struck me most forcibly was the contrast between the political rhetoric and the reality that this small state had suffered the highest per capita casualties in Vietnam.

I had been with the BBC only six months and was still exulting in the freedom offered by the documentary form. There were six reporters on the *Panorama* program, all at least as experienced as I. We worked in cycles of several weeks, dividing the world among us, my areas being American and European politics and British domestic stories. After years of making two-minute reports, to stretch to twenty or thirty-five or sometimes even fifty minutes was a great luxury.

The form permitted latitude in film technique and journalistic interpretation. We stretched both in the film we made in New Hampshire. I went there with a fixed idea, determined to find a body coming home from Vietnam so that we could contrast that private reality with the wider political reality engulfing the state as it does from January to March every four years.

We found the body; or rather, the Pentagon's supreme efficiency found the body. Its computers found it still in Vietnam, recently dead. They could predict when it would cross the Pacific to be transshipped from base to base until it got to New Hampshire. The Defense Department was totally obliging, but their computers underlined my obsession. I could imagine them chattering to each other through the night over the military communications network around the globe; the IBM ball darting with blurring speed from line to line; the rolls of paper quietly cranking themselves through the machines, until it came to the line which said, KELLER, RONALD JAMES, USN, HOSPITALMAN 3RD CLASS, EXETER, NEW HAMPSHIRE — KILLED 2.9.68

What the computer did not say was that awaiting the body in Exeter was a wife, aged seventeen, and a baby of ten months.

Eventually, Ronald Keller's body began its journey back to them, a journey halfway around the world, one of many identical aluminum coffins identifiable only by its tag, in the hold of a jet cargo plane.

At the same time, producer David Harrison and I set out from New York, where we had done our planning. Planes were grounded by a heavy snowstorm on the East Coast, so we drove all night to be in Manchester for a news conference called by George Romney. We got there just in time to hear Romney say he was pulling out. His campaign had never recovered from his admission that he had been "brainwashed" in Vietnam. Another, smarter politician, able to play the media more deftly, might have turned such a blunder to account by pointing out that the entire country was being brainwashed on Vietnam. It was no disgrace to discover it. But Richard Nixon made no such admissions and Romney's withdrawal made the first milestone easy on Nixon's march to the White House. Nixon at that stage trod a very careful line on Vietnam.

Eugene McCarthy gave the primary its drama, and, as it turned out, upset history. The Minnesota senator did a rare thing: challenging an incumbent president and commander-in-chief, when the nation was at war. Lyndon Johnson did not campaign in person. Instead, his face and voice were everywhere and the Democratic machine organized written pledges of support. The Johnson message was "Support your Commander-in-Chief. Don't vote for fuzzy thinking and surrender." "Fuzzy thinking" meant Gene McCarthy.

McCarthy carried his dry humor to platforms up and down the state, delivering his message in a strange rising inflection, so that when he finished his peroration with the key phrase, "the killing has to stop," it seemed not like a final judgment but a fragment of prayer torn out of his conscience. Thus it seemed to thousands of young people, who flooded out of the colleges and high schools of New England to follow this wry Pied Piper. If you felt as I did then about the war, McCarthy's was the only voice of sanity, putting Vietnam squarely where it belonged in the center of the political arena. All the others, including Robert Kennedy, were equivocating. Others had pleaded with Kennedy to challenge LBJ; they turned to McCarthy only when Kennedy refused.

A week before the election, it was still unclear whether McCarthy was leading a foolish, quixotic crusade or, as it turned out, he could actually force President Johnson to withdraw from the election: a stunning achievement for the austere senator whom regular Democrats had laughed off.

We filmed sequences showing all of these men campaigning over the snow-covered state, concentrating our symbolism on the way their voices and images saturated the media. It seemed that anywhere, amid the firs or the birches, you could have stuck an aerial into the pure, frosty air and snatched out the voices of Johnson, Romney, Nixon, McCarthy, and others, all shouting over each other.

Gradually it came to me how to marry this political babel about the war with our small piece of reality of that war, the returning body of Ronald Keller.

We went to see his parents and asked their permission to film the funeral. They agreed, almost eagerly, and only after they had agreed asked why, coming from Britain, we wanted to film it. We explained and then Keller's father said a pathetic thing. He was glad we were filming it. "It will give Ron's death some meaning."

There was the terrible indictment of Vietnam. This decent man had to bury his son, comfort his wife and a teenage daughter-in-law, watch over an infant grandson, and the state that had taken his son's life had given him no meaning for it, or no meaning he accepted. His son might as well have been run over by a truck outside their house. I felt outraged on his behalf and on behalf of all the Americans bereaved, wounded, crippled, hurt by this war. And the outrage went into the film.

Harrison and I went to see Ronald Keller before they buried him. His viewing room at the funeral home was empty. In the dim light and the thick smell of the floral tributes, we stood and looked at this youth, dressed in his number one navy blues, his face handsome and unmarked, his wounds invisible. Like all young dead, he looked as though the spirit could reenter him at any moment, and he would revive and be nineteen again, as in the fairy stories.

We went to the funeral and to the cemetery, keeping our distance so as not to intrude with the camera. The churchyard was deep in snow, surrounded with birch trees and tall pines. They repeated the military ritual etched on the nation's mind by John Kennedy's funeral, the Stars and Stripes folded upon itself into a triangle handed to the widow, the volley over the grave.

They went away, the young wife in her black veil, her legs barely able to support her. When they had all gone, the undertakers removed their equipment. A bulldozer started up, settled its blade behind the mound of freshly dug earth, and pushed it into the grave. In one thump, it was full.

Then it was quiet except for a strange, staccato tapping noise. There were several little flags fluttering above the snow, marking soldiers' graves. Above them flew a large U.S. flag and the halyard was tapping against the flagstaff with a noise like a distant machine gun. We recorded that too.

We opened the film with a symbolic sequence, intercutting shots of the winter graveyard, with its small flags, with an extreme close-up of an IBM ball rattling on a computer printout. The sounds were also intercut, the computer and the *tat-tat-tat-tat-tat* of the flagpole halyard.

We summarized the views of each of the contenders and heard excerpts of what they were telling New Hampshire voters about Vietnam. That took half of the film. Then we went to the funeral.

Over the sequences when there were no prayers, we sneaked into the soundtrack some of the political voices we had heard for Nixon, Johnson, McCarthy. In my mind the effect was as though those at the funeral could pick these voices out of the winter air around them. The last, as the coffin sank into the earth, was that of an announcer speaking for President Johnson: "The Communists in Vietnam are watching this primary closely. Now is not the time for weakness or indecision. On Tuesday, March 12, let's show Hanoi that Americans back their boys in Vietnam and support their Commander-in-Chief."

The last shot of the film was the bulldozer filling the grave. It seemed to me the final gesture of contempt, or indifference;

although, of course, the way that churchyard in midwinter chose to dig and refill its graves had nothing to do with Vietnam or the Pentagon or Lyndon Johnson.

It went too far. The irony I intended was too heavy. The film was a political statement more than a piece of journalism. I go into all this detail because I think it is the farthest I have ever been led into pure advocacy journalism.

As it happened, that week's *Panorama* was also shown in the United States, over National Educational Television on the Public Broadcast Laboratory (PBL). The film made PBL uneasy but they ran it, minus the bulldozer scene, which they asked me to cut.

I thought it was strong. I intended it to be strong. But the images fell brutally on eyes not yet prepared for irony that heavy, including my wife's. When I got back to London I found her very unhappy about the way I had depicted America to the British. Vietnam was one of the few controversies where I felt with absolute conviction that I was right; but the conviction was often shaken.

Just recently I was given the script of a documentary in preparation by Dutch television and it contained this observation: "But the Vietnam war not only lost the Americans. It lost the youth of the world. It became a metaphor by which other disturbing images of America could be interpreted."

It certainly became a metaphor for me. Vietnam was what was wrong with American television and how I earned my living. The world's most powerful nation was informing itself through a medium that was essentially flawed; a medium so potent, so much the captor of the national attention that it had become a form of psychic feedback that was shaping the nation's destiny. Democracy is still an experiment, still evolving; how it evolves is being shaped by its communications. Most of the time its institutions are running to catch up with communications. Like human scale in architecture, or human speed in transportation, human modes of communication have been outpaced by technology, whose very speed and reach may create unintended meaning. Communications did that to Vietnam, creating the irony that America's first war which technology could bring into citizens' homes every night should have been a war so inexplicable to the citizens — a war of so little cheering. Television was blamed for making the war unpopular by showing its horror every night. But, inevitably, television sanitized the horror, domesticated and tamed it as suitable for family consumption at suppertime; not through any conspiracy to deceive but simply because television passes everything through a bland taste filter.

Occasionally, it did not; when it showed Marines with Zippo lighters burning the homes of Vietnamese peasants, or a naked little girl aflame with napalm, or the street execution of a bound prisoner with a pistol against his temple, the filter was torn and those images seared themselves into the national consciousness. In video terms, they burned into the orthicon tube — they would not erase. They became our history.

Those occasional images disturbed as the routine ones did not. They were shocking because they contradicted the routine story of brave Americans in action and positive official statements about progress. That was the only story television could sustain on a nightly basis because it was the only story for which there was a constant supply of action pictures. That made television — without meaning to be — a cheerleader for the U.S. side, as the news media have traditionally been when the nation is at war.

Finally, in 1968, during the Tet offensive, such contradictory images overwhelmed the reassuring ones, when the action picture reflected the political reality; when Americans could see their own embassy under siege; when Lyndon Johnson realized he had lost Walter Cronkite, and therefore the nation. That happened in the middle of the campaign for the New Hampshire primary. It swelled McCarthy's flock. It ultimately forced Johnson out and began the process that turned Vietnam into Nixon's war.

The disturbing images continued: Martin Luther King's assassination in April; Robert Kennedy's in June; and Chicago in August, where they chanted, "The whole world is watching."

What was the "whole world" seeing? What was the metaphor saying? It is now clear that it had many meanings. It revealed the bright as well as the dark soul of America, although the dark soul seemed to predominate. The metaphor seemed to be saying that America had become a blundering Leviathan too big for efficiency; that for all its overabundant communications, it was a society whose leaders could not explain their motives to their followers; that its government was reduced to databanks and binary codes that sucked the humanity out of official thinking and communications; that the world's principal idealists were turned into dumb killers; that the physical and moral distance between a humane president and the effects of what he commanded was so vast that he found himself inflicting terrible pain — like the Inquisition — deaf to all but his sacred, higher purpose.

Was not Vietnam also a powerful metaphor for the military power that shielded the Western world, revealing that the army which had produced generals of the greatest brilliance in World War II and Korea now had no inspiring leadership; that the armed forces defending the free world were tainted with political corruption and would falsify battlefield information and thus contribute to the self-delusion in Washington; that U.S. officers would permit the cover-up at My Lai; that U.S. pilots, freshly showered, clean-uniformed, sitting in jet fighters with nothing but the smell of their after-shave lotion in their nostrils, would unleash hell on the antlike Vietnamese below, while matter-of-factly describing what they were doing to a television camera?

Little of this was clear then. The images were too confusing, bewildering because they constantly contradicted each other. All of the news media wallowed in the confusion, but television was the preeminent image machine, poor at putting events in context in the best of times; capable of nothing but haphazard montage and accidental juxtapositions in times that began to have the flavor of an American *Götterdämmerung*. It left each American to sort out and explain the colliding images for himself, to make them fit some subjective consistency. It was hard: even the best informed of us were baffled.

Smack up against images like My Lai were reminders of American tenderness and fairness. They told the Americans that their army took better care of its troops in battle than any in history; that swift medical evacuation produced the smallest ever dead-to-wounded ratio. They told the world that this nation was not fighting for any ignoble goal — not territorial conquest, nor imperialist ambition, nor colonial expansion, nor command of resources; that it was a nation prepared to see thousands of its young men die so that one-half of an Asian nation should not have Communist rule imposed on it. The images said that America for all its terrible power was willing to fight with limited power, to let the more primitively equipped enemy dictate the conditions of battle. They said that this nation refrained from massive retaliation against the civilians of North Vietnam, yet was ambivalent about that restraint — the Old Adam of the American Right shouting, "Bomb them back to the stone age," the Left yelling, "Stop the killing," the men in the Pentagon fluctuating between humane restraint and rationalizing every violence short of nuclear weapons. Other images said to the world: in America a popularly elected leader struggled publicly with the moral battle all men struggle with privately, the struggle between ruthlessness and compassion.

What did the Vietnam images say about American power and leadership? Among the Western allies, applause that the U.S. was drawing the line gradually turned to pity, derision, and anxiety as the quagmire deepened. Was this their shield against communism, this huge war machine that fought so futilely, that oscillated so often between determination to prevail and hesitation to do so; a nation whose youth by the thousands responded loyally and went to die, while other thousands escaped through cynical influence, or conscientious objection? Would the American people, traumatized by Vietnam, ever be willing to fight on abstract principle again or would they defend only their own shores and homes? Did Vietnam show what Europeans had so long feared, that in the crunch the real American defense perimeter started at Boston, not Berlin? Was this ally so insensitive and inflexible that it could not extricate itself from an embarrassment? Were the managers of the world's greatest economy willing to go on bleeding depreciated dollars into the world money markets, exporting a massive inflation which, hindsight now reveals, helped inspire OPEC to transform the cost of energy?

And the images further said: this is an open society whose people can see and criticize all these things; a nation which would permit its journalists to point out uncomfortable truths; whose presidents tried but could not get correspondents like David Halberstam and Morley Safer recalled from Vietnam; a nation which permitted a distinguished journalist like Harrison Salisbury of the *New York Times* to go to the very capital of the enemy, Hanoi, and to give human credibility to their suffering and determination. It was a nation whose press reported that an anguished President Johnson crept off in the middle of the night to pray in a Catholic chapel and that another president, Richard Nixon, watched a football game on television and ignored the biggest political demonstration in U.S. history happening outside his window. It was that America was a nation where citizens could assemble peacefully to protest against official policy, yet where, on one occasion, Kent State, citizen soldiers could open fire and kill fellow citizens who were demonstrating. It was a nation which permitted a youthful army in Chicago to challenge the presidential nominating procedures and permitted the police to riot and savagely beat them up. It was a nation whose national myths were being ripped away like time-weakened fabric — myths of greatness and victory in battle, of brave soldiers off to glory and the grateful nation applauding; myths of good presidents, wise lawmakers, swift justice, incorruptible policemen, straight lawyers, selfless doctors, subservient blacks, submissive women, respectful children, and an automatic lump in the throat for "The Star-Spangled Banner."

Chicago was one of the "disturbing images," disturbing to many in the West because it almost totally distracted American attention from the savage Soviet repression of freedom in Czechoslovakia.

I went to the Democratic Convention for the BBC, having made a twenty-minute film report to run in London the Monday night the convention opened. On Sunday, the *Panorama* editor, Bob Rowland, phoned from London to say they needed to take seven minutes out. I protested: "Don't you realize how important this story is?"

And he said: "Don't you realize there are Soviet tanks in the streets of Prague?"

It shocked me to realize how much my news perspective was being distorted by my obsession with Vietnam and American politics. But 1968 was an obsessive year in the United States, and nowhere did that obsession burn more brightly than in Chicago.

The rooms assigned to the BBC were on the fifth floor of the Conrad Hilton Hotel, at the front overlooking Michigan Avenue. So the stage for much of the violence between the Chicago police and the followers of Senator McCarthy was directly beneath us. Since we had to stay late at the convention hall to feed a breakfasttime summary to London, we missed some of the worst clashes. But when we returned from the convention hall we hung out those windows watching as from a grandstand, retreating whenever the police, or later the National Guard, shouted through bullhorns to close the windows because McCarthy youths in windows on higher floors were throwing things at them. Sometimes the Guardsmen reinforced their orders by aiming their rifles at us.

The scene from those windows looked like a sound stage set for a sequence in a Cold War movie. The floodlit street was empty except for lines of helmeted troops in battle dress, with rifles poised. Jeeps with barbed-wire fences attached to their fronts formed barricades holding back a seething dark mass of chanting figures. The smell of Mace drifted up, a smell that pervaded the hotel lobby and corridors all week.

It is hard now to separate what I saw happening from what I think I saw. In December 1968, I made a ninety-minute special for the Public Broadcasting Laboratory on how the TV networks had covered the Chicago violence. The documentary was in response to the widespread public conviction that the networks had provoked and exaggerated the violence. Polls showed that public sympathies lay with the Chicago police more than with the peace demonstrators they assaulted. In preparing that program in New York, I spent many hours examining videotapes of what the networks had shown, and they quickly became as real to me as what I had witnessed myself.

Compared to the violence which I had seen French police using against student rioters a few weeks earlier, the violence of the Chicago police was not exceptional. But the TV pictures clearly showed, as the Walker Commission later confirmed, that the police were out of control, bludgeoning and clubbing and kicking with a grim and vindictive pleasure. Taken in the whole context of time devoted to the convention, the networks were in fact quite restrained about the violence. What created the enormous impact, and the outrage across the nation, was the timing. Because Mayor Daley's paranoid security measures prevented television from making live reports from Michigan Avenue, the riots had to be videotaped and rushed by motorcycle courier to the network tape machines in the convention hall. That caused them to appear on the air in accidental juxtaposition with other dramatic moments on the convention floor; as when, for instance, Mayor Daley tried to shout Senator Ribicoff off the podium. The total effect was to give the impression that despite a mass uprising of antiwar sentiment, the Democratic party regulars, backed by Daley's police force, were going to impose their candidate on the convention — Hubert Humphrey, the choice of the repudiated President Johnson. And in fact that was the truth. What live television, with its mixture of art and accident and journalism, portrayed were the dying moments of the old Democratic party. In the candlelight rally of McCarthy supporters after his defeat, Richard Goodwin spoke: "In another couple of years, we're going to take the country away from the Connallys, the Meanys and the Daleys."

My PBL documentary, *The Whole World Is Watching*, tended to exonerate the TV networks for Chicago. That had its irony because my book, *The People Machine*, had just come out and I was on the TV and radio talk circuit (Mike Douglas, William F. Buckley, Phil Donahue, etc.) telling anyone who would listen what I saw as the serious weaknesses of TV news. So I found myself having to do a lot of "Yes, but . . ." Both perceptions were true. Daily TV journalism was riddled with weaknesses but in occasional special coverage, like the Chicago convention, television could excel.

The fundamental asset is credibility. Survey after survey has shown television to be the most credible of all the news media. Yet in Chicago the American public did not believe what the networks told them. The networks got it right, but two-thirds of the public said they did not believe the network version. In self-protection, the networks recalled the Persian kings who executed messengers who brought them bad news. Was America turning irrationally on its messengers, or is there a more disturbing explanation?

Does the television news audience feel free to choose what it believes and what it does not? Has television news become another form of drama before which the audience can suspend disbelief or not, according to its whim? Has the news gone so far in making itself attractive as television entertainment, that it invites skepticism even while rolling up huge audience numbers? I cannot dispute the numbers. I dispute that they either demonstrate credibility or confer it.

The networks go out of their way to present the news in a diverting manner. They employ every entertainment device — rapid pace, short attention span, visual variety, fast action, dynamic presenters — to keep the news diverting. These devices often fight sense or comprehension or news judgment. Do they also fight credibility? They are used essentially not to serve the viewer, but to keep him awake, to keep the uninterested viewer from turning off. That may not serve the interested viewer very well, but these values are accepted as conventions of the medium.

I have no way of knowing how much the American people believe the television news they watch. The surveys say they find TV the most credible; if there were a conflict with newspapers, magazines, or radio, they would believe television first.

I do not know what that means. It may be a matter of dire concern to the democracy that its principal medium of public information invites disbelief. It may be a clue to the much-remarked alienation of the large parts of the body politic, or it may mean nothing at all. It may mean merely that millions of Americans who pay very little attention to events see some television news and therefore give positive responses about television to pollsters. It may only confirm what advertisers have long assumed: people tend to believe what they are told concerning matters about which they know very little. What Chicago revealed was that when events invaded their own lives and offended their view of society, they did not believe. In one respect that was understandable: in tearing the American social fabric, Vietnam exposed a dormant fault in the American psyche, a clash of culture and class.

The savagery of the Chicago police was a bellow of indignation from the lower middle class of America against the college kids of the McCarthy crusade who seemed loose in their morals and deficient in patriotism. A small incident in the Conrad Hilton revealed it.

Late one evening, with my wife and a group of BBC colleagues, I left the rooms on the fifth floor to go out. By the elevators was a middle-aged man with a gun jammed against a young man he was holding against the wall. The sight of the drawn gun indoors made us all shrink back to the elevator doors behind him. The man with the pistol was about fifty-five, wearing a leather jacket. He looked like an off-duty cop or security guard. Against the wall he held a tall youth of about twenty, blond, wearing a T-shirt and blue jeans, with a string of convention credentials around his neck.

The off-duty cop sounded drunk as he harassed the youth, forcing him to spread his legs wider and his hands higher on the wall. He was saying:

"You miserable little son of a bitch. I'm going to find out what you're up to. Get your legs apart. Dirty-minded little bastard. Look at those tight pants. Probably haven't got any underwear on under them. Have you? HAVE you? Is that how the girls like it? Probably haven't got any balls either. Goddamned college kids. I'll bet you're scared, aren't you? Listen, I'm cocking this gun. Do you hear that? I'll bet you're yellow, you Yippie."

That is my best recollection of what he said. If he mentioned the antiwar movement, I have forgotten, but the implication was there.

Somewhere in his muddled brain, the older man was fighting his own little crusade against promiscuity, foul language, the privileged education of these moral degenerates who would tear up draft cards and burn the American flag. Perhaps he envied them too, and was expressing that.

By this time no elevators had come and there was a crowd of about fifteen people pressed frightened against the walls. Worried about the youth, I ran down five flights of stairs to the lobby and persuaded a police sergeant to come up. With a group of policemen, he commandeered an elevator and, on the fifth floor, they casually disarmed their off-duty colleague and took him away.

One of the problems with criticizing television is that it has a way of suddenly redeeming itself with a flash of brilliance or sensitivity. There were a number of such moments in the Chicago coverage. Ironically, some of the most enduring images for me were created by a talent foreign to television, the famous war photographer David Douglas Duncan. NBC hired him to produce daily photographic essays. They made a stunning impact at the time and have been preserved in a powerful book, *Self-Portrait: U.S.A.* Duncan visited the Great Lakes Naval Hospital, thirty-two miles north of Chicago, full of wounded men from Vietnam. They were nearly all amputees, many with wounds still draining. They watched from another world, as television covered the convention, where rhetoric about Vietnam was the chief topic.

Juxtaposed with those haunting faces was a sequence taken in our hotel the night the police beat up the McCarthy kids, their bloodied bodies filling the bedrooms on the fifteenth floor, while suddenly maternal girlfriends tore up the hotel sheets for bandages. It was the first time middle-class kids had experienced any violence from the real world. The press paid a lot of attention to their understandable anguish. No one except Duncan, who had spent his life photographing war, paid any attention to the men the rhetoric was all about.

The last photograph in the naval hospital was of a paratroop major, paralyzed from the neck down. All you saw was the top of his head on the pillow. He was black. Above him was a card with the hours when his body was to be turned. Pinned to the bedstead was a picture of Martin Luther King, with the quotation from 1963, "I have a dream that one day this nation will rise up and live out the true meaning of its creed: 'we hold these truths to be self-evident; that all men are created equal.' "

As he left, Duncan asked the duty officer how many delegates or candidates had come to visit these men. The officer said: "Not one."

After the Nixon inauguration in January 1969 I was out of the United States for most of the year, making BBC film reports on a variety of social issues in Britain, like treatment of the mentally retarded, abortion, and secondary education. I also covered stories like President Eisenhower's funeral, Nixon's visit to Europe as president, a European summit at The Hague, and the Napoleon Bonaparte anniversary mentioned earlier. I was out of direct touch with the Vietnam story for most of the year. When I came back it was again an explosive domestic issue.

There was a clear pause while America gave Nixon a chance to fulfill his campaign promise that he could provide the leadership to end the war. In his first major report to the nation in May, he rejected a "purely military solution" and offered Hanoi fresh negotiations. In June, Mr. Nixon announced a withdrawal of twenty-five thousand troops and said more would come home as South Vietnamese forces took over more of the fighting. In September, he announced that thirty-five thousand more Americans would be withdrawn before Christmas.

But impatience was building in the antiwar movement now being joined by a growing number of congressmen. There were mounting calls for a cease-fire, and for withdrawal of all U.S. combat troops.

October 15 was named Moratorium Day and demonstrations for peace were planned across the country. Two days before, Mr. Nixon announced another major televised report to the nation but scheduled three weeks later. The October Moratorium disturbed the White House by its size and composition. More than five hundred college campuses took part, with fifty-six congressmen and twenty-eight senators declaring their support.

Anticipation of his speech became fevered. It was known that Mr. Nixon had retired to Camp David and had hand-written ten drafts of the speech, every word his own. He put more effort into it than anything since his acceptance speech in Miami in 1968. The nation felt it was a turning point.

In London, we felt the moment was important enough to warrant the whole one-hour program. We came out in advance of the speech and began building a documentary on what people hoped he would say and then how they reacted to the reality. I was teamed up that year with Frank Smith, a very talented producer. We made a lot of films together and had become good friends. It was one of those ideal working partnerships which make the best documentary journalism, in which Frank was as much the reporter as I and I as deeply involved in the filmmaking as he. We improvised rapidly and intuitively and we had this entire hour conceived, researched, shot, edited, dubbed, scripted, and on the air back in London, two weeks from the day we set out. It was an exceedingly satisfying professional experience and what made it possible was that we stumbled onto a remarkable story.

We again chose New Hampshire for a number of reasons; continuity being one. It was still the state with the highest per capita Vietnam deaths. It had deep currents of both conservative patriotism and outspoken liberalism. It was there that McCarthy raised the challenge that upset Lyndon Johnson. More recently, the state's notorious newspaper, the *Manchester Union Leader*, had attracted national attention by pillorying the antiwar movement. On Moratorium Day, above its front-page name-plate, it ran the caption: "Attention all peace-marchers, hippies, yippies, beatniks, peaceniks, yellow-bellies, traitors, commies and their agents and dupes: help keep our city clean just by staying out of it. Signed, The Editors." Across the front of its building, the *Union Leader* hung a sixty-foot banner saying: "America, Love it or Leave it: Victory in Vietnam."

And the paper knew its readers: One woman wrote to the editor: "If I were President Nixon, I would order that the leaders of the Moratorium be shot for treason."

A man wrote: "What is so immoral about killing off a few hundred thousands little Tongs who have the audacity to try to keep the U.S., the greatest nation in the world, from running their country?"

In short, New Hampshire had everything.

I interviewed a broad cross section of people in Manchester before the speech — veterans of several wars, a Marine colonel just back from Vietnam, housewives, newspaper editors, ministers, students, and draft-age young men. Although there were hawks and doves of all colorings, common to all their views was the hope that Nixon would do something more to end it, to get the troops out, to stop the killing.

Because part of Nixon's purpose was to reassure and buy time from those who opposed the war, we gathered a group of such people to watch the actual address on television. One of them was a pretty blonde of twenty-one called Brenda Genest. Her husband, Richard, had been killed in Vietnam eight weeks earlier. In the end her story became the framework on which we hung all the other people.

Journalistically, it was a perfect story. It needed no hyping. Often a reporter is tempted to "improve" the details of a story, to make the quotes crisper, to bend the facts a little to make them "better." It is a temptation that has to be beaten down even as you are trying to extract the maximum in dramatic impact from the facts as they stand. Brenda's story never led us into that temptation because, as it unfolded, it was a perfect and terrible parable for what the war was doing to the American people. In fact, when it was shown an American film director who saw it in London wanted to adapt it for a feature movie.

Brenda's family owned the local Chevrolet dealership, Richard's family the largest bakery in Manchester. She went to a small Catholic girls' grammar school, then to Manchester Central High School. Richard was a senior in Brenda's freshman year. She said, "I didn't really know him. I knew who he was, but he didn't know me. I finally met him through my best girlfriend, whose brother was a friend of Dick's."

I could imagine her there. There are a lot of American high school girls like Brenda, though few perhaps quite as beautiful. She had a classic oval face, framed in very pale blond hair. She spoke with a soft monotone, her voice slightly nasal; she sounded like little girls do when they have been crying. Her voice, like her face, was one color, as though to put more color on her face, or more colorful inflection in her voice, would add too much; as though she were afraid of her beauty and wanted to subdue it. Yet she was in no way insipid. She was a child of the '6os: earthy, funny, idealistic, and, until Vietnam, totally apolitical.

She and Richard were married six months after they met. She was nineteen and he twenty-two, and he went to work in the family bakery. Richard got a deferment from active service by joining the New Hampshire National Guard. Brenda became pregnant. Then, on May 1, 1968, his unit, the 197th Artillery, was activated. She heard about it on the radio. "I called him at work and I said, 'Is that you?' and he said, 'Yes.' And when he came home that night, I said, 'You didn't know anything about it until it was on the radio?' And he said, 'No,' and he just didn't want to talk about it. It was too upsetting to him."

Two weeks later he was on active duty at Fort Bragg, North Carolina. Even then, they did not think he would go to Vietnam. The last time the National Guard had been activated was during the Cuban missile crisis, and the Manchester unit had just stayed at Fort Bragg for ten months and come home.

"There were all sorts of rumors around about who was going and who wasn't going to Vietnam. We finally found out about two weeks before he left that he was going."

Their son, Dicky, had just been born. Richard talked with a friend about going to Canada to avoid the war, as thousands of young Americans did. But he decided he had to go to Vietnam.

"I would have much rather had him go to jail, but his parents and my parents thought that he should go — as the right thing. So he went."

They wrote each other every day. Once or twice a week they sent tapes. Brenda showed me some of the letters.

In one, Richard wrote: "I just get so mad at the United

States Government subjecting Americans to this type of life. Why don't we just mind our own business? I don't like to think about it because I just get so mad."

He thought the war was "ridiculous," she said; "that the South Vietnamese didn't want us there; that they were just stealing the Americans blind. They worked for us by day and the Vietcong by night. It was just a dirty war and he was really sickened by people being killed — for nothing. And he couldn't wait to get out of there and have nothing to do with the army."

The army kept trying to make him a sergeant but he refused.

Brenda wouldn't listen to the tapes with us. She let us listen by ourselves in our hotel. His messages to her were sweet and intimate; a little embarrassed when he came close to verbalizing what he longed for sexually. Played like this, when we knew he was dead, of course made them heavily poignant.

After six months, he was due for a week's R&R. Brenda flew to Hawaii. She was surprised to see him because she had been sure she never would again. "But when I saw him and told him how surprised I was, he said, 'Well, that just goes to show you that I'll be home.' "

His year was up in August 1969, and Brenda finally got word that he was coming home.

"They were landing at Pease Air Force Base in New Hampshire and I had spent the summer at York Beach in Maine, which was about ten miles from Pease. So I was going to pick Dick up and we were going back to the beach to spend a few weeks there. So I came to Manchester, which is about sixty miles from there, and got Dick's clothes and spent the night here. And it was then that I found out about Dick's death. A military man came to the house and all he said was that Dick was on a mission and the military vehicle went and hit a mine. That's all he told me."

The road had obsessed him. In January he wrote: "I told you that the infantry leaves this place around seven or so every morning and goes out with their tanks, etc., and checks the road for mines, etc., before they open the road for traffic, or I should say, for the United States trucks. Well, anyway, they were about nine to ten miles away from here and they got ambushed. So, anyway, 14 people were hurt and two killed, so you can see it was a real *bad* day."

Genest was stationed at an artillery base called Thunder III, sixty-five miles north of Saigon. The road was Vietnamese National Route 15, a vital link between the capital and the bases along the Cambodian border. It was known as "Thunder Road."

After he died Brenda got a letter: "I really will be glad to get to Fo Loy for once we are there, that will mean we have gone down the road and going down the road is going to be the worst part of the trip home. I just hate that road so much, just like everyone else. I wish we could leave here by helicopter but no such luck; we're going to go by truck."

Another soldier in the battalion told Brenda what happened. "There was a convoy of five trucks. They were on their way to a base camp to come home and Dick and the other four boys [killed with him] were in the last truck. And the driver of their truck was an inexperienced driver and new in the country. The South Vietnamese farmers drive their trucks up the road and try to knock the American military vehicles off the road so that they will hit mines. Well, the first four trucks, their drivers weren't frightened by this; they knew that the South Vietnamese farmer wouldn't hit them, that he would — you know — chicken out. But the last driver got scared and he went off the road. When he went off the road, he started spinning the wheels and that's when the mine went off; and they were just like, maybe, halfway between the field where they had been all year and the base camp where they would be leaving for home."

All five dead were from Manchester. They brought them back together and there was a ceremony at the airport. On the tarmac the five coffins were lined up, each covered with the Stars and Stripes. Standing with the bereaved families were the governor of New Hampshire, the mayor of Manchester, senators, congressmen, and the Roman Catholic archbishop of New Hampshire, who recited the Twenty-third Psalm and sprinkled each coffin with holy water. A color guard saluted and there was a muffled drum beat.

The archbishop prayed: "Father of all pity and God of all consolation, you love us with an everlasting love. You turn the shadow of death into the dawn of life. Look, we pray you, on your servants in their mourning and distress."

The five coffins were loaded into hearses. Escorted by the state police, the motorcade drove through Manchester streets to various funeral homes. A local newscaster said: "Along the way, everyday citizens gathered in silent clusters, nervously trying to express their sympathy, but not knowing just how to do it."

The story does not end there.

The army planned military funerals but Brenda refused. When she saw Richard in his coffin, the military had dressed him as a sergeant, the promotion he had consistently rejected. The sight offended her.

"I couldn't have any part of a military funeral because Dick couldn't stand military life, and I just couldn't stand it, seeing him there in his uniform — all the stripes and everything. I wanted him dressed in his civilian clothes and I didn't want any taps or any of the funny military trappings."

With the help of a sympathetic priest, Monsignor Kenny, the funeral mass became a statement of conscience about the war. It shocked the community of Manchester as much as the deaths of the five soldiers. Traditional funeral music was replaced by popular songs with a guitar accompaniment. They were the songs of the sixties, of generational protest and the antiwar movement — "Blowing in the Wind," "Abraham, Martin and John," and "Where Have All the Flowers Gone?"

According to Monsignor Kenny, the greatest majority of Manchester people were "shocked and angered. They felt that the young lady was completely out of order, that she was flip; that she violated what they call the virtue of patriotism. That her manners were lacking."

Brenda said people "made a lot of snide remarks, not to me but to relatives and the family and friends. One person said

I deserved a good kick in the ass. Another person referred to it as a 'hippie funeral' because it was a confirmation of life and not death."

Monsignor Kenny got anonymous phone calls, late at night, some of them obscene.

The excitement eventually subsided and Brenda began life as a widow in the small apartment they had shared: having breakfast with the baby, giving him a bath, cleaning up, having lunch, going to see her mother or Richard's. She went on a bicycle, Dicky riding a small seat behind her.

At first we were concerned about intruding into Brenda's grief. She looked very fragile and we agonized privately over whether we were simply exploiting her and, even if we were not, whether the people around her would think we were. I interviewed her at length and she was happy to let us film parts of her daily routine. The most delicate part, which we shrank from as too intrusive, she herself suggested: a visit to Richard's grave.

It was a raw November day, too cold to stand around the cemetery while the film crew set up the lights and camera. To spare her that wait I drove her to a coffee shop and we had a cup of coffee. It was still too early to go back so we sat in the car near the cemetery. She was silent and I had run out of things to say, so I turned on the car radio. They were playing "Leaving on a Jet Plane." There was a little cry from Brenda and she began to sob uncontrollably, huddled into the corner of the seat and the passenger door. I wanted to take her in my arms and comfort her but thought she might misunderstand. So I reached over and patted her shoulder, deciding it was probably better to let her cry it out.

> *I'm leavin' on a jet plane*
> *Don't know when I'll be back again ...*

It was their song. It was the song of millions of other American kids of the late 1960s. It was the song of innumerable partings for Vietnam. They heard it on the last night of Richard's R&R in Honolulu.

I offered to call off the visit to the grave but she wanted

to do it. She said: "I can only go on sunny days because it's too depressing on any other day. I expect some kind of communication, or something. But there's nothing and I really get depressed when I go there and visit the grave."

"Why do you expect something?" I asked.

"Because when we were in Hawaii, I told him that if he ever got killed, to promise to come back to me, if there was any way possible that he could; and he hasn't, and I guess I'm still waiting for that." She laughed wanly. "I guess that's kind of far out but, you know, I was groping for something."

We filmed all of these sequences before Nixon's speech so that we felt we knew Brenda quite well when that evening arrived. But she continued to surprise me.

The president disappointed them. Brenda and her friends wanted immediate total withdrawal. Nixon said that would have been the easiest course for him politically, to blame the inherited war on Lyndon Johnson and come out as the peacemaker. "Some put it to me quite bluntly. This was the only way to avoid allowing Johnson's war to become Nixon's war."

Precipitate withdrawal would have been a "disaster . . . the first defeat in our nation's history . . . a collapse of confidence in American leadership . . . so we're going to stay."

Since all his efforts to negotiate had been rebuffed, he was introducing another plan, the "Nixon Doctrine," to help friendly nations fight their own battles but not to use American troops. Gradually, Vietnamese troops would replace Americans. He had a timetable but could not disclose it.

Then he turned to the peace movement.

The young audience had been listening respectfully to the president. Now they began interjecting sardonic remarks and it became a dialogue. "If a vocal minority, however fervent its cause, prevails over reason and the will of the majority, this nation has no future, in a free society."

"*You* have no future," someone said, and they all laughed.

Nixon said: "I respect your idealism, I share your concern for peace. I want peace as much as you do."

In the room they laughed bitterly.

Then Nixon said: "This week I will have to sign eighty-three letters for mothers, fathers, wives and loved ones of men who have given their lives to America in Vietnam. It's very little satisfaction to me, but this is only one-third as many letters as I signed the first week I was in office."

I looked at Brenda. Tears were forming in her eyes. She said to the image of her president on the television screen, "You bastard!"

We did not use it. It was so shockingly disrespectful of the president of the United States that, it seemed to us, to publish it beyond the private occasion was too much; she would not have said it knowing it would be used. But that is where Vietnam had brought America: that a twenty-one-year-old girl, of Brenda's sheltered background, would call the president a "bastard." A girl who had never given the slightest thought to politics had been deeply politicized. Like millions of other Americans, Vietnam had taught her contempt for a president and government she found unresponsive.

At the next Moratorium in Washington, Brenda joined a silent March Against Death, one of forty-thousand people parading past the White House, each with a candle and a placard bearing the name of an American killed in Vietnam.

I covered many other Vietnam stories until the war ended but the story of Brenda and her community never left me — the divisiveness, the anger, the bitterness it created; the chasm between the morally acute and the morally obtuse. One man wrote to the *Manchester Union Leader*: "If a war is necessary to stabilize the economy, then we shall have a war. It affects the everyday lives of most of us so little that we need hardly acknowledge the fact that it is going on. Surely the sacrifice of a son, husband or father by a hundred or so of our citizens every week is not that overwhelming. They will forget their losses in time."

SIXTEEN

Adventures in Fairness with Richard Nixon

ONE PLEASANT EVENING IN late September 1966, my wife and I went to call on Richard Nixon in his apartment on Fifth Avenue. Intermediaries had arranged a personal interview as background for the congressional elections that November. The former vice-president was campaigning almost as hard for Republican candidates that year as he had for the presidency in 1960. Quite visible beneath all that generosity was the springboard for his next attempt on the White House in 1968. I was covering his efforts for NBC.

Nixon had emerged from the shadows of his 1960 defeat by John Kennedy and his loss to Pat Brown in 1962 for the governorship of California. As everyone remarked, a sunnier, more relaxed and confident Nixon had successfully hung up his shingle in New York and was enjoying the Eastern Establishment prestige that had eluded him since 1937 — when the top New York law firms spurned the graduate of Duke Law School. He was making a lot of money and he lived in the same apartment building as Nelson Rockefeller; the same apartment building, ironically, where Rockefeller had exacted the famous "Fifth Avenue Compromise" on platform issues as the price for supporting Nixon's nomination in 1960.

Now the self-made boy from Whittier was Rockefeller's neighbor. In the mornings, identical limousines could be seen purring away at the two entrances, waiting to whisk these two possible presidents of the United States off to their daily chores.

This was my first meeting with Nixon and I carried to it the standard liberal journalist's baggage. It was like obligatory field equipment for the political reporter, this prefabricated set of attitudes about Richard Nixon — standard issue, like my battered Olivetti and grubby trench coat. It consisted of a collage of nasty Herblock cartoons, pasted over with scraps of headlines and impressions about red-smearing campaigns for Congress; the vengeful pursuit of Alger Hiss; the mawkish Checkers speech; the theatrical kitchen debate with Khrushchev; the furtive, haggard look of the first TV debate with Kennedy; and the bitter, "you won't have Nixon to kick around any more" farewell to the press in 1962.

From his personal to his political style, there was never a lack of disparaging material. Positive material took more finding. He was the classic villain in the melodrama of liberal politics. Now I was about to beard him in his lair and my wife, Jane, had come because I wanted to compare impressions.

The wood-paneled elevator served only one apartment on each floor. We were admitted by a Filipino butler. It did not feel homey, but stiff and formal, unlived-in, like a rented hotel suite. The butler in a white jacket showed us to Nixon's study and we had a few minutes to look at it before he came in. Parading across the mantel was a herd of elephants in jade and ivory. On Nixon's desk was a knight in shining armor.

Nixon came in and greeted us warmly. He sounded genuinely distressed that "Pat and the girls" weren't there to meet us. Yet Jane was sure they were there. She sensed something strained and unfriendly in the atmosphere, from the butler's greeting and Nixon's appearance. But he dispelled that quickly by talking about Washington, where she grew up, and asking questions about the pregnancy that was obvious from her clothes. He charmed her, in part because she had expected him to be socially awkward and stilted, unable to say the right thing. He said the right thing quite easily.

He did look awfully stiff, however, sitting in his own study at eight o'clock in the evening in a dark suit and black, lace-up shoes. Did he have another appointment, I wondered, or would choosing informal clothes have presented awkward choices of image? No, surely he had just come home from the office, or a late meeting with a client, and was dressed precisely as a lawyer with a big New York firm should be dressed. After all, I wasn't there to play poker with him. But that's the point: something made you want to speculate about his motives.

He did not have the notorious five o'clock shadow and he looked younger than his photographs; younger and lightly tanned, less fleshy. In person he radiated a distinct charm, not discernible in the photographs. There was more warmth, more twinkle in the eyes. It could vanish quickly. When he grew didactic, the brows lowered over the black eyes, the creases at the top of the flat-bridged nose stood out, the jowls deepened, and suddenly, the scowling Nixon of the caricatures was sitting there — the dark Nixon. But there was a sunny Nixon and it was sunnier than I had expected. My God, I thought, maybe he's a nice guy!

That face had betrayed him; it too frequently showed the world a scheming, wary, hostile man. But did it show the truth? Our faces after forty, they say, are what we have made them. Why, I wondered, was his face so much less threatening in the flesh? What did photographs do to Nixon that made even his smile look contrived? One explanation came to me several days later and with it the intuition that this man was far from washed up politically.

I was on the road with him in Florida and one of his stops was for a television interview in Miami. The TV station let the traveling reporters watch from a control room overlooking the interview studio. Some of the monitors were black and white, some color, which was just then being widely introduced. Suddenly it struck me that I was watching two different men. The black-and-white monitors brought out the dark Nixon, Herblock's Nixon; color made him far more personable and cheerful a character.

Considering the hairsbreadth loss to Kennedy, had a mere delay in introducing color television cost Nixon the presidency in 1960? Considering his narrow win over Hubert Humphrey, did color television give him the White House in 1968? Awful thoughts, yet not inappropriate about a man whose public career has been a staple of television for a generation. Richard Nixon and his family have been the longest-running continuous drama since television began in America. He was always there, with his triumphs and his tragedies. Nixon lived and died politically on television, from the Alger Hiss hearings of 1948 to the post-Watergate interviews with David Frost in 1976. A whole generation of Americans could measure their lives by the beat of Richard Nixon's TV career.

So, in his study that September evening in 1966, the first Nixon I ever met was the nice, affable "new" Nixon: confident, at ease with the press, expansive, even garrulous. That was my first surprise.

The next was his skill in sketching in the political situation that year. I had listened to a lot of American politicians the two previous years; my ear was "in" and my bullshit threshold pretty low. Nixon talked no nonsense and indulged in no wishful thinking. He was as incisive and well informed as if he had been pre-scripted and was reading off an invisible tele-prompter hung outside the Fifth Avenue window behind our heads.

He had scheduled visits to sixty-one congressional districts before the election, more than any other Republican, giving the candidates, the voters, and the press a sense that it was a national event. He went through the districts without notes, ticking them off, state by state — the candidates, the issues, and, sometimes, quite subtle background — all from memory. Six weeks later on election day, the voters proved him more than right. He had claimed that the Republicans, benefiting from an "LBJ drag," would pick up about forty house seats. They picked up forty-seven.

We were equally impressed with his candor about his own motives and pre-presidential tactics. Several years later, when the full cleverness of his assault on the presidency was laid bare, when the battle was won, it was apparent how little he told us, yet how much.

The battle for the Republican nomination in 1968, he said, would be a struggle for the center of the party, the GOP having rejected the Left in Rockefeller and Scranton, having tried with Goldwater and the Right in 1964 and failed. Four years later he proved himself right.

He said: "I am not looking for delegates. It would not go over with the congressional candidates I am campaigning for. It is not true that you can build up credit and later collect. But what the party will remember in 1968 is that I was loyal to the party — a party man."

At the time his views on Vietnam seemed to me only mildly cynical, as any politician's might be in private. Reading my notes of that conversation now, fifteen years later, knowing that the Nixon presidency was in a sense both made and broken by Vietnam, his calculation is interesting. In public he was all strength, patriotic fervor, calling on President Johnson to increase the pressure on North Vietnam; not to bargain a halt in the bombing of North Vietnam for a promise that Hanoi would deescalate the fighting. As we traveled that week in the South, Nixon accused Johnson of prolonging the war, giving an "impression of American weakness and confusion."

In private, Nixon was quietly calculating the political odds. Off the record, he told us: "By 1968, I assume that Vietnam will be out of the way. If it is not out of the way in 1968, it will be a disaster for the country."

"The guys running this year as doves are kooks. Doves represent maybe one-third of the country. But in places like the Midwest they are beginning to sense a 'get out' feeling. By 1968, if the war is still going on, the Democrats will be falling all over themselves to get out and the wrong kind of solution will result."

Nixon added: "I assume we can still settle it with a victory — if I may use an unfashionable word."

But he understood the bind Lyndon Johnson was in: "What can he do? There have been so many peace offensives that another would only create a flurry and have little impact." What would mean more to the voters, Nixon thought, was a "more vigorous war effort."

The sentence that rings with irony now he uttered in another off-the-record session for several reporters the next day flying to Jackson, Mississippi.

"The difficulty with Lyndon Johnson," Nixon said, "is that he deals with the politics of the problem rather than with the problem."

There were only a handful of reporters along and the game all week was deciding whether each speech or press conference or interview was the "old Nixon" or the "new Nixon," or, as someone said, "Which new Nixon?" — the "new New Nixon" or the "old New Nixon"?

Clearly, though, he was out to make a fresh start: considerate of the press; moderate of utterance; and cheerful of countenance. It behooved a smart political reporter to wipe the slate clean, to take Nixon at face value and prepare to build a fruitful relationship toward 1968. Since my "slate" was a grab-bag of acquired prejudices about Nixon from 1962 and beyond — not based on any reporting of my own — it was easy to wipe clean. Perhaps they had all misjudged him; perhaps he had changed. It didn't matter. What was important was to start afresh. So I covered that week with a positive attitude, thinking I was laying the foundation for a solid reporting effort stretching into the future. I interviewed him twice during that trip and I thought our relationship was becoming relaxed and easy. I determined to continue cultivating Nixon when I got back to New York. But he too was carrying baggage from the past — a burning hostility to the press, to believe his memoirs — that must have required colossal self-control to mask.

I never got that close to Nixon again. I never spoke to him directly again, and whenever I actually laid eyes on him in the future, he was unapproachable.

Back in New York, after the '66 elections, Nixon sent me a friendly note and a memento of the campaign. It was one of a special issue of crowns, the obsolete English coin worth five shillings, that had been struck to commemorate Winston Churchill. The coin bearing his likeness was set in Lucite with the caption: "Birdwatchers of 1966, Robert MacNeil Charter Member. Signed: Richard M. Nixon." Birdwatchers presumably meant Johnson watchers. The note, signed "Dick," said the coin was a reminder of Churchill's statement about the Munich settlement in 1939: "The belief that security can be obtained by throwing a small state to the wolves is a fatal delusion." So, it transpired, was the temptation to stretch Munich analogies too far.

Then, he went to earth; he hibernated politically. I was told by my contact that Nixon wanted to keep a low profile. It was so low that it was impossible to see him or speak to him again, through 1967, as he meticulously planned the 1968 campaign. By then I was going through the turmoil of leaving NBC, moving my family to London, picking up with the BBC. So I didn't refocus on Nixon until the New Hampshire primary in 1968, in which, as indicated, I was preoccupied with the politics of the Vietnam war more than with the presidential race per se. The one item that really stuck in my head was a remark made by one of Nixon's top aides as we rode his press bus in New Hampshire. He was my special contact, who had arranged the first meeting with Nixon. He said: "Nixon in his own mind feels that Vietnam is going to involve big face-saving on both sides." I thought that was one of the most sensible observations I had heard and I used the line in a number of BBC stories. I assumed, naively as it turned out, that if elected Mr. Nixon would get about the face-saving business rather swiftly and that face-saving meant life-saving, both for Americans and Vietnamese. It gradually turned out that what was needed was face-saving on only one side, the American side or Nixon side; and that proved to be very costly — to be precise, from Inauguration Day 1969 to the cease-fire in January 1973, 14,847 American lives. Increasingly, it appeared, the face they were dying to save was Nixon's, or some Nixonian abstraction of the national prestige.

Before the Republican Convention in Miami, I spent some time traveling around Iowa meeting delegates and came away convinced that, while the Republican fringes ached for ideological purity with Rockefeller or Reagan, the large middle wanted Nixon. His tactics had worked. The only shock at the Miami convention was the selection of Spiro Agnew as running mate. A few moments after it was announced, I was climbing the stairs to the Nixon headquarters in the Hilton Hotel and ran into Senator Charles Percy. He had clearly expected the nod himself, because he was in a state of shock, chalk-white, muttering, "Disaster, absolute disaster."

By nipping in quickly, I managed to snag the "disaster," the garrulous Mr. Agnew, for an exclusive interview for the BBC. He came to our room in the Eden Roc Hotel, and we filmed Agnew taking a call from Vietnam, telling his son, Randy, who was on active service, the good news. It made a charming introduction to an interview that made me believe Nixon had blundered badly. Agnew, not a shy man about sharing his opinions, obligingly unburdened himself of outrageous views on a number of topics, including the need for law and order. If the police saw anyone fleeing from the scene of a looting, Agnew said, and he would not stop, the police were entitled to shoot him, "because they did not know whether he was a looter, a rapist or whatever." There was a lot of similar talk that year but to hear such sentiments from a man trained in the law and selected by a presidential candidate who was also a lawyer seemed incredible to me. Spiro Agnew was a charming man, as sleek and well-groomed as an otter, but what was Richard Nixon up to? Was he insensitive to the reverberations of remarks like that? Was it unfair to Richard Nixon to point out that such insensitivity was disturbing in a man aspiring to the mantle of Jefferson and Lincoln? As widely remarked, it was a gesture of swift tactical expediency, a running mate acceptable to the South to prevent any bolt to Reagan before the nomination. That had to be noted. So did the fact that for Norman Mailer, who found in his liberal viscera an eloquent rationale for Nixon's election, Nixon "kept going in and out of focus, true one instant, phony the next."

I watched him, shortly before the convention, having his picture taken with delegates in Chicago, scores of them in an assembly line. Each stepped forward: Nixon would pump his hand, flash a smile, the camera flash would pop, the smile would fade, hand dropped, next please! What tolerance for the drudgery of politics! What talent for the organized petty flatteries it demands!

My next brush with the Nixon story was in January 1970, an hour-long report for the BBC on his first year in office.

Coming over on the plane from London, Frank Smith and I were groping for an idea, a framework. An hour is a long time in television. In topical reportage although you use documentary techniques you never have the luxury of the time consumed in making documentaries proper, in which six to nine months is not unusual. The various sequences can be built slowly and carefully and tested in montage; the whole piece rough-cut and put through a number of fine cuts, sometimes substantially rearranging the elements for better pace, or tension, or editorial clarity. In topical reporting, as we were doing for a weekly program, you have to crash in quickly both journalistically and artistically. Yet the finished product must abide by most of the values audiences expect from painstakingly produced documentaries. Finding a structure, or framework, is a big help.

Jet planes are wonderful places in which to think, especially long transatlantic or transcontinental journeys. You are freed from telephones and meetings and office interruptions that distract the attention. And it is my private theory that the pressurization system, by slightly enhancing the oxygen content in the air you are breathing and lowering the atmospheric pressure, stimulates the brain. Psychologically, there is something in the feeling of being so far aloft, the illusion that from those stratospheric heights of forty-five thousand feet, your mental reach is extended as is the reach of your eyes, that adds to the pleasant sense of thinking better. Further stimulated on that trip by British Airways scotch, Frank and I wrestled with ideas, until one of us, I don't remember which, said, "Well, isn't the big thing in Washington the dinner party? Isn't that where all the political gossip takes place? Why don't we give a dinner party — invite a good cross section of people and let them discuss the effects of Nixon's first year as president?"

The idea took many turns from there but it ended with us checking into the Hay-Adams Hotel across from the White House, and phoning Perle Mesta, the "hostess with the mostest" from the Truman years, now resting on her fame as the original of the Irving Berlin musical *Call Me Madam*.

I said: "Mrs. Mesta, I am a reporter from the British Broadcasting Corporation in London and I have a crazy idea I'd like to discuss with you."

She said: "I *love* crazy ideas. Come on over and discuss it."

So, without unpacking, Frank and I got a taxi to her apartment at the Sheraton Park.

Would she consider giving a dinner party for people who could talk about Nixon, if we paid for it and invited the guests? No hesitation. "Of course, I will. Things have been getting very dull around here recently." Within a few minutes the good lady was discussing menus, wines, and invitations. "I think we should have the Meissen china and the gold cutlery, don't you?" she asked as we were getting up to go.

"Of course," we said.

"Oh, and would you like to come to a little party I'm giving for Ethel Merman?" she asked. "You could bring your cameras. Some of the Nixon cabinet will be coming."

Ethel Merman was the original star of *Call Me Madam*. We accepted and the party provided a dazzling opening to our film, including Miss Merman belting out "There's No Business Like Show Business." As a top-flight Washington political hostess, Perle Mesta may have been passé, but everyone we wanted was intrigued by the invitation. It made putting our cast together much easier than it normally is to cozen a handful of busy people onto a television program that won't be shown in the United States.

Beatty Beale, the society columnist for the *Washington Star*, later called it "the unlikeliest dinner party of the year, if not the decade. Neither the hostess nor one of the guests would have put that combination together for a purely social reason — not, that is, without taking out explosion insurance first."

It wasn't that explosive, just provocative. One provocation was Chuck Stone, a militant black journalist and the first black, I was told, who ever sat down to dinner at Perle Mesta's. Another was Charles Goodell, the senator who had taken the seat of the assassinated Robert Kennedy and who was at the time the most outspoken dove in the Senate. Balancing him was Howard Baker of Tennessee, now the Republican Majority Leader. Congresswoman Margaret Heckler of Massachusetts, a modern Republican, Peter Lisagor of the *Chicago Daily News*, political analyst Richard Scammon, and liberal lawyer Peter Edelman filled out the table. The discussion was moderate and balanced, whether because of Mrs. Mesta's elegant surroundings or the presence of the cameras and microphones. I led the conversation through a number of prescribed areas: crime, the economy, and the Vietnam war. For each of the areas we then put together a film sequence so the effect was of a dinner-party conversation, interrupted by a factual package on that subject, narrated by me.

One of those packages was about the atmosphere around the Nixon White House and the way its press and public relations were handled. We made the ritual unsuccessful application for an interview with the president. Instead, we were allowed to film Ron Ziegler, his press secretary, giving a briefing to the White House press corps. In fact that nearly symbolized the reality. As I said in my commentary: "The White House press corps, including reporters who have covered four or five presidents, have rarely had such little contact with the man in the seat of power — about fifteen feet from this lounge. In one year he has given no on-the-record interviews to any reporter. He has had background chats with only two or three reporters known to be friendly. He has held only four press conferences — the fifth is scheduled tonight." I went on to describe Ron Ziegler as "the front man of an information machine so highly organized that reporters are not sure just what originates with the president and what comes from the apparatus they call 'Nixon Incorporated.' "

While we were in Washington, "Nixon Incorporated" obliged us with a spectacle worthy of Cecil B. de Mille. Vice-President Agnew arrived back from a diplomatic mission to the Far East and was greeted by the president and the cabinet as though he had just solved the Vietnam war. As Air Force One pulled into the hangar at Andrews Air Force Base, a red carpet was rolled out, klieg lights came on, cameras whirred, and Marine trumpeters with silken banners hanging from their trumpets sounded a fanfare. The event was so ludicrously out of proportion to anything Agnew had accomplished that it cried out for spoofing. So we used it to end the film, for two purposes: to make solid commentary points and to poke a little fun. As the sequence ended, we snuck up into the sound-track Ethel Merman's "There's No Business Like Show Business," and that carried over the closing titles.

The film was not shown in the United States but it was noticed by the *Washington Post* man in London, Alfred Friendly, who gave it a long and exceedingly bad-tempered review. In fact the tone and temper of our report, hung I'll admit on a rather lighthearted structure, stands up very well today. Apart from a little ridicule of Spiro Agnew, it comes out today as eminently balanced and fair. But there, you see, was one problem about being fair to Nixon. There were always people around who made it their business to decide that fairness to poor Richard meant applause, an assumption his press machinery assiduously cultivated. They did not want straight reporting; they wanted the press bending over back-wards. They wanted the imagined sins of the earlier press generation, which had lived through the Jerry Voorhis, Helen Gahagan Douglas, and Alger Hiss episodes, to be visited on this generation and continually atoned for. And when they considered the press too critical, they took it as personal criti-cism of Richard Nixon; they imagined a vendetta and they unleashed Spiro Agnew to bombard the press and the televi-sion networks with simplistic phrases like, "nattering na-bobs of negativism." The mass public loved it. They hated violence and dissent and change and loved to believe that it would go away if the media were not whipping it all up. They also loved the sophomoric alliteration.

The sad thing, as I discovered personally, was that deserved criticism of the news media got lost in the whirlwind of attack and defense caused by Agnew's excesses. It was no time to be promoting a book that tried seriously to examine the frailties of television journalism. I had to decide which side I was on: free press or repressive administration?

The administration hotly denied that it was trying to

muzzle the press, but it was clear to anyone objective that they were waging (and winning) a skilled propaganda campaign for the allegiance of what Nixon called the Great Silent Majority. Systematic denigration of the press and the war protest movement were the techniques. Impatience was mounting over the pace of Mr. Nixon's plan to extricate the country from Vietnam. He did precisely what he had accused Lyndon Johnson of doing four years earlier: he dealt with the politics rather than the problem. Was it unfair to Nixon to point that out?

The December Moratorium had brought the largest political demonstration in American history to Washington. It was overwhelmingly peaceful. Mr. Nixon ignored it. The White House was encircled by buses parked bumper-to-bumper as a shield against possible violence. The president announced that he was watching the Purdue–Notre Dame football game. There were skirmishes with a small group of Weathermen, who wanted violence and got it. But the next day a parade of administration spokesmen were out saying Washington security forces had saved the city from greater riots than after the death of Martin Luther King. As the *Washington Post* observed: "The Nixon Administration was less interested in trying to keep the march peaceful than in trying to make it seem less large and more violent than it really was and in trying to scare the daylights out of the putative Silent Majority at the same time." More egregious than that was the calculated effort by the White House to relate dissent over Vietnam to treason. It might have been "fair" to Nixon to ignore that. It certainly wouldn't have been fair to the American public.

In a sense my job in those years was easier than if I had still been working for an American network. With the exception of a few specials for public television, all my reporting on Nixon was for British consumption. In other words, I was a foreign correspondent again and in that form of journalism you can inevitably be freer with interpretation than in domestic reporting. You have to simplify America for a foreign audience as American reporters do from abroad. So I was freer to simplify and generalize; and to watch as Nixon's relations with the American press deteriorated.

Two years later, buoyed by his landslide reelection in 1972, and at the lifetime peak of his popularity, Nixon confided to Saul Pett of the AP: "I don't care what they write about me. I know I haven't got any friends out there. They have always been out to get me."

All three statements were untrue: he *did* care; he *did* have friends out there; and the press was not always out to get him.

At first even the most liberal columnists put aside the old prejudices and gave Nixon the benefit of the doubt. Herb Block, the cartoonist, who as much as anyone planted negative images of Nixon in the national mind, also decided to wipe the slate clean. Putting away the unshaven, menacing Nixon that had peopled his cartoons, Herb Block gave Nixon a shave out of respect for the new president. But as time passed, and Nixon's plan to end the war did not end it; as the economy turned down; and as the president retreated into deeper solitude behind a phalanx of smooth PR men; the honeymoon with the new Nixon began to sour (as it does with all presidents) and he began to draw criticism from editorial writers, columnists, and network commentators. The White House responded by letting Agnew out of his cage to bark at the media, and the media, not surprisingly, barked back.

This reached a crescendo when Nixon suddenly announced the Cambodian incursion at the end of April 1970. I went back to Washington to cover the explosion on the campuses which followed, including the killings at Kent State. Mr. Nixon was widely criticized for having characterized the student war protestors as "bums"; some commentators felt he had thereby contributed to the Kent State tragedy. Evidently, Nixon felt the charge because he went out of his way in a television address to answer it. But Spiro Agnew was out three days after Kent State saying the campus demonstrators were "paranoids . . . tomentose [hairy] exhibitionists who provoke more derision than fear."

Once again the Nixon tactics worked; according to the polls, the majority of Americans stayed with him, although with perceptibly less enthusiasm.

And for the rest of 1970, I went back to London to concentrate on domestic British stories.

These forays into America's deepening economic and political crisis made very good "stories." The basic stuff of journalism, after all, is to be able to tell your audience colorful and important stories that will hold their attention. For the British, the spectacle of their great ally tearing herself apart over an unpopular war was riveting. For a reporter it made very good "copy" and, like all reporters, I felt a certain affection for the source of it all.

As a reporter, I had separate mental compartments. In one compartment was my professional objectivity about Richard Nixon: he was the president of the United States and I would report what he said and did impartially. No moral or political judgments leaked into that compartment. They belonged in the second compartment, where the cauldron of my own personal attitudes to Nixon bubbled and hissed, the flavor turning relatively sweeter or more sour as I adjudged his behavior. I privately thought that through some lack in his own personality, some need to appear macho, akin to his obsession with football and winning and being tough (the really tough never talk about being tough), was causing him to stray farther and farther from the pragmatism he exhibited to get elected. Words like "defeat," "second-rate power," "peace with honor" seasoned his talk more and more.

In a third compartment my curiosity played with Richard Nixon, like a strange object, trying to understand the mainsprings of his psyche because he symbolized so many of the ambivalent values of this country. Yet he was a slippery object because he seemed to stand for nothing except dog-eared bromides — and getting elected. Much better clues came after Watergate — like the suggestion that Nixon needed the presidency to complete the development of his personality and that once he had it he didn't know what to do with it. He needed the reassurance of his worth that it brought, but when he had it he continued to need more reassurance, and more.

Since my personal contact with him had been so slight, Nixon became largely an abstraction to me, a curious phenomenon, an idea — not a man. Viewed in that way, he was fascinating to me, and still is; as though the latent playwright keeps obsessively turning this complicated piece of human machinery over and over, trying to come to terms with it.

Then, in 1971, I got personally drawn in. The Nixon White House began a campaign that directly threatened public television and my own career. It reached a point where I felt obliged to throw off my objectivity and resist. It became my personal corner of Watergate, and it is a story with a supremely ironic ending.

What gives it added piquancy is that I now have the rare satisfaction of knowing not only what I saw and heard but what they were up to in the White House at the same time. Their true motives are more brazenly documented than any other part of the Watergate saga; even while cautioning each other to be discreet, because disclosure would be embarrassing, they wrote it all down. But first I record what I knew as it was happening.

In August 1971, public television announced the creation of a centralized news operation in Washington. It was kind of embryonic "PBS News," although the steamy politics of the day precluded saying anything remotely like that. So a title was concocted that was so gloriously stilted that it seemed almost to be seeking anonymity in the Scrabble wasteland of Washington acronyms — NPACT, National Public Affairs Center for Television. Try saying that over the telephone fifty times a day when the person at the other end has never even heard of public television!

"It's the network that carries *Sesame Street*," you'd say, and get a vague, "Oh, yes?"

But anonymity was not its fate — not yet. To give NPACT some instant identity, its founder, Jim Karayn, decided to hire recognized television journalists. After a search, he settled on Sander Vanocur and me and called us both Senior Correspondents. Sandy was just making a disillusioned exit from NBC. I was with the BBC in London and got a leave of absence to see the experiment through the 1972 election year. Our mission was to cover the presidential election in a more coherent and consistent fashion than was expected of commercial television.

I came over from London. We had press conferences; they took our pictures; we gave interviews; and we made some modest claims about trying to cover news and politics differently. Sandy was far better known and attracted most of the publicity. I didn't realize until much later that he was a lightning rod — a lightning rod that nearly burned down the barn.

The political rumblings began almost immediately. Before we had even gone on the air, the *New York Times* reported that White House aides were unhappy with Vanocur's appointment. Then Nixon's policy man for television, Clay T. Whitehead, stunned us all with a speech to a public television convention in Miami. Whitehead was director of the newly formed White House Office of Telecommunications Policy (OTP), in itself a little sinister because it was a gathering-in of power over broadcasting to the very door of the presidency. For public television, still nervously negotiating the paths of Washington's power jungle, Whitehead was a figure to be feared and courted. He held the key to Nixon's decisions about future funding.

Whitehead amazed everyone by openly attacking the centralized concept of NPACT as alien to the spirit of localism intended for public television. Quite discernible was a veiled threat that funding for the entire system would suffer as a consequence of hiring people like Vanocur.

The future began to look a little dodgy, as the English say. It looked at the very least as though the White House was trying to drive a wedge between us and the local public stations.

Then we began to pick up rumors of a whispering campaign on Capitol Hill about our salaries. That buzz went around for several weeks until the Corporation for Public Broadcasting suddenly made them public. The fact that Vanocur was being paid $85,000 and I $65,000 a year caused a storm among some congressmen, whose own salaries at that time were $42,500. Representative Lionel Van Deerlin, a California Democrat, said he was afraid the revelations would not help the public television funding situation in Congress. Even sympathetic congressmen said they were shocked.

It was very upsetting. I had no reason to be ashamed of what I was earning. It was what I had made in my last year at NBC, five years earlier. I was perfectly comfortable at the BBC and $65,000 was my price for giving that up. But having it published, the subject of gossip among our friends and neighbors, was a very painful invasion of privacy.

The pressure continued. A few days after the salary storm, Whitehead made another speech attacking the drift toward centralized network structures. In mid-December, the Corporation for Public Broadcasting caved in and voted to give very low funding priority to news and public affairs programs. A month later it voted not to fund network news analysis and commentary programs at all.

All this time we were trying to produce programs. Our first effort was a special broadcast a year to the day before the 1972 election. It explored the political mood of the country and I summed up my impressions with the observation that Nixon looked a pretty good bet for reelection. Scarcely the conclusion of a hostile commentator out to get the president.

In January our weekly series, *A Public Affair — Election '72*, began and we originated one of the first programs from Illinois. With much care we had chosen a suburban family as "average" Americans whose views we would sample periodically. We filmed the couple, Mr. and Mrs. Richard Johnson of Rolling Meadows, Illinois, watching television as Edmund Muskie entered the presidential race. The Johnsons watched and shook their heads. They were lifelong Democrats; if Teddy Kennedy were running, they said, it might have made a difference. As it was, ten months before election day, our "average" Americans thought they would vote for Richard Nixon. That was a pretty significant conclusion for January 1972; again, difficult to interpret as hostile to the president.

The series went on. For the most part, the mechanics of producing it, traveling, ironing out professional frictions and weaknesses in a new organization absorbed us. The mounting political trouble was like distant thunder. We were too busy to pay close attention. Yet we were affected; at the very least I know I was determined not to give the Nixon people any ammunition. That editorial sensitivity was inhibiting but not paralyzing.

One of the most poignant episodes of the year was the brave but futile attempt by Congressman Pete McCloskey to challenge Nixon's renomination. McCloskey was a dove on Vietnam and he tramped forlornly through New Hampshire telling groups of six or seven voters why Nixon should be dumped.

Nixon himself was seven thousand miles away in Peking. It was the historic moment when the arch Red-baiter of old was reopening the forbidden door to China, with half of American television there to beam back every winning picture. Nixon never went near New Hampshire but he blanketed the airwaves. I filmed a sequence with McCloskey watching a TV set in his New Hampshire motel room asking: "How do you compete with that?" You didn't, and that was the point.

The half-hour was pointed but fair. The fact was that Nixon was using his incumbency to maximum political advantage. But that I had even to consider what the reaction might be when the piece was viewed in the White House was to some degree inhibiting. Why were we devoting a half-hour to McCloskey's challenge, they might ask? Were we not magnifying his chances to make a dent in Nixon's advantage? Were we exaggerating the importance of McCloskey, and therefore of the antiwar movement itself? Those were all legitimate editorial questions for us to ask ourselves; it was oppressive to be asking them over and over because of what we thought the effect might be in jeopardizing the wider future of public television.

The political pressures were not restricted to Sandy and me. I also became the host of *Washington Week in Review*, already a popular and well-established PBS program. It then enjoyed a cadre of talented regulars: Neil MacNeil of *Time*; Charles Corddry of the *Baltimore Sun*; and Peter Lisagor of the *Chicago Daily News*. Peter was one of the brightest lights in the Washington press corps, a witty and penetrating journalist, with a knack for the funny, demolishing phrase. On the program he pulled no punches with the Nixon administration, any more than he had with Johnson before. But the Nixon

White House found him intolerable. They called Karayn more than once to demand that Lisagor be taken off the program. Karayn refused, but the incident shocked us because the hypocrisy was so blatant: on almost any day Whitehead or some other Nixon aide was saying how inappropriate it was to fund public affairs programs with tax money because of the risk of political interference. It was like the fox warning the chickens they were in danger of being eaten.

Lisagor remained on the program until he died of cancer, a long ordeal he faced as cheerfully as he faced everything politically. And *Washington Week in Review* was one of the first places you might have heard about Watergate's true dimensions. In October 1972, Neil MacNeil emphasized that it could grow into the biggest scandal Washington had ever known — a scandal that could bring down the administration.

When the public television battle was not being fought in public speeches and through the newspaper columns, it went on behind the scenes; Nixon appointees controlling CPB tried to eradicate news and public affairs; PBS and key stations fought back. All the sets of initials, the nuances of power at stake, the bureaucratic ephemera of these battles made tedious fodder even for those of us whose livelihood was at stake. For the press at large, they were arcane and irrelevant. It wasn't a big story but there was a steady flow of comment which added to our growing feeling of persecution.

In April 1972, *Broadcasting* magazine summed it up this way: "From the Administration's point of view the salaries alone were bad enough; that they were paid to former network newsmen was worse; that they were paid to these newsmen — described vaguely as 'liberal' but perceived by some as a balding yippie and his icy blond sidekick — was intolerable."

We also had strong supporters, like Lawrence Laurent, syndicated TV critic of the *Washington Post*, who wrote: "What has been put on the air has generally drawn high praise from the published critics, a breed that is rarely celebrated for its kindness or its generosity. Complaints about what has been put on the air have been few indeed, and with six months of weekly and special events broadcasting behind them, Vanocur and MacNeil have a record of meticulous fairness and an unquestioned capacity to pay attention to all contenders in the national political controversies."

By the summer of 1972 the whiff of gunpower began to penetrate our editorial offices. Cutbacks by CPB had killed plans for us to provide continuous coverage of the political conventions. We went through the tumultuous McGovern nomination by the Democrats doing a half-hour each night. Then, for his own political reasons, Karayn decided to provide gavel-to-gavel coverage of the Republican Convention, using limited pictures of the action on the podium; eschewing all the razzle-dazzle that makes commercial TV coverage attractive to viewers and irritating to its critics. It was announced in the press that Sandy and I would anchor that coverage.

Sandy and I refused. We felt it was quite inappropriate for a news organization under attack by the Nixon White House to cover his renomination convention in full when we had not covered McGovern's. I totally approved of an attempt to provide an alternative to network coverage, but this was not the time. Whatever NPACT's motives, I felt it would be widely perceived as an act of abasement. We had very fierce arguments but stood our ground. Karayn persuaded Bill Moyers to anchor the coverage while I covered the convention for the BBC. It had begun to be pretty obvious that public television was not going to be a very congenial place for me.

Then the White House began shooting itself in the foot, not once but repeatedly.

First in June Mr. Nixon vetoed a generous two-year funding bill passed by very large majorities of both houses of Congress. Immediately the disparate forces of public television, divided by the bait and poison of funding threats, began coming together.

Then in September the White House engineered the appointment of Henry Loomis, number two man at the United States Information Service and former head of the Voice of America, as president of CPB. Already trailing the smell of officialdom about him, Loomis committed two serious gaffes. He admitted he had never seen any public television, but in the same breath announced he knew certain programs, like

Washington Week in Review, should go. How did he know if he were not listening to his master's voice?

Then in November, Loomis casually suggested that public television preempt all programming to carry continuous coverage of the Apollo space shot, coverage incidentally supplied by NASA, which was known to be unhappy about commercial TV plans. The conversion of public broadcasting into the feared domestic Voice of America seemed at hand. There was such an outcry that Loomis was forced to withdraw the proposal.

We completed our forty-seven weekly programs on the election. Mr. "Average" American, Richard Johnson, firmed up his resolve to vote for Richard Nixon because "he kept the bombs off our roofs." No, he said, the stuff beginning to come out about Watergate didn't disturb him. It seemed a lot of fuss over nothing. He joined Nixon's irresistible landslide.

I got particular satisfaction from one half-hour. Nixon made one of his very few campaign appearances in Atlanta, a triumphant progress through thousands of cheering Southerners, the motorcade almost engulfed in a blizzard of ticker tape.

We had heard that the *Atlanta Constitution*, one of the great liberal organs of the nation, was agonizing over whom to endorse. The editor, Reg Murphy, let us film one of their deliberations, the small editorial board sitting under the portrait of their famous editor, Ralph McGill; a ghostly conscience overseeing them.

Those men enumerated the negatives about Richard Nixon and then about George McGovern with such conviction that you wondered how they could ever contemplate either man as president. Then they listed the positives — and there Nixon's foreign accomplishments easily outweighed McGovern's assets and they made the decision: Nixon. Each of those men left some blood on the table in doing so.

Our program alternated scenes of Nixon's glorious and triumphant ticker-tape procession with the agonized, conscience-tearing discussions of the *Constitution* editors. To me the total effect conveyed a lot of the reality of that fall. There was the contrivance in some of the outpouring for Nixon. For example: we had shots of the ticker tape, not being thrown by delirious voters, but blown from the rooftops by large machines. We had shots of the crowd, not lunchtime Atlantans only, but thousands systematically bused in — not even by local Republicans, but by the Committee to Re-elect the President. And we had the awful dilemma of America's Democrats, following their heads and not their hearts and dismissing McGovern for Nixon. The piece was flattering to no one. It conveyed reality.

After the election, we went sailing for two weeks in the Caribbean, an experience which effectively washed away the politics of public television and my inhibitions about them. I returned feeling it was time to fight back.

Almost immediately, I had the chance. Just before Christmas, the Corporation for Public Broadcasting, now thoroughly controlled by Nixon appointees, announced that they were "deferring" any decision on funding programs like *Washington Week in Review*. In closing the program one night I told the audience that its funding was in jeopardy and asked them to write what they felt. Their letters overwhelmed us. In three weeks, more than thirteen thousand were received, of which precisely twenty were negative.

When we announced this, Henry Loomis responded sarcastically that "the number and emotional content of letters is not necessarily a good measure of audience size or interest."

In January I was asked to speak to the Consumer Federation of America, an organization with branches all over the country. It seemed an excellent forum to lay out our case that Nixon's men were turning public broadcasting into a government broadcasting service. I strongly denied bias: "Bias in their minds is apparently any attitude which does not indicate permanent genuflection before the wisdom and purity of Richard Milhaus Nixon."

I said that many people believed in a form of television journalism independent of the commercial networks, yet insulated from interference by the government of the day: "Today they are sadly disillusioned people as they watch their dream being perverted before their eyes and their ideal of independence being made a travesty by Mr. Nixon's appointees."

The speech received very wide press coverage and the text was printed in the *Congressional Record*. I see, on rereading it, that even then I was leaving open the possibility that "This whole furor may have been quite unfair to [Nixon] personally. It is unlikely that he wants to be remembered among other things as the man who set out, in the words of the *National Observer* last Sunday, 'to strangle the national public broadcasting network.' If he wishes to change that impression, I would with the greatest respect, and full recognition of his many more urgent priorities, suggest that he take half an hour to see what his people have been doing."

I urged the Consumer Federation to encourage its vast membership to write their local stations with their views on public broadcasting and they did. *Variety* reported that thousands of people wrote CPB complaining about White House interference with public broadcasting.

All the same, in March, CPB confirmed its December decision not to fund the controversial programs *Washington Week in Review, Bill Moyers' Journal*, and William Buckley's *Firing Line*.

But by then, such tumultuous things were happening that the decision seemed almost irrelevant. Sandy had resigned, partly out of personal wounds at the vendetta against him, partly to remove himself as a provocation. He was replaced by Jim Lehrer, a newspaperman from Texas who very soon became my close friend. We launched a new weekly series, *America '73*, using a documentary magazine format to examine one theme each week. And while we were busy with that, the Nixon defense on Watergate began to unravel.

Then the announcement came that the Senate was setting up the Ervin Committee on Watergate, whose proceedings would be televised. No commercial network made any announcement about coverage. The way was open for public television to win the kind of credibility that the new ABC network had by preempting all daytime programs to cover the Army-McCarthy hearings in 1954. A small group of us at NPACT and PBS strongly urged that public television announce immediately that it would cover the hearings in total, with no interruptions, and cancel all evening programs to run them when commercial television would not. Cautiously, PBS questioned the local public television stations. Fifty-two percent said, "Yes," and on that basis the announcement was made, still well before any commercial network had revealed its plans.

There were other developments. Quite unexpectedly Tom Curtis, the former Republican congressman whom Nixon had appointed chairman of CPB, resigned and publicly charged improper White House interference with the board.

The Watergate hearings began, with Lehrer and me teaming up to anchor the coverage. In many cities in the East, our gavel-to-gavel coverage was carried live in the daytime and again at night. We not only carried the hearings but included substantial commentary and analysis with legal and constitutional experts. While commercial television went in and out, covering some days and not others, breaking away for commercials, PBS stayed with every minute of the hearings and did not go off the air during the committee's dramatic recesses. We filled those with more analysis and on-the-scene reporting from Peter Kaye outside the committee room.

The response was incredible. For the first time in its brief history, it seemed the entire nation knew what public television was. Viewers spontaneously sent money and took out memberships. The memberships of some stations, like WNET in New York, trebled because of the hearings. But the coverage served another, deeper purpose: it revealed to doubters that public television journalism could be vital, fair, and trenchant when dealing with the most sensitive political material. Perhaps the most important people to discover that were the managers of local stations who had long doubted that we should be in the news business at all.

By a curious turn of fate, public television, one of the victims of the Watergate mentality, had been saved by it.

To Lehrer and me, the moment seemed supremely ripe to take what we both considered the next logical step, a nightly national news program to put public television firmly in the business of regular journalism and to give the PBS network a sense of cohesiveness. I argued in many meetings that however wonderful they were, all entertainment programs were ultimately dispensable. Only news would give PBS programs an air of *indispensability*.

Unfortunately, not enough people saw it our way just then. Nor were we able to secure the untrammeled editorial control we felt we needed to launch such a venture. I had been marinating in the politics of public television for nearly two years, and my whole being began to smell of it. I could not face another year of that bickering. When the Senate hearings adjourned in August, I resigned and gratefully moved my family back to England and the creative environment of the BBC.

Now, through all our travails at NPACT, I was never quite certain how much the Nixon men were really out to get us and how much we were imagining. We often asked ourselves, "Are we being paranoid, or is there a conspiracy afoot to defame us?" Even if there were, was it credible that Richard Nixon himself could be involved?

The answer we now know is that we were not paranoid; there *was* a conspiracy and the president himself was directly involved.

In February 1979, the Carnegie Commission, using the Freedom of Information Act, secured the release of thousands of White House papers documenting their relations with public television.

They are quite simply damning and, when I want to get worked up about it, damnable.

Here is staff secretary Jon Huntsman in a "confidential, eyes only" memo to Peter Flanigan and Bob Haldeman, dated September 23, 1971, quoting the report of the Vanocur/MacNeil appointments to NPACT, and adding: "The above report greatly disturbed the President who considered this the last straw. It was requested that all funds for Public Broadcasting be cut immediately. You should work this out so that the House Appropriations Committee gets the word."*

Then follow many memos between Whitehead, Flanigan, John Ehrlichman, Charles Colson, and others as they debate what course to recommend to the President. The options they consider range from "take over the management [of CPB] and

---

* I am grateful to David Stone, whose Princeton University thesis, "A Poetic Symmetry, Nixon's War on Public Television," has made a coherent narrative of these documents and greatly helped me to understand them.

thereby determine what management decisions are going to be made" (Ehrlichman, October 6, 1971) to "carefully prepared public embarrassment (which might be arranged for Vanocur)" (Whitehead, October 20, 1971).

Here is a memo from White House staffer John Rose in November 1971: "In spite of what it may seem, no one participating in this exercise has ever been unclear as to the President's basic objective: to get the left-wing commentators who are cutting us up off public television at once, indeed yesterday if possible."

The Whitehead memo to Haldeman of November 24, 1971, constitutes as much of a "smoking gun" as I shall ever need to demonstrate that we were not paranoid: there was a conspiracy to undermine our credibility with Congress, the press, and the public television system:

EYES ONLY

EXECUTIVE OFFICE OF THE PRESIDENT
OFFICE OF TELECOMMUNICATIONS POLICY
WASHINGTON, D.C.   20504

DIRECTOR

November 24, 1971

MEMORANDUM FOR

Mr. H. R. Haldeman
The White House

With the controversy between the Administration and the Corporation for Public Broadcasting becoming more visible, you might be interested in what we are doing behind the scenes on the Vanocur/MacNeil situation.

After Vanocur and MacNeil were announced in late September, we planted with the trade press the idea that their obvious liberal bias would reflect adversely on public television. We encouraged other trade journals and the general press to focus attention on the Vanocur appointment. Public television stations throughout the country were unhappy that once again they were being given programs from Washington and New York without participating in the decisions. My speech criticizing the increasing centralization of public television received wide coverage and has widened the credibility gap between the local stations and CPB. It also has brought more attention to the acknowledged liberal bias of CPB and NPACT.

We then began to encourage speculation about Vanocur's and MacNeil's salaries. As a result of the increasing public controversy, several reporters and Congressman Lionel Van Deerlin asked CPB to release the salaries. Macy refused, but after pressure increased, quietly made it known that Vanocur receives a salary of $85,000 a year and Robert MacNeil $65,000.

We plan to do two things in the next few weeks to continue to call attention to balance on public television, especially NPACT. We will quietly solicit critical articles regarding Vanocur's salary coming from public funds (larger than that of the Vice President, the Chief Justice, and the Cabinet) and his obvious bias. We will quietly encourage station managers throughout the country to put pressure on NPACT and CPB to balance in their programming or risk the possibility of local stations not carrying these programs. Our credibility on funding with the local stations is essential to this effort.

Clay T. Whitehead

cc: Peter Flanigan
EYES ONLY

One other document intrigues me. It is a memorandum for the record made by Whitehead from notes he took during a meeting on June 22, 1972, between the president and thirty executives from independent commercial broadcasting stations.

The President opened the meeting by referring to meetings he has had with broadcasting executives and said he wanted to have similar meetings with individual station owners. He is aware of their concerns, cable television, and the like. He wanted to start the meeting off by asserting some principles: the first, was his belief in the private enterprise system — particularly in the media. It is in the interest of the country that we have a strong and independent private enterprise broadcast system for two reasons: (1) principles of the First Amendment — free speech, free press, dangers of government control; (2) he has traveled abroad extensively and seen what government-run or government-sponsored broadcasting is like; and in spite of the growing reports of many people that government-controlled broadcasting produces high-quality programming, no commercials, etc., he stated that no one should be fooled — that that was a bunch of crap.

The President then turned his attention to public broadcasting in this country. He stated that his country would benefit from the public broadcasting system, that most of his advisers disagreed with him on this subject, and urged him to support the larger funds for broadcasting [sic]. He thought that the biggest danger, however, was not that it be too big, but that it be kept under very careful control as to size and what it was allowed to get into because it would inevitably be subject to Government control, and would inevitably become a political force in our country. He felt that we had to give serious consideration to the fact that you never know who's going to be sitting in his chair next and that some presidents might be inclined to use Federal support of public broadcasting to their advantage, that that was a risk not worth taking; and, therefore, public broadcasting, particularly the use of Federal funds, should be kept under the strictest of control and not be allowed to become too large.

Eight days later, Nixon vetoed the public broadcasting funding bill passed by Congress. The meeting is significant because of Nixon's brazen hypocrisy: warning that "future presidents" might do what he was in fact doing. It was, incidentally, five days after the arrest of five men burglarizing the Democratic headquarters at the Watergate, and the White House cover-up was in full swing.

The other significance to me is that the meeting explains why so few commercial broadcasters shed any tears or made any protest while the White House was trampling on their colleagues in public television.

Although I moved back to London and the BBC in August 1973, I spent most of the succeeding year back in the United States, reporting for *Panorama* on the continuous drama provided by the Nixon story: the resignation of Agnew and appointment of Gerald Ford as vice-president; the Saturday Night Massacre, the House Judiciary Committee hearings; the release of the damning transcripts of Nixon's tapes; the Supreme Court ruling that he had to hand over sixty-four more tapes; the vote for articles of impeachment; Nixon's resignation and his subsequent pardon by Gerald Ford.

All of this had a curious sequel.

After his resignation, the BBC began to consider devoting an entire evening to a program on the rise and fall of Richard Nixon. I was asked to prepare an outline for a program which David Frost and I would both host. I produced a thirty-page outline, but after some preliminary discussion, we all decided that a long interview with Nixon himself would be essential, so we had better start there. So I was dispatched to California to try to secure Nixon's consent. I carried with me a very carefully written letter arguing that the BBC was probably in a better position to be objective about Nixon than the American networks. I alluded to our relationship in 1966. I did not duck, but did not dwell on, our more recent history. A BBC colleague who read it said it was "a very smarmy letter, the smarmiest letter I've ever read." It was certainly the smarmiest letter I have ever written.

A friend got me the private phone number of Nixon's retreat, the Casa Pacifica at San Clemente, a reminder of one of the minor scandals of his presidency, the major improvements carried out at public expense. I reached the aide who had stayed with him, Marine Lieutenant Colonel Jack Brennan, whom the nation had last seen in full dress uniform almost defiantly announcing the "President of the United States" as Nixon took his emotional farewell from the White House staff — like every other crisis moment in his life, in full view of national television.

I got Colonel Brennan on the phone and explained my mission, and he said that if I brought my letter to San Clemente he would give it to the president for consideration. I didn't quite believe I had gotten that far.

I rented a car and drove down the Pacific Coast, trying to imagine what Richard Nixon must be thinking about as he stared out at the ocean these days. Did he still walk on the beach, as in the photographs I had seen, in his black lace-up shoes?

The entrance to the Casa Pacifica was close to an exit from the San Diego Freeway. The house was hidden by trees. A long driveway ended in stone posts and a metal gateway. There was no one in sight. When I stopped the car by the gate post, there was a whirring sound and a combination microphone-speaker unfolded itself from the gate post. A voice asked me what I wanted. I explained I had a letter for Colonel Brennan. The voice said, "Wait there!"

I waited and presently a car came from the house by the long drive, going very fast. It stopped at the gate and a Secret Service agent got out and took the envelope. The feeling was decidedly creepy, as though the man in the Spanish-style house behind the eucalyptus trees was their prisoner, or a man with a disease that might infect the world. The car drove off toward the house and I headed back to Los Angeles and the Beverly Wilshire Hotel to await developments. I was so anxious for the call that I scarcely left the hotel for five days, passing the time writing and reading. Eventually it came. Colonel Brennan said Mr. Nixon was "quite interested" in our proposal and wanted me to get in touch with his agent, Irving Lazar, in New York. I could hardly believe it: the "smarmy" letter was working.

Since New York was on the way back to London, I packed up and flew to New York by the next flight. Irving Lazar, better known in the trade as "Swifty," was the agent who had sold Nixon's memoirs to Grosset and Dunlop for two million dollars. He was very easy to reach and very direct. I offered to come to see him in person, but he said there was no need. He had discussed the proposal with the president and they agreed to give me, on a world exclusive basis, four or five one-hour interviews with Richard Nixon, to be recorded in the summer of 1974, between the time he finished his memoirs and the date of their publication. The price would be one million dollars. I said: "Thanks, I'll be back in touch."

I flew back to London that night amazed at how easy it had been. I did some crude calculations. An asking price of one million dollars, with very gentlemanly bargaining, could come down to seven hundred and fifty thousand dollars. If the BBC then sold rights for showing in other countries — the United States, Australia, New Zealand, Canada, France, Germany, etc., etc. — it could come out costing the BBC nothing, yet it would remain a BBC program.

Back in London, the BBC confirmed Lazar's offer but then had second thoughts. Aubrey Singer, the controller of BBC 2, the second network, finally refused, saying, "I don't want to be remembered as the man in the BBC who paid a pardoned felon a million dollars for his memoirs."

So, too bad. I forgot it and went on to other things, notably a long trip to Pakistan for a documentary on the origins of the immigrants to Britain.

I thought nothing more about the Nixon interviews until midsummer 1975, when two things happened. A BBC friend in Toronto, who knew about the dealings with Nixon, called to say he had some businessmen who were prepared to put up the million dollars for the interviews. He said they would call the next day. Before they called, I read in my *New York Times* that David Frost had made a deal to do the Nixon interviews for six hundred thousand dollars, and, of course, he subsequently did them.

I had mixed feelings; the interviews would be so enormously newsworthy that they meant an important career milestone for the interviewer. I hated having that slip away.

But I also felt relief, which grew when I saw the actual

interviews. The ground rules were that only one hour was devoted to Watergate, the rest to other more flattering parts of Nixon's reminiscences. Frost recorded the Watergate interview last but showed it first. It was a courageous and well-calculated try at an impossible task.

Since Nixon had refused to explain himself in any other manner, to appear before any court of any kind, the television interview became the court of world opinion. How appropriate to our age, to the career of this ever-televised politician, to the enormous power of television, that he should choose to explain himself only there — and for money. How fitting for our time that the only man in the world who got to ask Richard Nixon all the unanswered questions should be a television personality — not a lawyer, not a judge, not a journalist, nor even an American, but an international television personality.

This extraordinary circumstance required of Frost to play many roles at once, to assume a persona which somehow embodied all the unsatisfied moral outrage of those left frustrated by Nixon's swift exit. He handled it very well, but I found myself thinking, "Thank God, as it turned out, I didn't have to do that myself." As a journalist, I could not have played prosecutor of the Western world as Frost did — yet it needed that somewhat theatrical approach to meet Nixon on his own unreal ground. The interviews inevitably became further stanzas in Nixon's lifelong epic of self-justification.

Even in retirement, Nixon has continued to test my journalistic objectivity.

Late in 1978, he scheduled an appearance at the Oxford University debating society, the Union. It was to be the first major public appearance since resignation and disgrace. We taped the event and transmitted an edited half-hour on the *MacNeil/Lehrer Report*. The student questioners were untypically gentle and respectful to Nixon and he was back in form, Nixon the elder statesman in full bloom. Put simply in TV terms, it made him look very good. That prompted a lot of people to complain bitterly: "Why are you putting *him* on? Why are you making Nixon look so good?"

SEVENTEEN

The MacNeil/Lehrer
Report

WE HAD A WONDERFUL HOUSE in England, a Tudor barn attached to an Elizabethan manor house, much rebuilt. Our barn dated from 1483 and the oak beams may have been even older, possibly taken from broken-up ships. The exterior had exposed timbers filled in with tawny brick, set in a herring-bone pattern. Where the cow stalls had been was our library. It looked out through leaded windows on a little courtyard formed by some outbuildings that had been connected in modern times. Beyond the courtyard was lawn and flowers. It was only twenty miles from London, yet centuries away from television and the jet planes I practically lived on.

I remember sitting in that courtyard writing a letter one morning in June 1975. June is the sweetest month in England and when the fine days come they have a transcendental purity; the beauty of the light and the length of the evenings toward the solstice in those high latitudes gives the time an other-worldly quality. Under that light, the growth is so luxuriant, the effect so bosky, that you feel as if ancient pagan divinities are pushing the scenery around. You can believe in forest spirits and the ghosts of others who have used that land.

Around me the climbing roses I had planted several years before were now established and profuse. In another walled garden behind the barn were espaliered fruit trees I had been nursing for six years. By walking through a small gate in the manor house wall, down a lane, through a wooded pathway, I could come out on an Elizabethan village green. On the far side was a pub where I could drink bitter beer and play darts with the locals.

The letter I was writing committed us to move back to the United States, and I stopped many times to look around and wonder if I were doing the right thing to leave all this. The children were in excellent schools. We had a close group of friends. The BBC was as stimulating a place as you could find in which to pursue the television craft. London was close at hand; France close enough for casual weekends. But I was forty-four and restless. I needed to do something different. I needed to run something myself, and that was the opportunity I was being given in New York.

I was writing to accept an invitation to launch a nightly news program for public television, just what Lehrer and I had been trying to arrange in Washington two years earlier. This invitation came from WNET in New York, the largest PBS station. I was still leery. My exposure to public television had been pretty disillusioning. I stalled WNET for a year before finally agreeing, with some reluctance and very mixed motives.

Thus I backed into my smartest decision yet, to take a risk on something that has proved to be the most liberating and satisfying thing I have done, *The MacNeil/Lehrer Report*.

One of the reasons our program works is that the timing of its birth was right: something like it was clearly needed in 1975 — and politically possible. The timing was the inspiration of WNET, as was another critical decision, to place the program in New York immediately following the news programs on the commercial networks. That half-hour, 7:30–8:00 P.M., was full of rubbish, a wasteland for intelligent viewers. Our placement there also let us try to capture some of the people who had just finished watching NBC, CBS, or ABC news, and who might want something more. It strengthened our initial argument that we were a complement or supplement to commercial television news and it helped to give us an identity.

Identity was a particularly difficult commodity to acquire on public television. On a commercial network, a new show is launched with such a hurricane of publicity that you feel no living creature on the planet can avoid knowing about it. Public television publicity is a small mew in comparison. You could do great things on public television and know no one would know about it. If you wanted to be noticed in the competitive media clamor, you had to try a little harder from a public television base. It was easy to be ignored.

I was convinced that we had to be noticed simply to survive. Public like commercial television had shown a distressing tendency to devour its young. In its frantic search for permanance and relevance, it kept permitting programs to be born and then killed in their infancy. Many had no confidence in their own judgment: in place of judgment they formed committees to ascertain this or that audience impact. Public television showed far more ingenuity at the politics of survival in the nonprofit world, playing the welfare game at the high end of the social spectrum, than it ever demonstrated in programming. That was because its various bureaucracies, national and local, seldom found time from their own busyness simply to invite in the creative people, give them money, and let them go to work. Public television often resembled an ant hill: with nothing much happening on the outside, inside it was seething with a mysterious and pointless activity of its own.

There have been exceptions, windows of clarity and purpose, and, fortunately, one of those windows opened for us. Jay Iselin, the president of Channel 13, and Robert Kotlowitz, the head of programming, simply asked me to start a half-hour nightly news program in New York, which they hoped could develop into a national program. They told me how much money I had to work with — 1.4 million dollars for nine months — and then left me alone. Nobody told me what the program had to be or what it had to achieve. They did not ask what I intended to do and they did not come and look over our shoulders, as we began to put it together.

It was the perfect environment in which to try something out of the ordinary. It is rare, partly because most people in television do not want something out of the ordinary. They define television by what they know and they expect to see something that resembles what they know. Good television is a program that looks familiar. Public television is suffused with that thinking. Many of the people in it still ache to do programs in the formulas made successful on commercial television. So they make parodies or pale imitations. The programs that have been successful on public television are those which have broken the molds.

It was a clear article of faith with me that if public television had any justification in America it was to make programs different from or better than those plentifully available on the commercial channels. It seemed so obvious as not to be worth repeating, let alone having to argue again and again. But it is not obvious because in their hearts many public television people pine for the "real world" of commercial television.

So a distinct identity was essential for two reasons: to fulfill my understanding of the public television mandate to be different, and to be noticed by the other media.

The idea which lent us that distinctiveness — to do only one story a night — just appeared as the simplest and most obvious answer because, apart from the tactical calculations, it perfectly suited the journalistic opportunity.

Even if we had been given forty million dollars it would have been pointless to spend it as the three networks did on their nightly news programs. Whatever one thought of them, viewers already had three to choose from and by long habit they commanded vast audience loyalties. It would have been silly to produce a fourth. And, of course, we had only 1.4 million dollars. Besides, while the network programs were brilliant and successful in their way, I had thought for years that they were inadequate. They were prisoners of their own commercial success, of formulas which had evolved from two parent strains — movie newsreels and radio news bulletins. Like anything else in show business, if it "worked," they kept it in. This worked wonderfully and its chief commodity quickly became the commanding ethos for all American television, the short attention span. The dashing pace of the newsreels, with their hugely oversimplified and sententious view of the world, and the breathless urgency of the first radio news reports set the tone. Hurry, hurry, hurry. Don't waste people's time, this ethic said; America is on the move, everyone is busy; you can't expect them to stop for long; you mustn't bore them; better leave them wanting more. So hustle on, move on, keep them distracted, keep them amused, and don't dwell on anything too serious for long.

As time itself, on radio and television, became more valuable, as minutes and even half-minutes could be sold for thousands of dollars, the motive to compress and hurry grew stronger. That bred the television commercial, a highly creative art form on its own, a miniaturized documentary, like a bonsai tree, the biography of a headache sufferer beautifully shrunken to thirty seconds. What happened to the rest of television necessarily kept happening to news. Even when the networks expanded to half an hour in 1963, extreme brevity remained a virus in their bloodstream.

So the public was conditioned to expect news to come with a rush; to expect to be hit with a bewildering kaleidoscope of images and stories, confusingly interrupted by commercial messages. In the words of a Montreal newspaper, *Le Devoir*, it was *"mitraillant de bribes,"* machine-gunning with scraps. It was lively and entertaining. At climactic moments in recent history, the nightly news programs provided the visual images which moved the nation and were frozen into our memories. Each of us carries in his head an instantly retrievable picture bank, like a family album of the past, of the key moments of our time. Each has a private cataloguing system with keys like "the year I graduated from high school," and television news has largely created that picture bank. But what it has not often contributed is the linking material to make the images comprehensible. There is no contextual memory except the personal. So the nation lives from one instant visual sensation to another.

If television were to lay claim to be, as the pollsters said it should, *the* mass journalism of our time, I felt it needed to do something more. It needed to slow down, take its time and pick its way a little more coherently through the complexities of the day. It did not have to be in a rush everywhere. There should be one place where information could be absorbed at a different pace and, I hoped, presented in a manner that made it absorbable. So, we set about creating that "place."

The most rewarding part was the luxury of sitting around for a few weeks and exploring what a television program does, and why it does it, from scratch. I arrived with a lot of prejudices about things I had liked or disliked in the TV programs I had encountered in various countries. For instance — sets: so we spent a long time talking about sets.

"Why does a television program need a set? What does it do?" we would ask.

"It creates an environment."

"Well, what kind of environment should be creating?"

"Should it be literal, do we create an identifiable place, like a mock newsroom with men in shirt sleeves and the sound of teleprinters?"

"No that's too corny, too much of a cliché, and too phony."

We discussed the vogue for futuristic news sets, particularly at NBC where they joked that the News Department had been turned over to the Vice-President for Interior Decorating. That produced sets like the flight deck of the Starship *Enterprise*.

We discussed every possibility from a mock library for a thoughtful tone, to a study, to a table in a cozy bar, where I would hang out every evening and interesting people would drop in. We even considered a set of inflatable figures representing well-known personalities, like Brezhnev or Castro, who would encircle the area for our talk and be watching and listening. The ideas sound absurd, but they were necessary to let out a free range of ideas, until we finally realized that what we needed was a set which created an abstract, nonspecific environment that was hospitable and gave us an identity without being distracting. After several attempts, the designer, Robert Wightman, found inspiration in the wooden box sculptures of Louise Nevelson and designed fiberglass panels suggestive of those forms. Although some people complained that the result looked like the tomb scene from *Aida*, we thought it worked.

One of my prejudices was the convention that news program sets all faced one way, with the various anchor people all looking in one direction, like the board of directors at a share-holders' meeting, while all the cameras could shoot were shallow angles from the front. If the newspeople wanted to address each other or interview a guest, they had to turn, stiff-necked, like someone wearing a neck brace, so as not to lose eye contact with a camera while trying to look the other person in the eye at the same time. The TV directors would say: "Just cheat your look around this way, will you, so we don't lose your face?"

And you would say, "But if I cheat my look towards the camera, I can't see the person I'm talking to. He's over there."

"Well, just fake it, will you?"

Television does many silly things for its own convenience, and I insisted we were going to have a setting conducive to easy conversation. The chief commodity of our program would be the news sources coming into our studio to talk. "Talking heads," as they say contemptuously in television, were going to be our stock in trade. We would not only make no apology for talking heads, we would make them respectable again in television. To do so, we had to extract from them the maximum in information and television value at the same time.

First, we made the set "in the round." The cameras surround us and shoot from anywhere in the 360-degree circle, so that interesting visual values in a conversation can be seen: the listening, the revealing reaction.

That requires interviewers and guests to be very close to each other, so that the cameras can catch them in relation to each other without making the interviewer look like a referee in a tennis match, his face wagging back and forth. Another prejudice: I have done hundreds of interviews where, to suit the camera, two or more chairs are placed so close to each other that the knees and legs of the participants are almost touching. They prevent them from touching only by taking conscious evasive action that makes people uncomfortable. Strangers do not want to sit in that intimacy with each other. It is distracting. But television insists because it makes a good shot, and people submit to it because they think that is television, like the need to put on makeup. It is hard enough to make ordinary people relax when you bring them into the totally alien and forbidding television environment with very bright lights and swarms of technicians. Yet, putting the guests at ease should be the first consideration, since what they have to give you is the essence of your program. Television often takes a perverse delight in imposing its artificial constraints because it appears professional. The result often appears artificial too.

As part of our environment we created a desk that permits the hosts to sit very close to as many as four guests without any feeling of being too near, yet well suited to good pictures of all groupings. It is a horseshoe, with the host in the middle and the people being interviewed around the outside. The horseshoe shape is reminiscent of the editor's desk in a newspaper, and, since we are the editors of the program, that symbolism is appropriate.

These matters are very simple and obvious, but it is surprising how much resistance had to be overcome to change the conventions. The hardest mind-set to change is that production values come first and the editorial content second. In television news much of the time, the production tail wags the editorial dog. I determined that was not going to be the case on this program. The editorial material came first. Television production would serve that material and not dominate or overpower it.

Production usually predominates because it has the lion's share of money and personnel. It gobbles up the budget. I made two changes which, I believe, explain why *The MacNeil/Lehrer Report* is different.

All television programs are run by a producer. If it is a big program or a series, it has an executive producer with a number of line producers who follow his orders. In television news, the executive producer may be a trained journalist or he may come out of the show-business side of television. Depending on his background and on how strongly he leans one way or the other, production concerns will take more or less precedence over editorial concerns.

In Britain, the executive producer of a news or current affairs program is called, significantly, the editor. It is a valuable distinction because it affects everybody's attitude. We went one step further and made the people who would be on the air, the anchormen, Jim Lehrer and myself, the editors. Because the program originated in New York and was called for its first year *The Robert MacNeil Report*, I became the executive editor. When the program became a co-production with WETA in Washington and was renamed *The MacNeil/ Lehrer Report*, Jim Lehrer became the associate editor.

We have an executive producer, Al Vecchione, who shares in our editorial deliberations while taking responsibility for all the logistics, administration, and budget. We think it is a good division of labor.

But the most important change was in editorial staffing. When I arrived in New York WNET had worked out a notional budget for the program. Based on common experience, they told me, "We thought you would probably need an executive producer, so many producers, so many associate producers, so many production assistants, and two or three researchers."

To me researchers have always been the dogsbodies of the television business — entry-level jobs with no status.

Television was typically top-heavy in production people, very light in editorial. I turned the pyramid upside down. We used the limited salary money to hire six, later nine reporters; we dispensed with associate producers and hired only two producers and one production assistant. Eventually, because we were killing the two producers, who had to do a half-hour program every other day, we had to create more. But the point was made in the beginning: the reporters were the backbone of the program.

It was exhilarating, at each step, when faced with the next decision, to say to ourselves, "Well, to hell with the way it's usually done! Let's do it this way!" We could not hire established reporters; so we hired very young people, a few straight out of journalism school, with only two criteria in mind: how bright and how keen they were.

We gave them "beats" or assignments, not in the usual way to cover institutions, but to cover issues. We had a few false starts about this because our own habits died hard, but we pretty quickly saw the sense of not wasting a body by sending it to sit around the White House press room all day waiting for handouts. So we have never had a White House correspondent. We cover the issues, not the buildings.

Having set this up, we then sat down to ask ourselves, "If we're going to be bold and brave and resurrect the despised 'talking head,' how can we do it so as to show the rest of television that it is not dull, that it needn't turn viewers away — that in fact it could be the most absorbing television you could put on?" We knew television viewers were conditioned to expect pace, action, visual variety, tension, and minimal demands on their attention span. In short, the essence of what are usually called production values.

Those are qualities seldom associated with programs produced in studios. Production values to most TV producers mean a lot of lively pictures whizzing by. If the average TV producer or studio director hasn't got moving pictures on the screen in front of him, something in his soul dies. The result is that television uses any excuse to put lively pictures on. We called it "wallpaper," this obsession with moving pictures, usually edited so that the cuts come very rapidly. Left to their own devices, TV people will wallpaper anything with pictures. If Jesus Christ reappeared on Earth and began to talk to the multitudes, TV would cut away from him for livelier pictures.

Example: Several years ago NBC produced one of its three-hour spectaculars on American foreign policy. One sequence had their economics correspondent, Irving R. Levine, talking about the fate of the dollar and its impact on foreign policy. The piece lasted three minutes or so. You could see from what appeared on the screen what went through the producer's head: "We can't just have Irving talking for three minutes. We'll have to illustrate it — get some action into it."

The result was a farce. Because Levine was talking about dollars, they had to show pictures of dollars. So they took him to the Treasury Department where banknotes are printed. They put Levine next to a printing press with continuous sheets of dollar bills rushing off. The noise of the printing was incredible; you could barely hear Levine's words above the din; and the pictures of new dollar bills zipping by were so distracting that you couldn't pay much attention to what he was saying anyway.

Another example in the same program: Edwin Newman, NBC's resident essayist, critic, and wit, wrote a satirical piece on the vocabulary of international diplomacy. Like anything of Newman's, it was precisely written and dryly funny. Not good enough. The producer hired a cartoonist to illustrate what Newman was saying. The result was absurd: apart from the style gap (the cartoonist's work was considerably less sophisticated than Newman's) it was a piece of botched communication. Yet it solved the problem of having to look at and listen to one man talking for several minutes.

Such dumb tricks are a staple of U.S. television, and we were determined to avoid them. We were determined to give the talking head its value.

The human head is almost the only thing that appears on television close to life size. The TV screen is perfectly adapted to carrying the talking head. The rest of the human figure is going to be diminished in size, because it appears in your living room at less than life size. Landscapes, battle scenes, car chases, anything in medium or long shot on television — unlike the big screen in the movie theater — is going to be much smaller than life. It is reasonable to me that in a primitive part of our psyches making things appear small diminishes them, trivializes them, an observation I credit to *The New Yorker*'s subtle TV critic, Michael Arlen.

That is how primitive man dealt with his obsessions and hungers in art, by enlarging or diminishing the relative size. I have a primitive painting from the Congo, depicting a hunt. The quarry is a bird; its importance is shown in its huge size relative to the much smaller hunters. I do not believe that we are so far removed from the primitive that we do not share those childish relativities, and subconsciously consider less important that which appears smaller than life on our TV screens.

The human face is still the principal means of communication in our lives. No electronic wizardry, no satellites or computers can displace the talking head as a communicator when it comes to the things that matter to us. When someone says, "I love you . . . I hate you . . . Will you marry me? . . . I want a divorce . . . You're hired . . . You're fired . . . ," that talking head usually doesn't have a window frame over one shoulder, with cartoons whizzing by to distract you. TV does. Paradoxically, it hires the most expensive communications talent it can find to talk to America, then deliberately distracts attention from them by flashing pictures on a screen behind them. If you asked why, the answer would be, "After twenty seconds, you need something different to look at." In my view that is merely a confession of fear that unless they continuously distract with fresh visual images, the audience, like a baby, will begin to fret and switch channels. It is an assumption that is profoundly insulting to the American public.

That said, we still recognized the need to extract what production values we could from a half-hour of talking heads. The set I have described was part of the solution. It arranged the guests in positions where their conversation with us could be interestingly shot.

Next we decided to originate the program each night from two cities, in the manner of NBC's *Huntley-Brinkley Report.* That served several purposes. Journalistically, Washington is the news capital of the world. Most national stories and many foreign stories lead there and it would be the biggest pool of potential guests. Second, having another city and another anchorman/editor to switch to would create pace and variety and, curiously, a kind of dramatic effect.

The switching back and forth also helped us toward another goal we established — coherence and lucidity. We threw out the usual practice in talk shows of introducing all the guests at the beginning, giving the host an impossible struggle to keep the various strands of thought distinct.

We chose guests as a newspaper reporter or documentary maker chooses quotations — introducing them as the editorial logic required. When we had extracted from each guest the points we knew he wanted to make, we moved on to the next. The advantage of two interviewers alternately asking questions is that one can listen and think while the other is on. He can adjust his questions to the next guest by the context of what has gone before. When it works well, I believe it makes the progression of ideas much easier to follow.

There have been some refinements of this procedure, but the fundamentals were all in place when we went on the air for the first time in October 1975. I am surprised now to remember how confident we were that it would work, when it went against the grain of so much television practice, and there were so many things that could have gone wrong.

I was not certain that we would be able to sustain one story for half an hour every night. Some nights we might have to do two or more. In fact we were never forced to do so. Once or twice we have done it because two such compelling stories presented themselves that we felt the audience would have felt it strange if we did not touch on both. It was a mistake. The audience quite understands our one-story rationale. The audience has understood our experiment far better than the professionals in television. By listening to the audience, we are gradually coming to understand what we have created.

We began by thinking of ourselves as a supplement, a complement to commercial television. At the beginning a few of our ads said tentatively, "Watch Walter Cronkite, then watch us . . . watch John Chancellor, then watch us," hoping to lead some of their viewers into the habit of switching to us at 7:30. That worked; early surveys showed that about one-third of our regular audience came to us fresh from one of the network evening news programs. We never presumed to think of ourselves as anything but the dessert, never the main meal. More recently, the growth of our audience nationally and the feedback we get has made us bolder in claiming to be an alternative to the nightly news. I think there are several reasons.

One was explained to me by David Halberstam, the writer, only a few months after we began, and I have seen the truth of it grow. He came into my office and said he really liked our program.

I said, "That's nice, but it isn't really meant for people like you. You don't need it."

But Halberstam said, "You're wrong. I'm not in daily

journalism anymore. I'm writing my books and they take four to five years each."

Angola was the big running story at the time and he went on: "I don't need the *New York Times* or anyone else to give me every day a sentence of something new, or contrivedly new, about Angola, with the *Times* computer printout of background tacked on. All I need is for someone, anyone, every few weeks to tell me what I need to know about Angola and then leave me alone until something important has changed and I need to know again." Since then we have discovered an ever-growing number of people like Halberstam, who want to take their news at a different pace.

Besides that, we have also, quite accidentally, tapped into the widespread disenchantment with other features of commercial news. We are extravagantly praised, sometimes with an air of astonishment, for being fair, because people perceive the commercial TV news as unfair, as giving only one side. Our stock in trade is giving a number of views of an issue simultaneously. It is perceived that we do not quote people out of context, as many Americans believe all the news media do: we cannot, because our interviews are live and unedited; our guests create their own context. We are praised for our civility of manner by viewers who dislike the bullying style of interviewing fashionable today. Our viewers congratulate us for the quality of our questioning, because they witness a lot of unprepared and uninformed interviewing elsewhere.

Some of this praise is deserved: we did deliberately set out to do things differently. Some of it is an overreaction to the imagined sins of our commercial colleagues. But it took me nearly six years to stumble on the explanation of why *The MacNeil/Lehrer Report* satisfies a growing number of people.

Without intending to, we have created a new form in journalism, not just in television but for print as well. In basic mechanics, we have resurrected the oldest forms. We are structured like a small newspaper. Our reporters find stories and tap the best sources they can to give them facts and interpretation. That is common to journalism anywhere. The more exhaustive and searching it is, the better the product. Often, however, today's journalism is based on the revelations of one source, and it takes other views several news cycles to catch up.

Where our product differs from the traditional form is in what happens when our reporters bring us the story as they see it, reported and backgrounded, and with three or four of the best sources prepared to come and talk. We complete the reporting "live" on the air, with the viewer able to watch. What is skipped is the last phase of the conventional journalism, where the reporter himself sits down at the typewriter and produces a synthesis of all he has picked up, slipping in quotes and facts from various sources as he considers them relevant. In our form, the viewer at home makes the synthesis himself. What we have done is remove one of the filters between the facts and the consumer. Of course we retain many other journalistic filters: our choice of what stories to air; what angle of each story we pursue; what facts our reporters think fit to include; what sources they select; and finally what questions we think it relevant to ask them. By eliminating the last filter, the reporter's own synthesis, however, we have created a slightly different form. It is enhanced by the simultaneity of different views, heard in the same time frame. It is further enhanced because we allow enough time to let these opinions develop. What you have in the end product doesn't have to be labeled fact, opinion, analysis, interpretation — it is all of those together. It is the nearest thing to making each member of the viewing public a reporter himself, able to seek out facts from the sources who know them and to discover what they mean.

All that said, we recognize that *The MacNeil/Lehrer Report* is still a modest exercise, a small corner of the nation's journalism. It was never intended to be anything but that. We have the added satisfaction of seeing it imitated on commercial television. But, it was never intended by us to be anything more than a foot in the door, a demonstration of one different way of using the marvelous instrument of television as a medium for journalism.

It is very satisfying to me professionally to see this simple exercise, put together quite unpretentiously, develop into a national institution. It is one thing to become well known, win awards, and be praised simply because your face is on television. In fact, it is a little embarrassing. To achieve the same thing, quite easily, by putting into practice a lot of ideas you believe to be right is not embarrassing at all. It is gratifying not to have anything to be ashamed of when you go home at night.

Much of the easiness is due to my partnership and friendship with Lehrer. People tell us it is unique in the business and I suppose it is. Although our backgrounds are very different, our taste and judgments coincide remarkably. We trust each other; one of us is not trying to upstage or outshine the other, and we recognize that our different styles and habits of mind are complementary.

I was at a party a few years ago and a woman darted into the conversational circle, pointed at me, and exclaimed dramatically: "Lehrer is a laser and you are a catalyst!" I think she was right. Lehrer is the single most intelligent person I have ever worked with. His mind is like a laser. It penetrates rapidly to what is important in anything — staff problems, internal politics, human relations, as well as news stories. It is a very American mind, totally free of cant and pretension. It is a matchless asset to have in a colleague.

Our entire team takes its tone from the relationship Jim and I have and share with Al Vecchione, Charlayne Hunter-Gault, and the rest of the staff. It has created such a congenial working atmosphere that we have turned down a number of attractive job offers in commercial television. So far, the pleasure of working together on what we want to do outweighs the higher salaries we have been offered outside. Besides, I learned a valuable lesson in leaving NBC in 1967 for one-third as much money at the BBC. Freedom from frustration and tension is worth a lot of money.

The only frustration in the *MacNeil/Lehrer Report* is that it has forced me to grow up and become responsible for a lot of people, instead of running around the world having adventures. I miss that. I miss the irresponsibility of traveling. I miss the hundreds of casual opportunities I had in the past to drop in on places tourists would drool over. Now I get such opportunities less frequently and have to refuse many because the program requires me to be in New York, five nights a week, for much of the year.

There have been exceptions.

As part of our routine coverage of foreign affairs, we had, by 1977, begun to notice the revolutionary stirrings in Iran. We interviewed the shah in Williamsburg on his last official visit to the United States and found him a stiff, withdrawn little man, who blandly maintained that all who opposed him were Marxists:

SHAH: . . . if you go and inquire about the nature of those who demonstrate against [me] you would find that they are mostly Marxists. . . .

LEHRER: . . . are there 100,000 political prisoners now in Iranian jails, as they charge?

SHAH: There are 2,200.

LEHRER: What are their crimes? What are these 2,200?

SHAH: Mostly terrorists; and all of them Marxists.

As the year 1978 progressed, we developed very good contacts with Iranians who were close to the Ayatollah Khomeini, who was still living in exile in France. While the U.S. government was putting all its confidence in the shah, these people were appearing on our program predicting, with total assurance, that the shah would soon be overthrown by the followers of the Imam. One of them was Ebrahim Yazdi, who later became foreign minister.

Another was his son-in-law, Shariar Rouhani, a Ph.D. candidate at Yale. After one program Rouhani asked Lehrer what the American people would feel about the government they would set up after the shah.

Lehrer said, "Well, if you go lining people against the wall and shooting them, the American people aren't going to approve of that."

Rouhani said: "Mr. Lehrer, eight members of my family were arrested by the shah's secret police, Savak. All of them had their fingernails pulled out. We are going to find the people who did that."

Late in November, through these contacts, we were offered the first extended television interview with the ayatollah. We never have enough money to do that sort of program casually. But this was a must and we took a small team to France. In the end we were able to make two programs out of the trip, because it coincided with Richard Nixon's appearance at the Oxford Union. I went first to London and introduced an edited version of Nixon, which we sent back to New York by satellite. The next morning I flew to Paris and drove twenty miles south to the village of Ponchartrain to join our group that had been preparing the Khomeini interview. The modest villa the ayatollah was using faced the road, the only street in the village. It was guarded by squads of heavily armed French police, because they expected the shah's assassination squads.

It is probably the most unusual interview I have ever done. I was shown through a throng of assistants and followers, most of them in Iranian robes, incongruous in the pale winter sunshine of France, into the very small living room of the villa. It had rather busy flowered wallpaper and a large whitewashed fireplace. Otherwise the room was totally bare of decoration or furniture except for the floor which was covered with overlapping Persian carpets. Each doorway of the room was blocked by a television camera, the only angles the director could manage.

In the Moslem custom we took off our shoes. For the interview, I sat cross-legged in my socks. After we had tested the microphones and settled the camera shots, the ayatollah was brought in, wearing dark robes and the black turban worn by those who claim direct descent from Mohammed. Immediately, I felt myself in the presence of an extraordinary personality. He settled himself cross-legged on a large cushion and looked at me as Dr. Yazdi, the interpreter, relayed my instructions. Khomeini's brown eyes and black brows seemed more youthful than the rest of his sallow face, framed in the white beard. He exuded total composure, total confidence, as though all of him, his organs, nervous system, bloodstream, were completely at rest, except for those few parts needed for that amount of concentration. He exhibited neither curiosity nor indifference. He looked at me as though Yazdi were indicating a set of steps the ayatollah would have to negotiate. He made no small talk and he invited none. He received information and asked no questions. I thought him devoid of humor until, during the interview, an ironic curl appeared around his lips. I was told afterwards by my colleagues in the recording truck that his followers, crowding around to listen, laughed delightedly at the mordant turns of phrase he employed, particularly when describing his disgust with the United States.

In a sense, the interview was very easy. I asked all the questions I wanted and he answered directly. When I pursued a point, he elaborated.

What I drew from it was the sense of a man who was not improvising. He had the clarity and simplicity of a scholar who has done his thinking.

MACNEIL: What have the Americans done to you that you object to?

KHOMEINI: The American government, they have committed the biggest crime by imposing on our people the Pahlevi dynasty. Through this support they have plundered our natural resources and instead, in return, they have given us things that do not help our people in any way. They have dominated our army in order to support their cause, to stand against our people. They have made bases in our country which are contrary to our independence. With this shah we don't have any life in our country and this is the American government who supports the shah.

KHOMEINI: We are the supporters of any oppressed people. The Palestinians are oppressed by the Israelis, and Israel is the oppressor, so we are sympathetic with the Palestinians.

MACNEIL: If the shah were overthrown and the kind of government you want came to power in Iran, how would Iran's relations with Israel change?

KHOMEINI: We will cut all relations with Israel; Israel is a transgressor and is our enemy.

MACNEIL: Does that mean Israel would no longer receive oil from Iran?

KHOMEINI: No. It will not receive the oil.

His moral and political absolutism was dismaying to a Western mind. But he was clearly not some stage-swami, invented to utter frightening imprecations, which was about the way the Carter administration was treating him.

MACNEIL: Has anyone in the American government or representing the American government been in touch with you recently?

KHOMEINI: Not at all.

MACNEIL: Is the American government ignoring you?

KHOMEINI: I don't know.

I came away with a much stronger impression that his forces would win; the uncertain shah could not withstand the whirlwind of that conviction, multiplied millions of times by the ayatollah's followers — unarmed or not. This was fervor coupled to intellectual certainty of a kind the West had not known collectively since the Crusades. Then, ironically, the Christian world thought the Moslems the infidels the ayatollah now found us. The West had known isolated pockets of such absolutism in more recent times; but to our flexible minds it was a disturbing retreat to the Middle Ages.

On two grounds the ayatollah stimulated a certain sympathy in me: if their claims about the shah's atrocities were even partly true; and their intense desire to protect their culture from the decadence of ours.

I had spent almost five months in the winter of 1974–75 studying the Moslem mind in Pakistan and among Pakistani immigrants in Britain. The first effort at understanding involved trying to distinguish what the Koran requires of Moslems as their faith, from the customs and style of life that go with it. The role of women is a good example. The Koran teaches that men and women are equal partners in life, that neither is a shadow of the other. Yet in Moslem countries, the role of women remains where it has always been, a kind of purdah or seclusion. The modesty of women before strangers is as fiercely imposed as it was in the Old Testatment.

So interwoven are religion and the social codes that immodest behavior by a woman, like wearing revealing Western clothes, seems a violation of her faith, an affront to Islam. The more Western values penetrate the big cities of the Moslem world, the more the fundamentalists see their religion threatened by a culture which encourages, not only promiscuity, but materialism, greed, acquisitiveness, the erosion of family life. To a mind like the ayatollah's the clock could still be stopped. The shah could be overthrown; America, the Great Satan, could be sent packing with all her corrupting ways; and innocence restored. In one sense it was a sweet vision, like a glimpse into the cloistered garden of a medieval monastery. It was amazing that this one man, sitting with me, had the power to make time stop for sixty million people.

A small footnote to that interview became significant later. Our translator was the same Ebrahim Yazdi who had been on our program several times in the United States. He had arranged the interview. But, in Paris, our reporter, Rob Hershman, kept getting calls from a man called Sadegh Ghotbzadeh, who insisted that he should do the interpreting. He was very persistent but it made every sense to us to stick with Yazdi, who was our contact and whose English was perfectly adequate.

After the revolution, both Yazdi and Ghotbzadeh returned to Iran with the triumphant ayatollah. Yazdi became foreign minister in the first government and Ghotbzadeh the director of Iranian television.

We continued to follow the Iranian story closely but were as stunned as everyone else when Iranian students seized the American embassy on November 4, 1979, and took its staff as hostages. In groping for ways to keep abreast of the story and remain competitive with the vivid picture coverage mounted by commercial television, I suggested, just for the hell of it, that we ask for an interview with the ayatollah. Nobody had spoken to him. No emissaries from President Carter could get through. The Imam stayed inscrutably in the holy city of Qom, while in his name radical students held up the world's most powerful nation to ridicule, demanding an impossible ransom, the return of the ailing shah, still under treatment in a hospital in New York. Perhaps because we had been the first to interview him at length, he might regard us as a suitable vehicle to carry his intentions or demands or whatever to Washington. Perhaps. In those circumstances you try all the long shots, then forget them and get on with the things that are practicable.

Incredibly, a few days later they said yes. Word came back from the Foreign Ministry in Teheran, through the embassy in Washington, that we could have an exclusive interview with the ayatollah. We practically fell off our chairs. The attention of the entire world was focused on this man. An exclusive interview now was the scoop of a lifetime. It would pay off enormously in publicity and prestige for the program. But how could we do it? Public television had no camera crews in Teheran like the commercial networks. It was well beyond anything we could spend to send a crew from New York. However, the chronic poverty of public television had accustomed us to humbling expedients. The only way we could tape our exclusive interview would be to ask the help of one of the commercial networks and offer them first access to the interview after we had run it. ABC had long been the most cooperative network and they quickly made a deal. We could use an ABC crew and ABC facilities to feed the interview out of Teheran by satellite.

Word of my trip quickly reached the special Iran crisis task force at the State Department. The U.S. government had tried every possible means to communicate with the ayatollah without success. Henry Precht, the official in charge of the task force, asked me if I would take a message to the ayatollah. I thought about it overnight. It was tempting to think of playing what might have been an historic role. But, with my colleagues I concluded it was too compromising to my journalistic independence. Instead, I suggested to Precht that he tell me what questions the U.S. government urgently wanted to have the ayatollah answer, which is the kind of background information reporters frequently seek and then decide for themselves what to use. He did and there were none that I would have had any trouble in asking Khomeini.

The Iranian consulate in New York, closed since the beginning of the crisis, was specially opened to put visas in our passports and three of us, producer Jo Franklin, field producer Mike Saltz, and I, set off for Teheran via London. On the flight, I began to have uneasy feelings. On the ground in Teheran, ABC would be bound to want to trade the use of their crew for shared access to the ayatollah. I had known the ABC correspondent, Peter Jennings, for years. He was very competent and competitive. I began to imagine scenarios of how to fend him off to keep our interview exclusive.

After some eighteen hours traveling we got to Teheran in the early evening. The omens were not good. There was no one from the Foreign Ministry to meet us at the airport as promised. No helicopter to Qom. Zealous guards of the Revolutionary Committees made me open my luggage and seized the scotch I had bought at London airport, knowing that the hotel in Teheran would be dry.

"Alcohol is forbidden in Islam," they said, smugly.

"But I am not Islamic," I said. "I drink alcohol."

"Here is Islam," the young guard said, pointing at the floor. "No alcohol."

I argued until I saw it was pointless and watched sadly as they opened the bottle and emptied it into a large oil drum in the corner of the customs area.

The Intercontintental Hotel was swarming with newsmen of all nations, and many seemed to have heard that we had an interview with the ayatollah. They wanted to know where, when, with whom it had been arranged, and so on. Then a producer from CBS told me that Mike Wallace was on his way and that he had an interview lined up too. My uneasiness mounted.

There were no messages from the Foreign Ministry so we telephoned immediately. They were sorry they had not met us and provided the helicopter to fly to Qom as arranged. Never mind, the interview was still on. It would probably take place on Saturday. It was now Wednesday night. Friday was out because of the Moslem sabbath. For our program schedule, it had to be Thursday, or the following Monday.

The phone calls went on. Our Foreign Ministry contacts grew more and more evasive. By Friday morning they were talking about several interviews. We protested. We had come all this way because we had been offered an exclusive. The officials were exceedingly polite and apologetic but "other arrangements" had been made. We waited all day in my hotel room for the calls. Through the open window we could hear the rhythmic chanting of the Iranian mobs outside the U.S. embassy. We stayed put for fear of missing a phone call and an immediate summons to Qom.

Late Thursday evening, still in our hotel room, I was asked to submit questions, so I dictated a long list to a lady at the Foreign Ministry.

On Friday morning we were told that nothing would happen until Saturday but to stand by the telephone for instructions. Finally, late on Friday evening, the Foreign Ministry told us there would be interviews with the ayatollah in Qom on Sunday morning, by CBS, ABC, NBC, and ourselves. It did no good to protest. Our exclusive had been spiked.

I lay awake for hours wondering what to do. Finally it seemed the only sensible thing was to refuse to join the parade. If Mike Wallace interviewed the ayatollah on Sunday morning it would be on *60 Minutes* that night. *60 Minutes* had the largest audience of any television program in the United States. ABC and NBC would mount news specials and command the rest of the audience. Even if PBS geared up to put on a special — a very creaky procedure — who would know and who would watch it? Equally pointless would be to have a me-too interview with the ayatollah and run it twenty-four hours after the three others on *The MacNeil/ Lehrer Report* Monday. By not doing the interview in such uncompetitive circumstances we would save our budget all the satellite costs. To refuse to join the pack seemed the right course. But in the middle of the night, after very little sleep, I couldn't be sure I was making a rational decision or refusing out of pique. It went against the reporter's grain to walk away from any interview like that, especially when it had been widely publicized at home. Yet clearly they were going to be assembly-line interviews. There would be no chance for subtlety.

By then it was clear what had happened. Our contacts in the Foreign Ministry had acted in good faith. But the commercial networks quickly went their own route. Their contact in Teheran was Sadegh Ghotbzadeh, director of Iranian television. He was also close to the ayatollah and obviously he had stepped in to argue the case for the commercial networks. Oh, yes! Ghotbzadeh, the gentleman we had spurned a year earlier in Paris. Our man, Foreign Minister Yazdi, was now in disgrace — fired.

Early Saturday morning we decided on one last ploy. We packed all our gear, checked out of the hotel, and got a taxi to the airport. From there we phoned the Foreign Ministry to say we were leaving. We had been asked there for an exclusive interview and had found ourselves instead at the end of a parade of networks. It was no good.

We had already gone through customs and passport control when we were paged over the loudspeaker. Our Foreign Ministry official, with profuse apologies, begged us to come back into the city; arrangements would be made today. A helicopter would take us to Qom. We would have our interview well ahead of the others. We were dubious but we had to take the gamble. Mike Saltz, who knows all about airline schedules, satellite times, and studio logistics, calculated that if we went to Qom, completed the interview, got back to Teheran airport by 3 P.M., we could fly to Rome and transmit from there by satellite. If alerted, PBS could run it as a special Saturday night and still beat the others by a day. With our competitive spirit revived we went back through passport and customs control (my luggage sporting a growing collection of Persian writing in thick felt-tip pen) and took another of the suicidally driven Teheran taxis to the Intercontinental. We checked in again and resumed waiting by the phone.

At noon, they phoned back. Nothing could be done today. Only on Sunday. All interviews would happen on Sunday. We said, "No thank you."

There was nothing more to be done, so we went out to a

quiet part of Teheran and ate a Persian meal, sitting on large cushions around a low table. We were the only customers in the restaurant.

We went back to the airport. With my Canadian passport, I went through the control easily enough, but our producer, Jo Franklin, with an American passport, was given a hard time by the Revolutionary Guards .After the regular customs inspectors had passed them, the young Guards reopened her luggage and inspected everything minutely. They found telex messages that had passed between New York and our hotel and got quite excited. They made an important show of running them the entire length of the airport to consult some higher authority. I wandered back to protest that this was pointless. The Revolutionary Guard in charge was a supercilious fellow of about twenty, cradling a rifle in his arms as he sat on the customs table swinging his legs.

I said to him: "Do you realize when all of this is over, you are going to need to be friendly again with the United States? Isn't this a bit silly, what you're doing?"

The young man looked at me and cocked his chin up. "Are you afraid of me?" he asked. And his scornful manner suddenly made me understand the extraordinary piece of surreal theater that was happening in Teheran. The pleasure this young student was experiencing in discomfiting us was a microcosm of the joy that millions of Iranians were feeling at having the great United States of America in their power. And I could imagine millions of others around the world, enjoying their own vicarious pleasure at the spectacle. Rendering the giant impotent was a powerful human myth and here it was being played out day after day on the world's television screens. It was the theater of frustration given vent; of South against North; undeveloped against developed; the ragged masses of the world against the affluent West. No matter that it violated centuries-old traditions of diplomatic immunity; it had in their eyes revolutionary legitimacy. It was legitimized by the Imam himself. It legitimized the supercilious young man who was sneering at me in Teheran airport.

A reporter's life is full of frustrations. You miss as many stories as you get, which is why there are so many "almost" episodes in this book. No episode has ever been quite as frustrating as this and nothing as difficult as the decision to refuse to do a fourth interview with the ayatollah. It was one of those decisions that you are sure is right but which your unconscious keeps re-presenting for confirmation, so that you find yourself endlessly replaying the argument, like a needle stuck on a record.

We stayed Saturday night in Rome. Early Sunday morning Saltz and I went for a long walk through the deserted streets until it was time to leave for our plane to New York. We drank in sights of that great old city slowly awakening on a mild winter morning: waiters putting out café chairs in the Piazza Navona, the watery winter sunlight rising over the Colosseum; the smell of fresh coffee and newly baked rolls, the startled immobility of the figures in the dry fountains waiting for the play of water to make them live again; the Romans emerging to enjoy their day off. The sights revived our spirits and restored some perspective.

I got back to New York in time to see *60 Minutes* and Mike Wallace's interview with the ayatollah. The relative positions of their bodies made Wallace look like suppliant, while the Imam uttered hollow diatribes against the United States. There was no useful communication. I felt better about the decision not to take part. I found myself being praised for a motive I did not have: refusing to take part in a propaganda exercise.

What the incident revealed to us once again was the overwhelming power of the commercial networks: power of resources and personnel to staff big stories like Iran. ABC, NBC, and CBS each had a presence in Teheran alone roughly equal to the entire staff of *The MacNeil/Lehrer Report*. To cover the hostage story, each network was probably spending in one week the equivalent of our entire year's budget. And every evening each network probably reached twenty-five to thirty million people, about ten times what our nightly audience was then.

Those differences are staggering when you stand on our side of the fence. They explain why in the broadcasting industry and in the press which covers it, commercial television is the "real world" and public television something else. There is what science fiction might call a time warp between that world and ours. In some modes we simply do not exist.

In 1978, ABC News asked me to become one of the anchormen on their nightly news. We discussed it for about two months before I decided to stay with public television. While we were talking, there were newspaper stories saying I was going to replace Barbara Walters. *People* magazine called me and said they wanted to come out to the house and do a profile of a man and his family, as they supposed, torn by indecision about the prospect of becoming rich and famous.

"Do you *do* anything?" the reporter asked.

"What do you mean?"

"I mean do you jog, or anything?" Jogging was very big with *People* that year.

I suggested that we wait until a decision was made and then consider a story. When it was announced that I had chosen to stay at PBS, *People* decided that it was not a story.

So did the Associated Press: an AP reporter called and said "I hear you've reached a decision." I said that ABC was preparing a statement and I would talk when it was out. The reporter said, "Well, if the decision is not to go to ABC, don't bother to call." In other words, I was not entering the "real world" of mass appeal that had whetted their appetite.

With all that reinforcement, the networks have had little motive to look beyond the staggering reality expressed by their numbers: viewers, ratings, budgets, revenues, profits. It reminds me of Detroit. For years, Detroit told Americans, in effect: "That big shiny thing out there that weighs two tons, with all the fins and grilles and chrome, is an automobile, America." In the American consumer consciousness, automobile was defined by Detroit; that was what Americans craved and worked for. Detroit has recently discovered that there is another kind of automobile which is less of an affront to common sense; which brings into a more rational equation the relative importance of transportation, consumption of fuel and raw materials, speed, safety, and yearnings for status.

The new reality in automobiles puts greater value on quality of workmanship, on reliability and durability. Detroit had fallen into the facile assumption that you could sell Americans any old rubbish as long as it was dressed up in "new" styling and marketed by creating images and fantasy. As Ralph Nader, spiraling oil prices, and foreign competition forced Detroit to recognize, they had also been denying the American public many advances in automobile technology widely used overseas, such as disc brakes, radial tires, and front-wheel drive.

Automobiles and television are important manifestations of modern culture, pervasive in their influence economically and culturally. They have altered many aspects of the society. Cars and TV programs say a lot about the nations which produce them. The cars and TV produced here say a lot about America. Until recently they have said that this is a society which puts marketing skills first and quality of product second. They said that this is a people whose dominating commercial ethic is "whatever will sell."

The shock of a changed commercial environment is modifying that ethic in Detroit; I see it also being modified on Sixth Avenue in New York, the headquarters of network television. Quality is going to acquire greater value as the new video technology erodes the networks' comfortable monopoly and splinters their captive mass market.

The search for quality will demand programs conceived as having some artistic or journalistic integrity of their own, and not merely as vehicles for commercials. Public broadcasting can claim some credit for pointing the way to that new reality.

I think we can claim the same in the field of television journalism; and as adventures in journalism go, that ain't bad.

EIGHTEEN

The Queen at
the White House

IN JULY 1976, in a nice Bicentennial gesture, Queen Elizabeth II visited the colonies wrested from her great-great-great-great-grandfather two centuries earlier. There was a state dinner at the White House. Public television secured rights to cover it and I was asked to host the program, a task that posed no professional terrors for me.

A few weeks before, I had had a medical checkup and the doctor had found that I had a double hernia which needed to be repaired by surgery. Within a few days I was in New York Hospital and emerged a week later, creeping and half bent over, feeling like a trussed turkey. By July 6, the day before the White House gala, I was walking straight again but still painfully, and when I sat down I couldn't cross my legs.

Since the broadcast was to last the entire evening, it required very thorough planning, and since whole chunks of the festivities were barred to the cameras (you cannot take pictures of Her Majesty doing anything as vulgar as actually eating), some ingenuity was needed to hold the viewers' attention. The executive producer, Martin Clancy, supplied that. He had cameras and commentators everywhere the White House would let him put them. Julia Child, public television's French Chef, did pre-taped segments in the White House kitchens, going through the menu with the chef. I recorded an interview with Betty Ford and a long history of the royal family. Jean Marsh, the star of *Upstairs, Downstairs*, was to be on the South Lawn to talk about the guests in the receiving line, and Frank Gillard, a veteran of many BBC royal broadcasts, was to join her after describing the arrival at the North Portico. The whole thing sounded a little ambitious, but plausible.

The White House had its own jitters, as though it feared the queen might proclaim the Revolution null and void and take the thirteen colonies back if she didn't like the arrangements. So they were not as helpful as they might have been. They wouldn't permit cameras on the grounds until the day itself, and we weren't able to rehearse with the cameras until midafternoon.

And that is when things began to go wrong.

In any television program with long ad lib or unscripted sequences you must be anchored firmly in those parts for which you can write script and plot camera moves. You need these islands of certainty: with nearly four hours of very unpredictable programming stretching ahead of us, we needed them more than usual.

The script called for a technically elaborate opening: I was to say "Good evening" at the top of the curved stairs on the South Portico, to continue talking as I walked down the stairs, point out where the receiving line would be, and, still talking, walk into the large tent and describe the gorgeous setting for the dinner. This involved several fixed cameras and one portable minicam following me into the tent. It also involved my wearing both a wireless mike and a wireless earpiece through which I could hear the program and the director's instructions. They are notoriously temperamental pieces of equipment, since each involves a little radio transmitter and receiver, liable to interference from anything from air traffic controllers to pacemakers. It is wise to check them out very thoroughly in each position where you want to use them to make sure there is no interference.

As we got ready for the three o'clock rehearsal, I said to the soundman, "Shouldn't we try out the wireless mike?"

He said: "What wireless mike?"

I began to intuit what the evening held for all of us.

"There is supposed to be a wireless mike and a wireless IFB for the opening."

"I'll have to check."

Half an hour later, he told me that the wireless mike and IFB were in Seattle. Someone had neglected to put them on a plane.

The director appeared.

"Never mind. We'll string a mike cable down here."

"To walk down the staircase?" I asked.

"Perhaps we better cut the staircase bit," he said.

"What about the walk into the tent and all around the tables?"

In circumstances like that TV directors tend to sound like Bob Newhart keeping calm.

"We'll drop that, too," he said. "We'll open right here and you can talk to camera two."

"Where's camera two?"

"It's going to be right here," the director said.

"No camera two," one of the cameramen said.

"What do you mean, no camera two?" the director said. "Camera two goes right there." He pointed to an empty tripod on the South Lawn.

"They didn't bring a head that fits this tripod," the cameraman said.

"Jesus Christ," the producer said: "Okay. You'll do it to camera three, right over there."

At the point he was called away to deal with another problem and we never got to rehearse the much-revised opening. That was all right. The on-camera piece was much shorter, and I could read the rest, voice-over, while they punched up appropriate pictures. It sounded okay.

We then went inside the White House, to see the small room they had given us in the East Wing as our commentary position for the rest of the evening. There was a quick way from the South Lawn to this room and I wanted to be sure I made it in the shortest time. I needed to be in position, with microphone and earpiece fixed and tested, five minutes after finishing my opening on the South Lawn. And because of the hernia, I couldn't run. But the Secret Service for their own reasons wouldn't let us use the shortcut, through Jackie Kennedy's garden. We had to go a roundabout way which added about two minutes to the trip and a lot to my anxiety.

We all went back to the Hay-Adams Hotel just across Lafayette Park to change and be back for a dress rehearsal. As we left it began to rain — on the tent, on the South Lawn, and on the cameras. The rain became the alibi.

Since Jean Marsh and Julia Child were in long evening dresses and Frank Gillard and I in rented white ties, we were driven back to the White House.

I don't know why it is, but the more often I go there, the longer it takes each time to clear me through the gate. For several years I had a White House press pass, and I have been checked through the Secret Service computers scores of times, but they always start from scratch. This time it took half an hour, while I wondered how many villains trying to assassinate the president would dress up in white tie and pose as a television anchorman to fool the security system. In any case, the security system has that one covered.

The dress rehearsal fell apart. The rain had produced chaos. Cables were wet. Electrical circuits were haywire. Heavy studio cameras on portable tripod legs were sinking into the mushy lawn.

It was now thirty minutes before the live broadcast and more things were coming unstuck by the minute. I had just taken my position for the opening and was standing fully wired up with an earpiece and a microphone, when the director said in my ear, "Robin, camera three is out. We're going to have to do the opening inside. Get yourself in there as fast as possible."

I got unwired and headed for the shortcut, thinking the urgency would persuade the Secret Service to relent. It didn't. With my White House escort, it was back through the long way. With fifteen minutes to air, I got into the chair in the commentary room, was fitted up with a microphone and earpiece, and began to collect my thoughts.

About a minute before we went on the air, I heard Frank

Gillard, waiting by the North Portico to describe the arrival, saying desperately into his microphone, "I can't hear a thing. I don't know if my mike is working. Are they hearing me?"

The fatal moment came and the broadcast began. After the opening titles I did my introduction and was told to throw it to Frank because the queen was arriving. In my monitor I saw the big car drive up, but from Frank what went on the air was, "I don't know if we're on the air. Are we on the air? Is this mike working?" Eventually, he got a signal because he began describing the scene. The moment he began talking, the queen, Prince Philip, and the Fords disappeared upstairs to the family quarters to have a drink in private. We were four minutes into the program with nothing to show.

The director tried to show the scene on the South Lawn where hundreds of guests were beginning to arrive for the receiving line. But there was trouble with the pictures and Jean Marsh could not hear her instructions because she didn't have an earpiece. Nor had they given her a monitor to see what shots were actually on the air, so what she talked about did not relate to the pictures viewers were seeing.

To get themselves out of what was turning into a classic shambles, the director and producer decided to run some of the pre-taped material, to give them a little time to breathe and regroup.

That filled in half an hour and it came back to me just as the official party were supposed to come out on the balcony of the South Portico overlooking the Washington Monument, descend the curved stairs, and start receiving the guests. But they didn't appear. I talked some more and they still didn't appear. So we switched back to the South Lawn where Jean Marsh, now plugged in, had been joined by Frank Gillard, who said he had been told that the receiving line had been canceled because of the weather. Consternation in the control room because the receiving line was one of the only activities they could televise. In desperation they came back to me and I filled for another fifteen minutes or so, saying anything I knew about the British royal family, what the British people thought of them, their institutional role, what they cost a year, what occasional calls there were to get rid of them — all the trivia about royalty I had amassed during sixteen years as a journalist in Britain.

They got Julia Child in to sit with me and that helped enormously, because she is a wonderfully enthusiastic talker — about anything.

Finally, the president and the queen did appear. Frank Gillard, who had a good view of them, gave a description worthy of the BBC outside Buckingham Palace. Unfortunately the view he had from the South Lawn was not shared by the only camera working on the wet grass. Just as Frank intoned: "There is a scene for history to remember, what a glorious picture!" the only picture the director could shoot was of a tree branch and leaves almost filling the screen, with a few faint yellow spots of the queen's dress showing through.

They descended and the receiving line began. It was a good chance to watch the queen close up, smiling and shaking hands, but for the television commentator it was fraught with danger. The first TV remote I ever broadcast was for the CBC in 1954. I managed to wrongly identify every person in an official group because I didn't know them myself and was being handed a file card with a name as each face came into view — the wrong file card.

I had argued strenuously for a foolproof spotting system this time and I was told it had been arranged, but it disintegrated too. We had no list of guests in the order of their being presented.

From outside, Jean Marsh talked on valiantly, identifying those whom she knew, like movie stars, but with no monitor she was talking about people the viewers at home weren't seeing. I had a monitor but recognized only one-tenth of the people, missing in the confusion such obvious faces as Julie Harris and Dorothy Hamill. I even failed to notice David Brinkley, who had been a colleague for years.

Elvira Ruby, an associate producer, who knew everyone in Washington, tried to improvise a spotting system by lying on the floor just off camera, looking at the monitor, and whispering names to me. But I couldn't hear her and she couldn't talk louder or the viewers would have heard. As it was, the sound connections were so crude that across the nation viewers clearly heard the director's instructions that only we were supposed to hear through our earpieces.

That ordeal ended and they went in to dinner. Our viewers then saw the best part of the program, Julia Child's delightful pre-taped pieces on the dishes the royal guests were eating. She had arranged that portions of the same food they were gorging "upstairs" would be served to us "downstairs" and appropriately Jean Marsh joined us. But the promised food never came and Julia Child began to sound a little testy. The four of us talked about anything we could think of vaguely relevant to the royal family, and Jean Marsh bubbled on, as though she were Rose, the maid in *Upstairs, Downstairs*, who had just caught a glimpse of Queen Victoria.

Eventually, the royal party came out of the tent, and the cameras caught them going to the East Room for the official entertainment. Bob Hope told some off-color jokes, at which the queen was not amused, or if she was, kept it primly to herself. The Captain and Tennille sang even more off-color songs, including "Muskrat Love."

To fill, as the queen left the East Room before the dancing began, we all said what we thought of the entertainment. Julia Child exploded: "I think it was terrible, disgraceful, with all the talented people there are in this country to have to show them that — I was expecting a more dignified evening." I'll bet very few viewers have heard anything as forthright as that on national television.

The dreadful evening finally ended when President Ford and the queen led the dancing. We weren't the only ones goofing things up. Just as the president led the queen to the center of the dance floor, the Marine Band swung into "The Lady Is a Tramp."

It was over. The only thing that gave us any satisfaction is that we had kept going, through several moments when it seemed I was going to have to say to the audience: "I'm sorry but too many things have broken down and we're going to have to stop."

Amazingly, public television stations got very high ratings and sustained them all evening. There must have been a lot of Americans who just wanted to see the queen and were prepared to put up with anything to do so.

They put up with a lot. Professionally, it was probably the worst piece of live television ever produced on a national network. The critics thought so. The *New York Times* called it a "technical farce." Referring to the loss of cameras, the *New York Post* said: "The preferable loss would have been Robert MacNeil." The *Post* critic said I was "pretentious" and had "botched the job."

As we staggered back to the Hay-Adams, Jean Marsh said in Rose's cockney accent, "Well, if nothing else, I got to see the queen. I've never seen her in person before. And now I have."

Which was more than I could say. This encounter with Her Majesty had just nearly wrecked the career that had begun so dazzlingly that morning in 1952, when I stumbled onto the bulletin announcing her father's death — because I was on the way to the men's room.

Clearly, there were limits to my lucky knack of being in the right place at the right time.